GENIUS GUT

'*Genius Gut* demystifies the science of gut-brain signalling and offers a wealth of practical solutions for individuals hoping to increase their overall well-being' Prof. John Cryan, neuroscientist & co-author of *The Psychobiotic Revolution*

'Apart from being an exceptional academic, Emily's talent and passion for disseminating the science into digestible nuggets is second to none. I devoured this book' Alana Macfarlane, founder and author of *The Gut Stuff*

'Dr Emily Leeming masterfully distils emerging and complex science into easy and actionable reading, dispelling common myths along the way. Everyone should own a copy!' Angela Foster, *High Performance Health Podcast*

'An essential and refreshing read about an important topic' Joshua Fletcher, the Anxiety Therapist, author of *And How Does That Make You Feel?*

'This truly is a gut-health bible' Kaitlin Colucci, gut-health dietitian

'In an ocean of much-needed books on health, I'm so glad I've got Dr Emily's *Genius Gut*. As a fellow ex private chef, I love how she writes practically and deliciously on food. Congrats Emily. Thank you from me and my gut' Melissa Hemsley, chef and cookery writer

Dr Emily Leeming, PhD MSc RD, is a microbiome scientist, registered dietitian, and chef. She is a Research Fellow at King's College London. Dr Emily writes for the *Daily Mail* and frequently appears in media outlets such as BBC Radio 4, the *Sunday Times*, *Telegraph*, and *Guardian*. She authors the popular weekly Substack newsletter *Second Brain* and regularly gives talks, translating new research findings into actionable everyday advice. *Genius Gut* is her first book.

www.emilyleeming.com
Instagram: @dremilyleeming
Substack: Second Brain

GENIUS GUT

The Life-Changing Science of Eating for Your Second Brain

DR EMILY LEEMING

MICHAEL JOSEPH

PENGUIN MICHAEL JOSEPH

UK | USA | Canada | Ireland | Australia
India | New Zealand | South Africa

Penguin Michael Joseph, Penguin Random House UK,
One Embassy Gardens, 8 Viaduct Gardens, London SW11 7BW

penguin.co.uk
global.penguinrandomhouse.com

First published 2024
006

Set in 11.25/18pt TT Norms Pro
Typeset by Jouve (UK), Milton Keynes
Printed and bound in Great Britain by Clays Ltd, Elcograf S.p.A.

The authorized representative in the EEA is Penguin Random House Ireland,
Morrison Chambers, 32 Nassau Street, Dublin D02 YH68

A CIP catalogue record for this book is available from the British Library

ISBN: 978–1–405–96442–5

www.greenpenguin.co.uk

Penguin Random House is committed to a
sustainable future for our business, our readers
and our planet. This book is made from Forest
Stewardship Council® certified paper.

This is for you

Happiness – it's a gut feeling

Contents

APPENDIX - YOUR GUT KIT

Preface

How are you?

'Hi. How are you?'

You're asked this often; the same familiar pattern of saying hello.

'I'm *great*, thanks! How about you?'

You say, '*great!*' or '*good!*' even on those days when you don't feel particularly great, or good, or fine. It's a reflex response more than sharing how you truly feel.

But really, though. *How are you?*

Like a jigsaw puzzle, your life is made up of many thousands of days. Imagine each day as a jigsaw piece coloured by your mood. Uplifting happy days in vibrant orange and jazzy yellow. Sad days in muted blue. Days where you're tired, low and running on empty in grizzly grey. Now step back from your theoretical jigsaw puzzle and take a look. What colour makes up most of the pieces?

Your happiness baseline is your default mood setting – where you find your mood settling after highs or lows. It's also closely related to your emotional balance too; how you handle life's bumps without losing control and veering off the road. Raising your baseline happiness and your emotional stability is the key to contentment in life, rather than chasing the extreme but less frequent highs of, say, relaxing on holiday or going to a once-in-a-lifetime event.

Forty per cent of why you feel happy or not is down to your genes.[1] The rest is influenced by where you live, your life experiences, your relationships with friends and family and now – based on the latest scientific research – what you eat too. This is where your gut-brain connection comes in.

Your gut and your brain are intricately and powerfully connected. What you feel in your mind, like your mood and emotions, you can often feel in your gut too. We've been casually talking about it for far longer than you might think.

You get *butterflies in your stomach* when you're nervous about giving a presentation at work.

You feel *punched in the gut* if your partner breaks up with you out of nowhere.

When you buy a lottery ticket, you get a *gut feeling* that this time, you'll win. Even if it's only a fiver.

Or you might listen to your *gut instinct* to trust someone you only just met.

The latest revolutionary science is now uncovering just how much this relationship between your gut and your brain goes the other way too – how your gut communicates with your brain, influencing your mood, happiness and emotional stability.

- When you're hungry, you get tired and angry.
- When you're on a sugar rollercoaster, your emotions are all over the shop.
- When you don't eat well, you're irritable and sluggish.

> - When you're stressed, you dive for the biscuits and chocolate.
> - When you're running on coffee fumes all day, you feel anxious and wired.

Sounds familiar?

Your gut and your brain are constantly talking to each other. And it's your gut that's the chatty one. Ninety per cent of your gut-brain talk is your gut communicating to your brain.[2]

Your gut is more like your brain than you might realise.

Like your brain, your gut produces molecules that shape your mood.

Like your brain, your gut is a hub of neural activity, housing an extensive network of nerve cells called neurons, known as your enteric nervous system.

And like your brain, your gut is a hormone command centre releasing hormones that influence how your body works, like how full or hungry you feel.

Not only that – your gut is also home to your gut microbiome – a newly uncovered vast and complex community of micro-organisms that are fundamental to your health and well-being. Your gut microbiome is involved in every aspect of your health, including your brain – influencing your mood and how well you think.

Feed your gut, feed your brain

Our medical system has separated the mind from the body, going all the way back to a philosopher in the 1600s called René

Descartes. Descartes was also a mathematician and scientist, and dedicated much of his life to studying medicine. He insisted that the mind and the body are so different that it's impossible that they work together, that the brain is unconnected and separate from the rest of the body. A concept that's been surprisingly persistent across the centuries.

> *'The difficulty is not merely that mind and body are different. It is that they are different in such a way that their interaction is impossible.'*
>
> René Descartes

The brain and the body aren't simply strangers tethered by fleshy neck muscle alone. Descartes' philosophy, however, has left its mark. Even the language we use reinforces the brain and body as distinct and different. We use phrases like 'mental health' and 'physical health', rather than just 'health'. Problems with the brain are still often treated separately from the rest of the body. Thankfully, there's now a growing understanding of how important the gut-brain connection is in both health and disease where disruptions in the gut can manifest as symptoms in the brain and vice versa. Signs that the two are intricately related. For example, up to 80 per cent of people with Parkinson's disease also have constipation, a symptom that can appear as much as twenty years earlier than other warning signs.[3] And a third of those with irritable bowel syndrome also have depression and anxiety.[4]

Disruptions in your gut-brain connection can manifest in various ways beyond noticeable digestive symptoms – like your mood, energy and brainpower. Scientists are rapidly bringing to light how the trillions of microorganisms that live in your gut, called your gut microbiome, influence your health too. They aren't simply bit-players in your digestion – they have main-character energy, producing special molecules that traverse your body like explorers navigating a complex maze without a map. These molecules influence every aspect of your health, including your brain, playing a role in your mood, your emotional stability and how well you think and problem-solve. Twenty years ago, we didn't even know the microbiome existed. Now, it's recognised by scientists and clinicians as a fundamental pillar of health. You wouldn't be the same without it.

The secret to understanding your gut-brain connection is recognising its two-way nature. No longer is your brain separate from the rest of your body. And no longer is health 'physical health' alone. By changing what you eat, you support your gut and gut microbiome to function at their best, providing your brain with the nutrition it needs to thrive – to think fast and clearly. To have more energy and feel happy. But we shouldn't ignore the power of the brain – your thoughts and your feelings. Your brain also exerts influence over how well your digestion works. When you're stressed, your digestion can slow down, but for others it can speed up – needing to urgently dash to the loo. And your thoughts and emotions can have a powerful influence over what foods you choose to eat. Your gut-brain connection – it's a two-way street.

How's your gut-brain connection doing?

The Gut-Brain Quiz

For each of the following questions, score 1 for yes, 0 for no.

- Is the shape of your poo either a smooth sausage, or a sausage with cracks?
- Do you 'go' between three times a day and three times a week?
- Is your poo dark brown?
- Does your poo exit smoothly and easily?

For each of the following questions score 0 for yes, 1 for no.

- Do you often get stomach pain, or pain when you try to 'go'?
- Do you often get other uncomfortable gut issues like being bloated all day or frequent, terrible-smelling farts?
- Do you often feel sad or down?
- Do you struggle to concentrate and think well?
- Do you feel tired often?
- Are you stressed often?
- Do you struggle with craving certain foods?
- Do you feel anxious or worried a lot?

Score:

12 I'm unstoppable!
10–11 I feel kinda all right for the most part
8–10 Hmmm. Meh.
5–7 I've had better days.
0–4 I'm really struggling.

In the pages that follow, I'll share with you the latest science of how food, your gut and your gut microbiome can influence your whole-body well-being. There are two actionable sections – the first is called 'Eating for Your Gut-Brain', which guides you on how to rewire your approach to healthy eating, and this is followed by 'The Genius Gut Method' with 10 hacks on what and how to eat to boost your happiness, brainpower and to feel amazing.

This quiz is not a substitute for professional medical advice, diagnosis or treatment. If you're struggling with your gut or mental health please see a healthcare professional. Please note that while what and how you eat can support your mental well-being, this shouldn't replace or delay seeking mental health guidance or taking prescribed medication.

If you have a condition, syndrome, disorder or disease – you may have unique needs that I unfortunately can't cover in this book. If you have a condition, disorder or disease, please talk to your healthcare professional for advice.

PART ONE – GUT-BRAIN TALK

1. Your Genius Gut

What is your gut?

If I ask you where you think the gut is, what springs to mind? When we talk about the gut, we tend to think only about the stomach and the intestines. Your gut, however, starts at your mouth and carries on all the way down to your bum. It's the whole thing! In simple terms, it's a long hollow twisting tube. You put food in one end, and out comes the waste at the other.

Your digestion can kick-start into action before food has even reached your lips. Hunger strikes and it's time to refuel. Your stomach muscles and intestines start contracting, their movement making the rumbling sound you hear when your stomach gurgles with hunger. Your gut-brain connection is already at play, signals pinging back and forth between your gut and brain like a well coordinated dance. Your brain says – it's time to eat.

As food arrives in your mouth, the mechanical action of chewing helps to pulverise and smush it into smaller, more manageable pieces. Enzymes in your saliva break down the starchy sugars too, before it slips down your throat like going down a slide at a waterpark.

It arrives in your stretchy muscular sack of a stomach. Your stomach is full of acid – it's more acidic than lemon or vinegar.

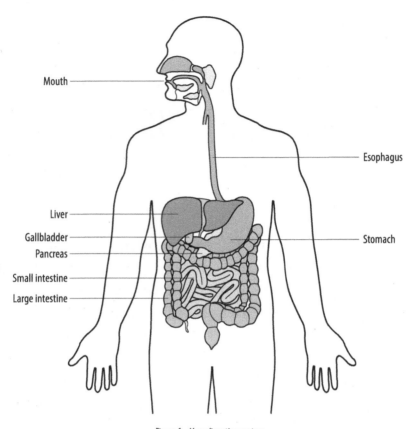

Figure 1. Your digestive system

The stomach acts a bit like a washing machine, churning and sloshing your food in acidic liquid. The dual action of acid and slop-slapping mechanics work to further break down what you've eaten into a thick fluid.

The stomach slowly empties its contents into your upper, or small, intestine. Small being that it's narrower than your wider large intestine that's lower down, but in fact it's actually the longest part of your gut. Your upper intestine measures about 6 metres, intricately and neatly tucked in your insides, and is where 90–95 per cent of the nutrients from the food you eat are absorbed into your body. For what's effectively a long narrow pipe, it's hard to believe that it can do such a big job. But looks can be deceiving. Your small intestine has the absorptive area the size of a tennis court!

Your small intestine pushes and squeezes food down the pipe rather like how toothpaste is squeezed out of a tube. Along the way your gallbladder, liver and pancreas help out with breaking down the food into smaller parts, so that it's easier for your body to absorb the nutrients it needs. Your pancreas is a long gland shaped like a flat pear and about the size of your hand which releases digestive juices to break down proteins, carbohydrates and fats. Your liver makes bile, a yellow-greenish liquid that is stored in the gallbladder, where it can then be released into the small intestine to help break down fats.

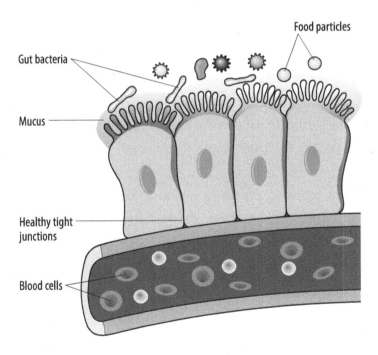

Figure 2. Your gut barrier lining

All along your intestines there's a thin lining that acts as your gut barrier. It's your internal skin protecting you from the murky matter within – the contents of your intestines. It acts as the gatekeeper that identifies which helpful molecules can pass through and into your body – like the nutrients from food – while keeping the harmful bad guys out, or even just stuff getting where it shouldn't. Your absorbed nutrients are then carried away, mostly to your liver first. Your liver acts like a processing factory, before distributing them to parts of your body to store or use.

Back in your small intestine, any left-over bits of food that you can't digest or absorb make their way to your lower or large intestine – the final 1.5-metre stretch. Your large intestine's job is to act like a sausage-packaging machine. It draws out the left-over moisture from the slushy mix, packs it down neatly, and pushes it in the form of a well-presented poo towards your back door. That's all your large intestine was believed to do. But it's also home to most of your gut microbiome. And what you weren't able to digest or absorb yourself, well, it's quite another matter for your gut microbiome. We'll dive into that later.

Your gut working properly is important because your body needs nutrients from what you eat and drink to work at its best. It helps you to break down and absorb proteins, carbohydrates, fats, vitamins and minerals to use for energy, growth and cell repair.

Proteins

Your body uses protein to build and repair, particularly your muscles and bones. There are many types of protein, each made up from differently put-together protein building blocks called amino acids. There are 20 amino acids, and they act rather like Lego bricks – you can make a different model depending on how those bricks are arranged or which bricks you use. Your body can produce some of these amino-acid building blocks itself, but there are nine essential amino acids that must come from the food you eat. High-protein foods are meat, poultry, fish and seafood, eggs, dairy, nuts and seeds, beans and legumes.

Carbohydrates

Fibre, starches and sugars make up carbohydrates. Carbohydrates are found in fruits, vegetables, grains and dairy. Your body uses carbohydrates for energy, and this is particularly important for your energy-hungry brain. Simple carbohydrates found in refined grains and sugary foods are digested rapidly and have the potential to dump quick bursts of sugar into your bloodstream. Complex carbohydrates found in fruits, vegetables and whole grains are digested more slowly, slowing the release of sugar into your body.

Fibre

While fibre is a type of complex carbohydrate, as it's a key feature of this book it's getting its own little section here.

After all, not all superheroes wear capes. Fibre is the plant roughage from whole grains, fruits, vegetables, beans, legumes, nuts and seeds. You can't digest fibre yourself – your body can't digest or absorb it. Instead you need your gut microbiome to help with that. Fibre isn't just one thing either, there are lots of different types of fibres.

Fats

Like protein and carbohydrates, there are different types of fats, too, that can have different effects on your health. Some are less healthy for your heart while others are protective. You can find fats in fat-rich foods like avocado, salmon, extra virgin olive oil and canola oil that help your health. Cheeses tend to be high in fats, but they seem to have a neutral effect on your health. Butter and fatty or processed meats like bacon, steak, hot dogs, sausages and meat pies are less healthy fat-rich foods. Fats provide essential fatty acids that are critical for your cell membranes, particularly in your brain and nervous system. Certain vitamins, like vitamins A, D and E, are better absorbed with the help of fats.

Why is your gut genius?

Your gut is the portal through which your body is supplied with the energy and nutrients you need to survive. It digests and breaks down the food you eat through a complex dance of enzymes, acids, moving muscles and much more. It shields you from its contents, while carefully extracting helpful molecules and nutrients and passing them safely into your body. It's home to your second brain, to 70 per cent of your immune system, and to your gut microbiome. It's directly linked with your brain, and able to produce hormones and molecules that influence your appetite, mood and energy.

It's so genius that it can work more independently from the rest of your body than your other organs. If your brain is the reigning monarch of a country, and your organs make up the different land areas, then your gut is the favoured region with the most independence to make its own decisions while remaining loyal to the central authority (your brain).

How do you know how healthy your gut is?

Gut health is your gut functioning at its best. It's where there's no disease or disorder, no gut symptoms, and a healthy gut microbiome. If your microbiome is unhealthy, you're likely to feel the same too – from feeling sluggish to low mood, and often digestive problems as well.

There's a free, easy way to keep tabs on how healthy your gut is, and that's by lifting the toilet lid. Your poo.

If you're a little awkward about poo, remind yourself that every single person on this earth does it, even the most impossibly glamorous movie star, and even the Kardashians.

What is poo?

If you thought poo was just left-over food, then think again. Your poo is only about a quarter solid matter. Three quarters of your poo is water helping to keep it nice and soft (and pain-free) as it exits your back end.

The solid part is made up of:

- 25–50 per cent gut bacteria – both living and dead
- Left-over undigested food as protein, fibre, fat and a little carbohydrate
- Some of your dead body cells
- Dried digestive juices

Your poo's shape, colour and how often you 'go' is a great way to see if your gut and your gut microbiome are in fairly good nick. If everything is working well, you'll likely have a nice, smooth, solid, brown poo that easily exits. If you don't, it's likely a sign that your gut isn't as healthy as it could be. So don't be shy, take a regular look to see how your gut is doing.

How often should you 'go'?

It's healthy to do a poo between three times a day and three times a week – whatever's your 'normal' in this range is right for you, even if that looks different from someone else's.

What does a good poo look like?

- A smooth sausage or a sausage with some cracks in it
- Leaves your body smoothly and completely, with no pain
- Tends to sink, though floating poos can sometimes be a sign of a high-fibre or high-fat diet
- A brown colour

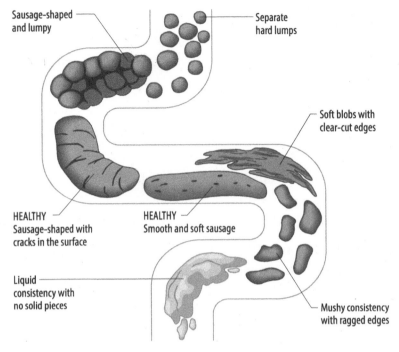

Figure 3. Poo guide

What does an unhealthy poo look and feel like?

- Sudden change in how often you 'go' that lasts more than three to four days
- Poo that's mushy and runny or hard pellets
- Discomfort or pain on going to the loo
- Even when you 'go', feeling like you haven't gotten all the poo out, or taking a long time to 'go'
- Red, black, yellow or green colour

Some of these can be a sign that you're not eating enough fibre, and can easily be changed through what you eat. Sometimes though it can be a warning sign. If your poo looks red or black, and you haven't just eaten some beetroot, this could be because of blood in your poo. This is a red flag symptom, and can be a sign of bowel cancer, ulcers or inflammatory bowel disease. Your healthcare professional can check if there's an underlying condition and can give you advice on sorting any digestive issues. I know it might feel a bit awkward to talk about your loo habits to a stranger even if they are a doctor, but I promise you, healthcare professionals all talk about body parts, fluids, poo, blood so regularly that it's a completely non-taboo topic – in fact we're more upset if you leave anything out. It's nothing we haven't seen or heard before, and it's a helpful, easy way for us to get a quick insight into how happy your gut is.

Why is poo brown?

The brown in your poo is from a pigment called stercobilin. Without it, your poo would be a pale beige colour. To help you digest fats in your food, your liver secretes a yellow-greenish liquid called bile into your small intestine via your gallbladder. Some of the bile breaks down into stercobilin, turning everything brown as it mixes in with your digesting food. When poo moves too quickly through your body, like when you have diarrhoea, the bile doesn't have time to break down to stercobilin and your poo can look more yellow or green.

Constipation

Constipation happens when your newly forming poo moves too slowly through your large intestine, allowing your body to draw too much water out of it, making it hard and difficult to pass, often looking and feeling like small, hard mini boulders. You can also be constipated if you do a poo less than three times a week, or if you're unable to get everything completely out. Being constipated occasionally is common and can usually be solved by changing what you eat and some of your lifestyle habits. Part Three covers tips on keeping your gut happy and helping you to 'go'. If you're often constipated or constipated all the time, visit your healthcare professional to help manage it and particularly if you've experienced unintentional weight loss, bleeding, or pain in your bum when you try to go. Constipation can be caused by a medical condition, but this tends to be rare.

Diarrhoea

You have diarrhoea when you have watery or mushy poos three or more times a day, or you 'go' more often than you normally do. This can happen for a number of reasons, including food poisoning or other infections, certain medications, anxiety, food intolerances and more. Infections from bacteria or viruses can irritate the lining of your gut, causing a flushing response with the release of fluids into your intestines increasing the amount of water in your poo and making it pass rapidly through. Food intolerances like lactose intolerance can interfere with how well nutrients are absorbed and may also cause diarrhoea, drawing water into your intestines. Some people also get diarrhoea when they're anxious, releasing stress hormones that speed up their digestion so that they urgently need to 'go'.

Bloating

Bloating is when your belly feels uncomfortably swollen as if you've gone up a waist size. It's very common and a normal response that most people experience now and again, so it's not necessarily something to worry about. You're more likely to get bloated, for example, after a big meal, just before your period (if you get one), or when you feel stressed or anxious.

Bloating can be a problem when it doesn't go away or gets worse. Being bloated can also be caused by having too much trapped gas, being constipated, or sometimes a food intolerance, allergy or a condition called irritable bowel syndrome where you have sensitive digestion.

Farts

When you eat or drink you can swallow small amounts of air that collect in your gut. Once the gas is inside you most of it needs to be released somehow, either up as a burp or down and out as a fart. The average person produces the equivalent of one large glass to four large glassfuls of gas and farts between 12 and 25 times a day, mostly in the hour after each meal. You also fart at night too when you're in bed asleep, as your anal sphincter muscle relaxes making it easier for gas to escape. If you share the bed with someone, at least that person is asleep and farting, too.

Everyone farts. It's entirely normal and is often a sign of a healthy digestive system, and particularly happy gut bacteria! When you feed your friendly gut bacteria the foods they love, they produce gas as a side effect. And that must go somewhere. Think of this extra fruity tooty release as a little like when a cat brings you a dead mouse as a present. It's a sign of love. So let it go, let it flow.

Most farts don't smell – but there's that 1 per cent that do. We all know the ones, they burn the nostrils and can clear a room faster than lightning. Most of the time this tends to be due to the foods you eat. A compound called sulfur, found in foods like meat, eggs, cauliflower and sprouts, is broken down by some gut bacteria into a gas called hydrogen sulfide – and it's this gas that smells like rotten eggs. If you naturally have more of these types of gut bacteria you'll (unfortunately) produce more of this stinking gas than someone else. If you're regularly dropping large stink bombs, though, it could be a sign of an imbalanced gut microbiome.

The Big Poo Review

A 2022 ZOE survey of over 140,000 people's loo habits in the UK found that:

- On average people poo 1–2 times a day
- 60 per cent of people poo after breakfast
- 92 per cent of people poo between three times a day and three times a week, the healthy range of how often to poo
- 20 per cent had constipation and this was more common in women than men
- No difference between how often men or women 'go', though men spend longer on the loo than women by nearly two minutes

What's the gut got to do with it?

- Your gut is one long tube from your mouth all the way to your bum
- A healthy gut is where there's no disease or disorder, no gut symptoms and a healthy microbiome
- Looking at your poo is a great way to see how healthy your gut is
- A healthy poo looks like a smooth or cracked sausage, is brown, comes out easily with no pain and happens between three times a day and three times a week
- An unhealthy poo is any one of the following: mushy or in hard pellets, not brown, causes pain or takes a long time to come out or doesn't come out completely, or happens less than three times a week or more than three times a day
- Your gut is genius – it not only digests your food and absorbs the nutrients, but houses your immune system and gut microbiome, and is intimately connected with your brain

2. Your Gut Microbiome

What is your gut microbiome?

Living in your gut are 100 trillion microorganisms – tiny living organisms that are too small to be seen by the naked eye. That's more microorganisms, or microbes for short, in your gut than there are stars in the Milky Way galaxy. Most of these microbes are bacteria. I know we've been brought up to think that all bacteria are bad, but lower the anti-bacterial spray and let me convince you otherwise. These bacteria, along with other microbes that live in your gut, like viruses, fungi and archaea, form your gut microbiome. A forgotten organ that we didn't even know existed a few decades ago, yet is now recognised as instrumental to your health and well-being.

The terms 'gut microbiota' and 'gut microbiome' are often used interchangeably.

Gut microbiota

Your gut microbiota is a collection of microorganisms (or microbes for short) that includes bacteria, viruses, fungi and archaea that live mostly in your lower intestine.

Gut microbiome

The gut microbiome includes all the microbes that live in your gut, but also their genes, the stuff they produce and their interactions with your body.

Gut microbes

An abbreviated term to refer to the collection of micro-organisms in your gut – they include bacteria, viruses, fungi and archaea.

Bacteria

Bacteria are microbes that make up most of your gut micro-biome. We also know more about them than other gut microbes.

Viruses

Your gut microbiome is also made up of viruses. They can interact with and influence your gut bacteria. We know less about them than your gut bacteria.

Fungi

There are different types of fungi in your microbiome and the term includes yeasts and moulds. The role of these fungi in your health is less understood compared to what we know about bacteria.

Archaea

Archaea are types of microbes that are similar, but different, to your gut bacteria. They are less common and less well understood.

While the largest number of microbes are found in your gut you're also covered in them. You have a microbiome in your mouth, called your oral microbiome. A skin microbiome. There's a vaginal microbiome. And a lung microbiome. You're covered in microbes from head to toe. They're all around you too, in the air you breathe and on every surface you touch. You're constantly exchanging microbes back and forth, picking them up on your fingers as you turn the pages of this book, up your nose when you inhale the scented summery breeze, when you touch your mouth as you're eating a sandwich, and let's not forget there's microbes on your food too. We've been rightly taught to fear the bad bacteria that can cause terrible food poisoning or worse. But in doing that we've forgotten about the many harmless and friendly ones all around us.

As far as bacteria are concerned, we humans are the invasive species. Bacteria were here way before us. Throughout evolution we've co-evolved with our bacterial friends, mostly in harmony. In fact, we're so entwined that for every human cell we have, there are roughly equal numbers of bacteria all over us and inside us too. If aliens were to land on earth, they wouldn't call us human. Based on our cell count we'd be classified as a hybrid breed, equal parts human to bacteria. And we couldn't live without them. Despite this, they're so small that if you bundled them all together from across your body and weighed them, they'd weigh less than 500g, about a can of beans. And if you weighed only your gut microbes, they'd weigh about 200g, similar to a mango.

Where did these hitchhikers come from?

Your own personal gut microbiome is seeded at birth. Depending on how you were born and who your mother is you might have started life with very different gut bacteria. If you were born through your mother's birth canal, your gut would have been seeded by bacteria from your mother's vaginal microbiome and potentially a little bit of gut microbiome-rich poo too, pushed up your nose and into your mouth on your way out into the big cold world, and all over your skin. If you were born by caesarean section the first bacteria your gut is seeded with tends to be types of bacteria commonly found on skin, from being held by your parents, doctors and the hospital nurses, and from bacteria commonly found on hospital surfaces.

Your gut microbiome isn't very diverse at this point. You only have a few types of gut bacteria that are in rapid flux as you quickly come into contact with other new bacteria around you. Breast milk contains bacteria that help to nurture your new-born microbiome as well as special Human Milk Oligosaccharides that feed your gut bacteria. As you start putting every single object in your mouth with pudgy grabbing fists you encounter more bacteria from the surfaces around you and not just from the skin of your parents holding you. It's only when you start eating solid foods that your gut bacteria become more diverse, with the range of fibres in food feeding many more different types of bacteria. Your first five years are crucial for the healthy development of your gut microbiome. When you reach five years old your gut microbiome starts to settle down and stabilise and contains gut bacteria types that are commonly found in adults – an adult-like microbiome. From this point your microbiome becomes more resilient to change, for better or worse, and fluctuates less. Your microbiome continues to develop though, after all, it's a living ecosystem.

Gut fact

What if . . . you didn't have a microbiome?

This invisible collection of microbes – you wouldn't be blamed for thinking, well, I can't see them, how important can they really be? If you didn't have a microbiome, you wouldn't be doing too well. Scientists have specially bred microbiome-free mice inside a sterile plastic bubble engineered to prevent any bacteria getting in and completely isolated from the outside world. If you don't look too closely the mice look like normal mice and in this sterile environment, they can live just as long. But they're not quite what they seem. They have problems with their immune system so that any tiny infection has the potential to be life-threatening. Their guts are grossly enlarged and don't work properly so they need extra nutrition and energy. Their brains don't grow properly either, changing their learning and memory centres.[1] And they behave oddly too.

What makes a healthy microbiome?

The more different types of gut bacteria you have – called the diversity of your gut microbiome – the more healthy you tend to be. It's kind of like how well (or not) you can play the piano when you only have two piano keys versus all eighty-eight. It also matters which types of bacteria you have too – are those piano keys in tune or do they make you wince? In your gut you have between 200 and 1,000 different types (or species) of gut bacteria. Each species of gut bacteria contains multiple different subtypes called strains. Which types and how many of them you have is as unique to you as a fingerprint. Even identical twins share only 35 per cent of the same species of gut bacteria.[2] Some of the bacteria in your gut we know are bona fide decent do-gooders. But much like us humans, apart from a few through-and-through bad eggs, most of our gut bacteria tend to be a bit situational in whether they're 'good' or 'bad'. They're either 'good-most-of the-time' or 'bad-most-of-the-time-but-occasionally-good'. Even the best bacteria with a squeaky-clean reputation like *Akkermansia muciniphila* that tends to be plentiful in people with great health, can occasionally behave badly. If *Akkermansia muciniphila* is starved, it gets hangry. I know we can all relate to that. If it's deprived of fibre, it can worsen an allergic response to a food allergy.[3]

> ## 'Good' gut bacteria
> Bacteria that produce molecules called metabolites that are good for your health. These bacteria are considered 'good' but their effect can vary depending on the person and situation.

'Bad' gut bacteria

Bacteria that produce molecules called metabolites that are harmful for your health. Whether they are considered 'bad' can depend on the person and situation.

Pathogenic bacteria

These bacteria can cause sickness and illnesses, ranging from stomach upsets to more serious health issues.

You and I likely have a very different gut microbiome. What we do have in common, though, are many bacteria that have the same jobs but different names. Like I have scientist colleagues called Kate, Asha and Ben – we all do scientific research, but we are not the same person. So just because you have one type of bacteria that I don't, doesn't mean that your microbiome is necessarily more or less healthy than mine. It's what they do that counts. Think of your microbiome like the workers in a big organisation or company – the company being you. The aim of the workforce? To keep you happy, healthy and alive. As a company you wouldn't want just a marketing department, no matter how many creative, brilliant ads they produce. You also need a strong product team, a kind and fair human resources team, and engineers crunching complex spreadsheets. You'd need cleaners to come and regularly clean the toilets so that workers don't get sick or grumpy. And there always needs to be at least one bubbly person who loves organising after-work socials. Some people leave, and other new people join. For the company to grow and thrive, you need workers with a variety of different skills just like we need from our gut microbiome. And no matter which workers you have – making the company a happy place to work is what helps them do a great job. And it's the same with your gut bacteria. By keeping your gut healthy and supplying your gut microbiome with the foods they need to thrive, your 'good' bacteria will flourish and the ones that have a bit more of a varied reputation are less likely to act out.

Blue poo

The shape, colour and frequency of your poo can help to tell you how healthy your gut and gut microbiome are. And you can take this one step further by measuring your gut transit time. This is the time it takes from when you eat something, to when it comes out the other end. To do this you'll need a food that you're pretty confident you'll be able to easily identify, like sweetcorn or a large amount of beet-root (just don't forget and panic that your wee and poo look bloody from the red staining of the juice!).

A few years ago I co-authored a scientific paper on transit time.[4] In the study participants were given two bright-blue muffins to eat, as blue as the cookie monster, and measured the time it took to surface at the other 'end', aka as blue poo. We found that the gut microbiome is more strongly related to transit time than the shape of your poo, or how often you go.

Fast gut transit time is less than 14 hours

Healthy gut transit time is between 14 and 58 hours (up to 2.5 days)

Slow gut transit time is more than 58 hours (over 2.5 days)

What we found

- The average transit time was just a little over a full day, at just under 29 hours
- People who had a fast or slow gut transit time had different make-ups of their gut microbiomes than those with a healthy gut transit time
- The slow transit time produced fewer of the healthy special molecules called short-chain fatty acids and had higher amounts of 'bad' gut bacteria

When your gut microbiome is unhealthy

Your microbiome can become disrupted with an unhealthy balance of gut bacteria. In an unhealthy microbiome you have a lower diversity of gut bacteria – you have fewer different types. You also tend to lose some of the 'good' bacteria and there can be an overgrowth of 'bad' bacteria. There are many ways your gut microbiome can be disrupted, like having an unhealthy diet for a long period of time, stress, taking too many antibiotics, or from an illness. Infections, like getting diarrhoea on holiday, inflammation and diseases, can also throw the balance of your gut bacteria out of whack. An imbalanced gut microbiome can cause uncomfortable gut symptoms for some people and can influence how you feel and your health beyond your gut. An imbalanced gut microbiome can cause excess inflammation that's linked to diseases like type II diabetes, heart disease and more.[5]

What does your gut microbiome do, exactly?

Your gut bacteria make their home in your gut, but they aren't freeloaders. They work hard and contribute to keeping their home, you, in good shape. Because without you, there's no them. Not all residents in your gut are as house-proud as others; some, you might say, leave the towel on the floor and don't seem to understand that just putting a dish in the sink doesn't mean it's going to wash itself. Other bacteria, though, really put in the hours, producing helpful molecules that influence your health and well-being across your body, including your brain and mood.

Metabolites
A metabolite is a small molecule produced by your gut microbiome as a by-product of breaking down the food you eat. Metabolites play a crucial role in your health.

Short-chain fatty acids
Short-chain fatty acids are examples of metabolites produced by your gut bacteria when they ferment fibre. They have been linked to many health benefits like your mood, appetite and more.

Immune system
The immune system is an intricate network of cells, tissues and organs that work together to defend your body against harmful invaders.

Inflammation

Inflammation happens when your immune system is trying to protect you from harm. It's a natural, helpful reaction that's part of the body's healing response. Inflammation, though, is meant to be a temporary response and can become harmful if it stays raised long term.

Probiotic

A probiotic usually refers to a supplement or sometimes a food that contains live bacteria. The definition of a probiotic is a type of microbe that, when you take enough of it, has a specific helpful effect on your health.

Prebiotic

A prebiotic is a substance that feeds specific 'good' bacteria in your gut, helping your health. Prebiotics are often types of fibre, but they can be some other food components too. Prebiotics are found naturally in food or as an added ingredient or supplement.

Digestive helpers

When you eat, you feed your gut bacteria. Most of what you eat is absorbed in the small intestine before it reaches your gut microbiome in your lower large intestine. What passes through to the dining hall of your gut microbiome are scraps your own body wasn't able to digest or absorb itself. One man's rubbish is another man's (or bacteria's) treasure. Your gut bacteria get to work, feeding on the undigested food. In return for you keeping them well fed, they give you back more than a few gifts. They give you energy – about 5 to 15 per cent of your energy needs. They produce vitamins for you, like vitamin K, some B vitamins and amino acids too. Your gut bacteria also help you to absorb more of certain nutrients like calcium and magnesium.

Why is fibre so special?

If fibre resembled anyone it would be Superman. Superman disguises himself as awkward and unassuming journalist Clark Kent to keep his true identity a secret. His love interest Lois Lane doesn't pay much attention to him at first. But when she realises that Superman and Clark are the same person her view of him changes. Fibre, like Clark, has been passed over too many times as boring, written off as simply something that 'helps you go'. But fibre does much, much more than that.

- It feeds your gut bacteria so that they can produce short-chain fatty acids and other helpful metabolites
- It acts like nature's toothbrush. The mechanical action of fibre moving through your intestines can help to sweep away any build-up in your gut, keeping it healthy
- It helps to balance your blood-sugar levels by slowing the absorption of sugars into your bloodstream

- It keeps you feeling fuller for longer due to its bulkiness slowing down the emptying of your stomach. It also influences hormones that signal to your brain to tell you you're full
- It helps your heart health by trapping the 'bad' type of cholesterol and preventing it being absorbed into your bloodstream
- It reduces the risk of many diseases, like colorectal cancer, type II diabetes and heart disease

Al's ode to fibre: The Unsung Hero

In the world of food, a hero stands tall,
A silent champion, the greatest of all.
Fibre, oh fibre, in grains and in greens,
A magical marvel, behind the scenes.

In veggies and fruits, it weaves its thread,
Through digestive pathways, it's widely spread.
A friend to the gut, it whispers, 'I'm here,'
Promoting good health, year after year.

It tackles 'bad' cholesterol, a worthy feat,
Keeps blood sugar steady, a nutrient elite.
With every bite of oats or bran,
Fibre dances through, a nutritional plan.

So let's celebrate this dietary star,
In lentils, in flaxseeds, from near and far.
For in the tale of wellness, it's a chapter,
Fibre, oh fibre, health's sweet captor.

Marvellous metabolites

Your gut microbiome isn't only involved in helping you to digest your food. Your microbes are like that fairy godmother from Disney that we all secretly wished we had. They produce special molecules called metabolites that have powerful health effects and can travel throughout your body, reaching as far as your brain.

When you eat fibre-rich foods you provide your gut bacteria with a smorgasbord feast. Your gut bacteria break down the food particles into a multitude of metabolites along with by-products like gas. These metabolites play a crucial role in supporting your health in many ways. They help your body to manage your blood-sugar and blood-fat levels, they help to look after your appetite and your energy needs, and they're quick to help act on any excessive and harmful inflammation. They get to work directly in the gut or they can be absorbed into your bloodstream to travel to different parts of your body – to your heart, lungs, brain and more.

Some metabolites, though, can be harmful. If you eat an unhealthy diet, 'bad' bacteria can start to dominate, producing damaging metabolites.

Short-chain fatty acids – metabolite royalty

Short-chain fatty acids are the movers, the shakers, the disco groovers of metabolites. They're the metabolites that we get really excited about and are produced by your gut bacteria when they feed on fibre. There are three main short-chain fatty acids: acetate, propionate and butyrate. Scientists think short-chain fatty acids are the main reason fibre and your gut microbiome are so integral to your health and well-being.

Acetate, propionate and butyrate make up 90 per cent of the short-chain fatty acids produced by your gut bacteria. A few stay close to home to help keep your gut barrier lining strong and healthy, the protective layer of cells that line the wall of your gut. Your gut barrier lining acts as a physical barrier between the wild west of bacteria, food and other components in your digestive system, and your body. Your gut barrier lining prevents the entry of harmful substances into your bloodstream, not too dissimilar to a castle with defensive walls and guarded gates preventing invaders from getting in but still needing to let well-meaning citizens and traders pass through. Like walls that might lose a brick or two or gates that start to get squeaky hinges after some use, your gut barrier lining also needs to be cared for to keep it in good repair. Short-chain fatty acids help to keep your gut barrier lining strong so that vitamins, minerals and other beneficial molecules can pass through easily, and stop bacteria trespassing through.

Aside from the few that stay in your gut, nearly all short-chain fatty acids are absorbed into your bloodstream and travel around your body. Your liver repackages your short-chain fatty acids so they can be used for different needs; they work with your immune cells by acting as fire-dousers to any lurking excess inflammation, they influence your storage of fat and they contribute energy to your brain by crossing your brain's blood-brain barrier – your brain's version of your gut barrier lining. They can signal to your brain that you're full and to lower your appetite,[6] and they're involved in your behaviour and mood too.

Hello, hello, an extra dose of vitamins

While you get most vitamins from what you eat, which are then absorbed in your small intestine, some vitamins are made or modified by your gut bacteria.

Certain gut bacteria can produce vitamin K. Your body uses vitamin K to help with clotting your blood so that wounds can heal, and it helps keep your bones healthy too. Your gut bacteria produce some B vitamins; 20 per cent of your B vitamin folate can come from your gut bacteria. B vitamins are involved in many of your body's processes, from helping your body to release energy from food to supporting your mood by helping you to produce neurotransmitters like your 'happy' hormone serotonin.

Your microbiome and your immune system

Seventy per cent of your immune cells live in your gut. That's most of your immune system, sitting almost elbow to elbow with your gut microbes. Your gut barrier lining is a crucial site for immune surveillance and defence. Immune cells are strategically positioned in your gut barrier lining to detect and respond to potential threats. Your microbiome is essential in how well your immune system functions, training and teaching your immune system to identify the 'good' bacteria from harmful pathogens, the through-and-through baddies that cause illnesses and disease. When this alliance is working well, your immune system and your microbiome help your body to defend itself against harmful invaders but also not to retaliate against an innocent bystander. It's rather like if you trained a guard dog, you don't want him to bite the postman.

How can you change your gut microbiome?

Your gut microbiome is constantly changing and evolving. What you eat is one of the greatest influences on your gut bacteria; they feed on the food you eat so that they grow in numbers and, over time, help to encourage new 'good' bacteria to take up residence in your gut. Food after all passes through your gut microbiome's home at least three times a day, and you can see significant changes in the levels of your gut bacteria in as little as three to four days.[7] Your microbiome rapidly shifting is likely to ensure that you're able to get the most nutrition possible from different foods. This could be an evolutionary response, harking back to when we were hunter-gatherers, perhaps spending days eating nuts and seeds before a sudden influx of meat from a successful hunt, and needing to make the most of the nutrition available.

Your gut bacteria particularly thrive on fibre, the roughage from plant foods like whole grains, fruits, vegetables, nuts, seeds, beans and legumes. You can't digest fibre yourself, so it passes through your small intestine to your gut microbiome in your large intestine lower down.

Besides food, what else can change your gut microbiome?

Stress: Chronic stress can influence the balance of your gut bacteria by encouraging the growth of potentially harmful bacteria while the 'good' bacteria struggle to thrive.

Excessive antibiotics: Antibiotics are life-saving medications. However, when they are not medically necessary (like for viral infections) or overused they can disrupt your gut

---

microbiome by killing or reducing the numbers of not only the targeted 'bad' bacteria, but also the 'good' bacteria too.

If you're a city slicker or live in the countryside: You're surrounded by microbes. Living in the city or the countryside can expose you to different types of microbes, influencing the types of bacteria in your gut microbiome. Soil is particularly rich in microbes.

Sleep: A poor night's sleep can affect your gut microbiome and is linked to changes in diversity and the types of bacteria you have in your gut.

Exercise: Regular exercise is linked to a more diverse gut microbiome and more 'good' types of bacteria.

If you own a pet: Those who own a pet have a different microbiome than those who don't. Pet owners share some types of bacteria in their gut microbiome with those of their cat or dog.

Food isn't the only influence on your gut microbiome either. Some factors that influence your gut microbiome you can't change, like how you were born, whether you were breastfed or not, or if you had many courses of antibiotics as a child. Your gut microbiome is constantly shifting and changing in response to you, the welcoming host, as well as its home life environment in your gut. It responds to how much exercise you do, to how stressed you are, to how well you sleep and to whether you live in a city or in the countryside. It's very intuitive as to how well you are doing mentally and physically, and in turn, you're also in tune with it, relying on it to thrive and feel your best. Not too dissimilar to a marriage between two people and the promise of "til death do us part', you are married to your gut microbes for better or worse. When this relationship goes wrong, both parties are fairly miserable. But when it's good, it's a sweet, sweet pairing.

Faecal microbiota transplants

There's no simple way to put this, but a faecal microbiota transplant (FMT) is when you take someone else's poo, rich in microbes, whizz it up into a poo-slurry and put it up someone's bum, transplanting the donor's microbiome into their gut. They can also be delivered in capsules you can swallow, so called 'crapsules' or 'poo pills'.

FMT is used as an effective treatment for a dangerous infection from a harmful bacteria called *Clostridium difficile*, or *C. diff,* that causes life-threatening diarrhoea. FMT is also used to help ease symptoms for some people with ulcerative colitis, a type of inflammatory bowel disease where your lower intestine and rectum can become inflamed.

It's important that donors are screened before FMT is performed, so that other health issues aren't passed on by mistake, in the same way that you would be checked before donating to a blood bank or for organ and tissue transplants. It's a new treatment that is not recommended outside of the supervision of a gastroenterologist.

Fourth-century golden soup

While FMT is now being explored as a treatment for other diseases and disorders, the concept isn't as new as we might think. In China in the fourth-century, 'golden soup' or 'yellow dragon soup' was a watery poo soup to be drunk by sick patients to treat diarrhoea and food poisoning. Tasty.

How long does it take to improve your microbiome?

While your gut microbiome can change rapidly, most of those changes are in the levels of the gut bacteria that you already have and in the metabolites they produce. You can quickly help your gut microbiome to produce more healthy metabolites through what you eat by providing them with lots of fibre-rich foods. At the same time, your gut microbiome is also resilient to any large changes. And this is a very good thing. If you were to have an infection from a harmful invading bacteria you would want your gut microbiome to be resilient, you wouldn't want that bacteria to completely change the make-up of your gut microbiome – that would be very bad news for your health. This goes both ways though – a fancy 'gut-reset' weekend will likely do very little, but if you keep up those changes over months and years you're consistently supporting your current 'good' gut bacteria to thrive, as well as encouaging any new 'good' gut bacteria to make your gut their home. So instead of thinking about one particular meal or day, zoom out and think big picture – about a way of eating that you can keep up over years.

The key to a healthy gut microbiome is not really about the names of which bacteria you do or do not have in your gut. It's how you support the 'good' ones you have to thrive and produce loads of healthy metabolites by feeding them a range of the foods they need. Even the best painter needs the right tools, and depending on which paints you provide your gut bacteria with they'll either paint something multicoloured and bright, or something more monotone and gloomy.

What's your microbiome gut to do with it?

- Your gut microbiome is made up of 100 trillion microbes including bacteria, viruses, fungi and archaea
- A healthy gut microbiome is one with many different types of gut bacteria
- What you eat is one of the greatest influences on your gut microbiome
- Your gut microbiome is crucial to your health, impacting how your body and brain work
- A disrupted microbiome is linked to many diseases and disorders

3. The Gut-Brain Conversation

If I ask you 'How do your gut and your brain talk?' you might say something about feeling hungry and tired, or full and energised. Before reading this book it would be entirely fair to assume that that's all that the gut does – provide fuel to your brain and other organs. As you'll see in this chapter and the rest of the book, that's not the case by a long mile. Considering how influential your gut and microbiome are, they deserve far more time in the limelight. And while yes, the brain already has superstar status, it hasn't been fully acknowledged for how your thoughts and mood can influence the biology of the rest of your body – and your gut and gut microbiome too.

The far reach of your brain

Your brain – that cauliflower-sized lump residing in your head – is unsurprisingly a complex organ. It's home to your thoughts, feelings and decisions, but also manages many other processes in your body that tick along without you even noticing (bar the fact that you're alive and breathing). Let's journey past your head and into your brain's connection with your gut. When you feel excited, you get butterflies. When you're sure you've won something, you get a 'gut feeling', and when you're scared or anxious you can end up with an urgent need to dash to the loo. A vaccine trial during the Covid-19 pandemic gave us a clear window into this connection. It was a stressful, horrible, scary time and then on top of that, imagine being one of the first people to take part in a trial for a brand-new vaccine. In the trial, one group was given the real Covid-19 vaccine and the other a harmless fake 'vaccine' injection of water into the arm. Neither group knew who was getting what. For those that got the harmless injection of water, but didn't know it, 30 per cent reported fatigue and headaches, 10 per cent had diarrhoea and others experienced vomiting and muscle pain. Their fear, worry and stress gave them gut symptoms. Your state of mind – your stress, mood and emotions – can change how you feel, and affect your gut.

Introducing your second brain

Your gut and your brain talk to each other. To start with, they're physically connected. Your brain and your spinal cord are called your central nervous system. They control your conscious decisions, like when you specifically want to walk somewhere, and also involuntary processes that happen automatically, like your heart rate, breathing and reflexes. You also have a second nervous system that covers the rest of your body and includes your gut. Like your brain and spinal cord, your second nervous system is also made up of a network of cells called neurons that act like communication pathways from your gut, other organs and limbs to and from your brain. These neurons communicate through electrical and chemical signals to each other, with chemical signals called neurotransmitters. This system is split into a number of parts, but let's focus on the sympathetic, parasympathetic and enteric nervous systems.

Your 'fight or flight' sympathetic nervous system is responsible for your body's reaction to danger and stress. It prepares you to flee or fight by diverting blood flow to your muscles and speeding up your heart rate.

Your 'rest and digest' parasympathetic nervous system acts like the brakes to the sympathetic nervous system's accelerator. It helps to bring your body back to a state of rest and relaxation. It lowers your heart rate and encourages your digestion through your vagus nerve.

Your gut's 'second brain' enteric nervous system is a network of neurons in the walls of your gut, from your oesophagus (the tube in your throat) to your bum. It can manage your digestion without direct input from the brain and is crucial to your gut health.

Your gut is your second brain. Yes, really.

While both your gut and your brain have distinct functions – your brain isn't going to start digesting your food for you anytime soon, and your gut isn't going to start writing poetry or solving maths equations – there are some surprising similarities between the two. While your brain contains 100 billion neurons, your gut contains around 500 million, more than any other part of the body, and more than those found in a cat's brain. Your gut can function with surprising independence – its own mini CEO of its own domain – while still being under the central command of your brain. That's why it's called your second brain.

To dive a bit deeper, your gut's nervous system:

- Controls the contraction of the muscles in the walls of your gut that help to push food and liquid through your gut
- Signals your digestive juices to be released to help to break down food in your stomach and upper intestine
- Helps to make sure there's blood flowing to your digestive system so oxygen and nutrients can be delivered
- Senses not only the presence of food when the walls of the gut are physically stretched, but also the nutrients in what you've eaten
- Interacts with the immune system, with 70 per cent of your immune cells living in your gut

As there are so many functions that your enteric nervous system has to coordinate, it contains many different types of nerves that each have a different function. This allows your gut's 'second brain' enteric nervous system to have complex fine-tuned control over every aspect of how your gut works down to the tiniest detail.

The gut, the brain and the vagus nerve

Your gut's 'second brain' enteric nervous system has a direct line to your brain through a long nerve called the vagus nerve. It's the crucial connector between your gut and your brain, physically linking both organs. This two-way system helps your brain to know what's happening in your gut, particularly during digestion, helping to control how your gut works. If you want to get hold of someone asap, you don't write them a letter. You pick up the phone and give them a call. For your gut and your brain, the fastest way for them to talk to each other is through the vagus nerve that links the two together.

The vagus nerve – your gut-brain connector

The vagus nerve is one of the longest nerves in your body, reaching down from your brain to your gut and other organs in the upper part of your body, acting as your brain's main communication pathway. It's the Robin to your brain's Batman, LeFou to Gaston, or Chewbacca to Han Solo.

It's not just one nerve, but a paired nerve, a twin. The left vagus nerve runs down the left of your neck and through your upper body, and the right down the right-hand side. Aptly, vagus means 'wandering' in Latin.

The vagus nerve reaches down from the brain, branching multiple times with tendril-like nerves reaching out to your other organs like a connecting road between a capital city and other towns. It weaves to your heart, lungs and gut. If your brain wants to check in on how your heart, lungs and gut are getting on, the answers usually come back via the vagus nerve. I like to imagine your brain and your gut as twin cities that never sleep, with cars, trucks and motorbikes travelling back and forth carrying supplies, information and trade, travelling between the two on the busy connecting vagus highway. Both cities rely on each other to thrive. And like any decent high-traffic road, there are two sides allowing transport to safely drive in both directions. While you might not be surprised that the brain as the CEO of the body is communicating to your gut, you might be intrigued to know that 90 per cent of this gut-brain chat is the gut constantly feeding back information to the brain. The party really does happen in Vegas, sorry, vagus.

On the vagus nerve highway

From brain to gut . . .

Messengers from your brain carry instructions, whether it's telling your gut muscles to contract to keep moving food along your digestive system or to release different chemical signallers.

. . . and back

These messengers pick up on how tight or stretched the muscles in your gut are, they listen and relay back information from cells that act like taste testers, sampling which molecules are present in your gut at any given time to report back to the brain.

The gut microbiome and your growing brain

To really understand the connection between your gut microbiome and your brain, we need to start right at the very beginning – at your developing brain. The first years of life are critical for the ongoing development of both the gut microbiome and the brain.

The mum biome

Your brain's relationship with microbes starts before birth. Your brain development begins about two weeks after conception, the big bang where your parents kick-started the making of you. At this point you're no bigger than a tadpole, a cluster of cells growing in your mother's uterus encased in the placenta.

The placenta is a temporary organ that develops during pregnancy and helps to support the baby's growth and development until birth and is attached to the wall of the uterus. An umbilical cord connects the baby to the placenta and it's through this cord that the baby receives a nourishing soup of nutrients, oxygen and gut-derived metabolites from the mother's bloodstream. The mum's gut microbiome changes in pregnancy and shifts through the trimesters, tweaking the cocktail of microbial ingredients and energy provided according to the baby's needs,[1] helping it to grow and develop.

Many of the integral parts of the brain develop before birth, like your neural tube, most of your brain cells and the major regions of your brain. A lot of our understanding of the relationship between the gut microbiome and the brain are from studies in mice. Mice born from mothers who've been bred not to have a gut microbiome have problems with their immune system, their blood-brain barrier doesn't form properly and they struggle to regulate their appetite and stress.[2]

Ye shall not pass! The blood-brain barrier

Like your gut barrier lining protecting your body from the murky contents of your gut, your brain has a blood-brain barrier. The blood-brain barrier acts as a physical barrier protecting your brain from unwanted invaders. It's a microscopic membrane containing tight junctions or gateways.

Imagine the scene in *The Lord of the Rings* where Gandalf stands on the narrow bridge blocking the path of the giant demon beast Balrog while the hobbits and the rest of the fellowship run on through to safety. It's not too different! What can pass through? The finest brew of metabolites the brain could wish for, yes. Problematic riff-raff, that'll be a no. It's highly selective, and very good at its job. Because the gateways in the blood-brain barrier are so tiny, only small molecules can make their way in. Some large molecules like glucose, your brain's primary energy source, are also allowed in but on an invite-only basis. They must go through special doors that only open for them.

Rapidly following birth, we start to grow and shape our own gut microbiome. The mum's microbiome during pregnancy, though, has a continuing influence on the baby's brain development past birth. Transfer of a mother's vaginal microbiome (that seeds the gut microbiome of babies born by birth canal) to the guts of babies born by C-section improved their brain development at three and six months old.[3] Scientists are able to tell more clearly how well a baby's brain has developed based on their mum's microbiome, than from the baby's own gut microbiome.[4] By the age of two, the brain will have grown to 80–90 per cent of its adult volume. Yet the impact of the mum's gut microbiome during pregnancy remains. Scientists have been able to predict whether a two-year-old child is likely to have early symptoms of anxiousness if the mum had a less diverse gut microbiome during her third trimester.[5]

Microbiome and the brain in the first years of life

Your own gut microbiome is important too, even at such a young age. We can get an early understanding about this from studies in mice. In baby mice that have been bred to not have a gut microbiome, their brains don't develop properly, and particularly a part of their brain called the hippocampus that helps with learning, memory and emotions.[6]

Your hippocampus – the learning and memory librarian

Your hippocampus helps you to process and store information. Like a librarian, it loves to read and absorb new knowledge, and then files that knowledge away ready for easy retrieval when needed. You don't want to get on a librarian's wrong side, however. The hippocampus plays a critical role in your emotional responses – if it's not treated well, it can impact your mood.

Your hippocampus helps you to:

- Form and file away memories
- Learn new skills and knowledge
- Handle your emotions and stress

At two years old, the make-up of your microbiome is linked to how well you're able to interpret visual information like recognising a favourite ball or teddy bear, and how well you can express yourself with a range of vocabulary and the ability to form sentences.[7]

By three, your microbiome is linked to how well you communicate and your fine motor skills – those that help you draw or put together simple puzzles.[8] In the microbiome of children from two months to ten years old, differences in gut bacteria have been related to both how well they think and the size of multiple parts of the brain, including the reward and risk-taking centre the nucleus accumbens.[9]

It doesn't end there though. The brain continues to grow dramatically and doesn't stop until the age of about 25. We already have the majority of our brain cells when we're born, but the connections between brain cells continue to develop. Then there's a process of pruning away the connections that aren't that useful and strengthening the ones that are that continues past adolescence.

Gut microbiome and your adult brainpower

Scientists continue to connect the microbiome to how well you're able to think in adulthood. In a small study of 26-year-olds, those who had higher levels of certain 'good' gut bacteria performed significantly better at mental tasks.[10] They found it easier to learn new information and problem-solve. Your gut bacteria likely support your brain to stay active throughout life too, and are a key factor in healthy ageing. As you get older, you start to lose the diversity of your gut bacteria. Giving old mice the gut bacteria from their younger, more sprightly counterparts reversed signs of ageing in both the body and the brain, and improved their memory.[11] Brings a whole other meaning to new poo, new you.

What clouds your gut, clouds your mind

A large study looked at data from over 110,000 men and women between the ages of 25 and their mid-seventies.[12] They found that those who rarely pooed (like from constipation) had significantly worse brain function, equivalent to an extra three years of ageing. Having frequent diarrhoea was also linked to worse brain performance. In a subgroup the researchers found that this link between how often they pooed and their ability to learn and memorise was related to the make-up of their gut microbiome – highlighting the gut-brain connection.

How your gut bacteria talk to your brain: the gut-brain pathways

Your gut bacteria and your brain talk in many different ways. Some are more direct, like knocking on the door to say hello. Other bacteria are less direct; the message can pass through multiple hands and sometimes change in nature – as if by post (where it needs to be picked up by the driver, sorted, then delivered by a postman) or by word of mouth, changing as it passes from person to person.

Mice aren't humans

To understand how exactly gut bacteria talk to the brain, scientists run experiments on mice or rats. We have to be a bit careful of scientific findings from mice and rats and how it applies to humans because – I don't think I need to state the obvious here – we're not covered in fur with a long tail.

Still, there are some close genetic and basic biological similarities between mice and humans, making many findings relevant to human health, which is why science often starts with mice before moving to studying humans. It's also incredibly useful to be able to understand through mice what we would find difficult or unethical to explore in humans. All findings, though, do need to be verified in humans where possible. It is worth remembering that this is a new and developing field of research – there's a lot we still don't know yet.

On the highway to heaven – the vagus nerve

Not only does your vagus nerve reach down from the brain to your gut, it reaches specifically to the lining of your intestines, home to your gut microbiome. This is partly how your brain can influence the make-up of your gut microbiome; it can directly control the secretion of digestive juices, the absorption of food and other factors which influence which bacteria thrive or die. And your gut bacteria communicate back, too. They can influence how stressed you feel, your energy levels, your mood and so much more.

Neurotransmitters

Neurotransmitters are the messengers of your brain and nervous system; they're chemical signals that allow your neurons to communicate with each other and with other cells. They're crucial for your mood, though they have roles in other parts of the body too – you'll likely already have heard of the most famous one: serotonin, the 'happy' hormone. What might surprise you, though, is that many of your neurotransmitters are produced in both your gut and your brain. In fact, 90 per cent of serotonin and 50 per cent of dopamine is produced by your gut with help from your gut microbiome.

'90 per cent of your "happy" serotonin is produced in your gut.' You see this all over social media – but it's not quite as simple as that. The serotonin made in your gut, with the help of your gut bacteria, can't cross the blood-brain barrier to reach the brain to directly influence your mood.[13] Neurotransmitters are too large and can't fit through the tight junctions in your blood-brain barrier. They're a bit like extra-large ready-made sofas – as much as you try and pivot, you can't fit them through your front door and into your living room. They just won't go. Instead, these ready-built neurotransmitters have different purposes in your gut than they do in your brain.

- **Brain's serotonin:** Known as the 'feel-good' or 'happy' hormone, serotonin not only influences your mood and emotions but also helps to regulate your sleep and appetite. It helps to curb cravings, making you feel satisfied. It's often targeted by many antidepressant medications.

- **Gut's serotonin:** Mostly produced by the cells that line your gut (with the help of your gut bacteria). It helps with your digestion by coordinating the movement of food through your gut thanks to muscle contractions.
- **Brain's dopamine:** Your 'I like it, do it again' hormone. Often linked with pleasure, motivation and reward, dopamine is released in anticipation of, or in response to, doing something you enjoy – like eating something tasty, listening to your favourite music or seeing an adorable puppy. It encourages you to do something again.
- **Gut's dopamine:** Dopamine is also produced by the neurons of your gut's second brain. In your gut, dopamine helps to encourage food to keep moving through, and helps with other parts of your digestive processes, like the secretion of gastric juices and blood flow.
- **Brain's GABA:** GABA is your 'zen' neurotransmitter. It helps you to feel calm, lowering your stress levels and helping you to fall asleep by stopping your neurons getting over-excited.
- **Gut's GABA:** In your gut, GABA acts like a balancing act. It calms down your digestive processes so that they're not overactive beyond what's needed – like the movement of your gut muscles and gastric secretions.
- **Brain's norepinephrine:** Operating as your 'fight or flight' responder, norepinephrine (or noradrenaline) is released when you're stressed or threatened. It makes you more alert, ramps up your heart rate and prepares your body to

respond quickly to danger. Because it mobilises the brain for action it can also help you to focus and feel more energised.

- **Gut's norepinephrine:** Like serotonin and dopamine, norepinephrine also helps to influence how your gut muscles contract and relax to move food through your digestive system.

While neurotransmitters made in the gut can't cross the blood-brain barrier into the brain, scientists think that they still influence the brain indirectly – gut-produced neurotransmitters are able to signal to the brain through the immune system and the vagus nerve,[14] and could influence mood that way. It's difficult to imagine that they have no effect at all on your brain and mood – though we need more research. Scientists are rapidly connecting the dots between the gut and the brain, so perhaps time will tell.

This is where it gets interesting though.

There's exciting new scientific evidence that your gut microbiome influences how your body uses the building blocks of your mood neurotransmitters. So think of a fully formed neurotransmitter as a piece of furniture, like a sofa – the building blocks are the arms, the seat, the back and the feet of the sofa, which need to be fitted together before it's made whole. Unlike ready-made neurotransmitters, these neurotransmitter components are small enough to cross your blood-brain barrier into your brain, where they can then be made into neurotransmitters by your brain. Some of the building blocks of neurotransmitters are amino acids, like tryptophan and tyrosine, that are found in protein-rich foods such as meat, fish, eggs, beans and legumes.

Your brain can't make your 'happy' hormone serotonin without tryptophan. And you need the amino acid tyrosine to make your 'I like it, do it again' dopamine. Most of these amino acids are absorbed in your small intestine, but some make their way to your lower large intestine – to your gut bacteria. Your gut microbiome plays its part in getting your brain the supply of tryptophan it needs in a number of ways. Some gut bacteria are able to produce a small amount of tryptophan themselves. Others break down these amino acids into metabolites that can signal to your brain – either directly or indirectly.[15] Amino acids like tryptophan are also used by the body for other purposes, with the different pathways closely controlled by your gut bacteria.[16]

Let's pretend that tryptophan is flour, like you have in your kitchen. Flour can be used to make different things, like bread, cookies and cake. There are three main ways that tryptophan is used by your body. And we can think of these like three different bakeries, all of which make products out of flour – tryptophan. One bakery uses flour to make cookies (your 'happy' serotonin). Another bakery makes cakes (metabolites that signal to your brain). The third bakery is the biggest, and uses most of the flour to make two different types of bread – one is good for your brain function, but the other can cause damage to your brain and is neuro-toxic.

Your gut bacteria oversee the balance of how much flour is distributed between the bakeries (and which type of bread is made by the big bakery). And this matters for your mood and cognition – how well you think, remember and make decisions. Disruptions in this balance have been seen in depression, irritable bowel syndrome and neurological diseases.[17]

Gut hormones

The gut also makes its own hormones that regulate your digestion and your appetite. Your gut bacteria change how many gut hormones are made and shape how they work too, affecting how much or little you eat, influencing your food cravings and potentially how you experience taste.[18] The cells in the gut that produce these hormones are plugged into the enteric nervous system, rather like phone booths that your gut hormones (nudged by your gut bacteria) can use to communicate with your brain via your vagus nerve.

Immune system

Your gut bacteria and their metabolites signal to the immune cells in your brain through a number of interconnected routes. Many of your gut bacteria are nestled into mucus lining the walls of your gut, putting them in direct or near-physical contact with nerve and immune cells embedded in and behind your gut barrier lining. These nerve and immune cells are like spymasters keeping close tabs on all the goings-on, and are quick to report back to the brain any sign of danger or suspicious activity. Your gut bacteria can act as informers in this spy network. They influence how well your immune system responds to danger across your body, and how your immune cells signal to your brain. Seventy per cent of the immune system's cells live in your gut, while 15 per cent live in your brain, called microglia – your brain's resident first-aid responders. Your gut bacteria have a significant influence on the microglia from birth and through to adulthood, and can influence how effective they are at responding in times of need.

Gut metabolites

Your gut bacteria produce over 50,000 types of metabolites. Certain metabolites can influence your brain, both directly by crossing your blood-brain barrier and also indirectly through signals to your immune system and via your gut's enteric nervous system.[19] They impact your mood, behaviour and how you think. They influence how tight or open the gateways are in your blood-brain barrier, protecting your precious brain within, and can even alter levels of neurotransmitters too.[20] Short-chain fatty acids are particularly important metabolites; they are powerful anti-inflammatory molecules that can help to fight excess inflammation in the brain. Lower levels of short-chain fatty acids have been found in brain diseases like Parkinson's disease,[21] and in mice studies of Alzheimer's disease[22] and chronic stress.[23]

Short-chain fatty acids can also influence what you eat. Brain-imaging scans have shown how the short-chain fatty acid propionate can ease food cravings by making foods, like doughnuts, cake, and biscuits, less desirable.[24] They can make you feel fuller, too, through their effects on your hunger and fullness hormones, as well as helping to balance your blood-sugar levels and supporting your metabolism.[25]

What's your gut-brain conversation gut to do with it?

- Your gut and brain have a powerful two-way communication system influencing each other in how they function
- Your gut is your second brain, containing a complex network of neurons – cells that are also found in your brain in bigger amounts
- There's exciting new science that highlights how your gut bacteria play a central role in the talk between your gut and your brain
- Your gut microbiome communicates with your brain through many different ways, influencing your mood and how well you think

4. The Female Gut-Brain Connection

We're learning more about the brain and the gut than ever before. Yet despite women making up half the world's population, only a tiny 0.5 per cent of neuroscience research is female focused. And only 2 per cent of all medical research* funding is on pregnancy, childbirth and women's sexual health. This lack of understanding of the female body has caused centuries of misdiagnoses, and likely many needless deaths.

For a long time, any woman's illness was labelled as female 'hysteria'. We have Hippocrates partly to thank for that. He thought female problems were due to a 'wandering uterus', the Greek word for uterus being 'hystera' from which 'hysteria' is now derived. The cure? Sex with her husband. I mean, of course. This sexual theory held on until the thirteenth century when it was then replaced with demonic possession requiring exorcism or torture.[1] Take your pick, either sounds delightful. Later, female

---

* Black, Asian and ethnic minorities and many other groups are also underrepresented in research.

hysteria morphed to describe disorders of the mind, though the cause and cure were still seen as sexual. In extreme cases, women were even forced to undergo a hysterectomy to remove their uterus. It was only in the 1980s, just over 40 years ago, that it was finally officially taken out of the medical lexicon.

Female sex hormones

Female sex hormones like oestrogen and progesterone ebb and flow throughout a woman's life cycle. They burst onto the front stage in puberty, rise and fall during the menstrual cycle and are in fluctuating decline through the menopause. Their main tasks are to thicken the lining of the uterus and the timing of egg release.

Oestrogen or estrogen refers to a group of hormones that play a crucial role in the development and regulation of the female reproductive system. Oestrogen levels tend to rise during the first half of the menstrual cycle, by around eight times.

Progesterone is another female sex hormone that works with oestrogen to help regulate the menstrual cycle. During the second half of the menstrual cycle progesterone levels rise before falling.[2]

Your gut microbiome recycles oestrogen

Your gut microbiome is an important regulator of your oestrogen levels. When oestrogen has been used up in the body, it passes into the gut as waste, ready to be shipped out with your other mish-mash of waste as poo. Your gut bacteria, though, have other plans. They can process some of the oestrogen back into useful components, like dismantling an old car for parts. While not all of it is suitable to be reused, some of the metabolites can be absorbed back into the body to be used again. Sex hormones can also influence your microbiome; when your oestrogen levels are high your microbiome tends to be more diverse.[3]

Is the female microbiome different from the male microbiome?

While everyone has a unique gut microbiome, as personal as a fingerprint, there are different factors that can influence the make-up of your gut microbiome, like your sex. Women's microbiomes tend to have different types of bacteria than men's. These differences may have developed due to different nutrient and energy needs for growth and reproduction. There are also links between certain types of gut bacteria and where your fat is distributed on your body, with women and men tending to have fat in different places.[4]

These differences aren't only in health but can be in diseases and disorders too.

Puberty

The age at which you reach puberty depends on both your genetics and cues like diet, exercise, how much fat tissue you have, stress and more. More recently your gut microbiome has been added to the list. Antibiotic use, which can disrupt the microbiome, is linked with early puberty in girls but not boys.[5] During puberty girls' sex hormones start to run riot and their microbiome changes too. Before puberty, girls and boys microbiomes are only slightly different. But during puberty, girls' gut microbiomes gradually shift more and more to being like an adult woman's microbiome, different to the microbiome of men.

The menstrual cycle

Female sex hormones subtly influence your neuroplasticity, with small differences in the structure and size of parts of your brain depending on where you are in your menstrual cycle. The hippocampus, vital for memory, emotional regulation and learning, is particularly sensitive to female sex hormones and contains more oestrogen and progesterone receptors than many other parts of the brain. Oestrogen does a lot for your brain, aiding in the uptake of glucose to use as energy. When your oestrogen levels are high like in the lead up to ovulation your hippocampus expands in volume and your brain uses more glucose as fuel.[6] It's during this time that you have more energy, feel happier, you're in your creative flow and as sharp as a tack.

You're more likely to binge or comfort-eat in the second half of your menstrual cycle, after ovulation and just before your period. Before and during your period you're more likely to eat more, feel hungrier and have more cravings.[7]

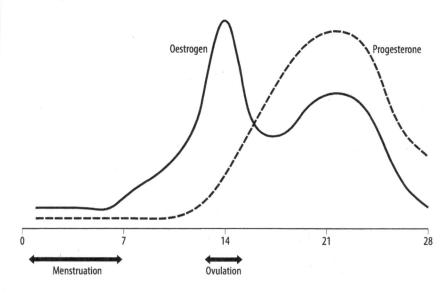

Figure 4. Sex hormones rise and fall during the menstrual cycle

Your dreams can change with your menstrual cycle

Before you ovulate, your dreams tend to be more surreal, happier and more erotic. When you're pre-menstrual, though, your dreams are longer and you're more likely to have bad dreams or nightmares[8] and this part of your cycle is linked to around a 25 per cent drop in deep non-REM sleep. This may be due to progesterone levels rising and then beginning to fall between ovulation and your period starting. Progesterone can raise your body temperature by 0.3–0.5°C, impacting your sleep when your core temperature normally drops a little. You may want to focus on staying cool during this time to sleep better.

Fertility and pregnancy

Getting pregnant seems to happen spontaneously for some, and to the sadness and frustration of many couples, with time, effort and difficulty for others. Fertility is a complex issue, and while there are many factors at play that determine how fertile someone is, we now understand that your gut microbiome is also involved in both male and female fertility.[9] If you do then fall pregnant, a mum-to-be's microbiome is linked to the baby's growth and health and whether the baby is born preterm or not.[10] Mums with a lower diversity of gut bacteria and fewer of certain 'good' bacteria are more likely to deliver their baby early.[11] Let's acknowledge though that being pregnant often includes changes in appetite and nausea – so if you're pregnant don't beat yourself up if you're struggling to eat many gut-friendly foods, and just do what you can.

Menopause

Menopause is the natural biological ending of menstruation and fertility, usually taking place between 45 and 55 years old. Officially it's defined as your periods stopping for at least 12 successive months, though this definition isn't the most helpful. The shutting shop of your ovaries rarely happens overnight; instead, women experience many years of bumpy erratic decline of their sex hormones. Seventy-five per cent of women experience symptoms during menopause, most of which affect the brain, including brain fog, fatigue, insomnia and hot flushes, which are thought to be triggered in the hypothalamus – the part of your brain that helps to regulate your body temperature. After menopause your brain's neurons grow used to not relying on oestrogen's helping hand with glucose uptake for energy, but in the lead-up to and during menopause hormones are crashing up and down leaving your brain cells temporarily deprived of oestrogen and so less efficient at uptaking glucose, but without enough time to fully adapt. While this could be a factor in some of menopause's brain symptoms, there's likely other factors too that we still don't fully understand yet – and this is probably why there's conflicting evidence whether hormone replacement therapy helps (or not) with cognition.[12] Though it can help improve menopausal mood swings, hot flushes and night sweats.

Like puberty, during menopause your microbiome shifts again. Whereas in puberty a girl's microbiome shifts to being more like the microbiome of an adult woman, in menopause the microbiome shifts to being more similar to a man's microbiome.[13] Women in Asia tend to experience fewer menopause symptoms than Western women, and this could be down to their gut microbiome. In Japan, 50–60 per cent of women have certain bacteria in their gut that are able to break down and use oestrogen-like compounds found in some plant foods like tofu and soybeans, compared to only 30 per cent of women from the US.[14]

Gut story

A newspaper featured a man who had faecal microbiota transplants from his mum in an attempt to improve his symptoms of inflammatory bowel disease. While his symptoms dramatically improved, he also started to experience his mum's menopause symptoms of hot flushes and brain fog.[15] Scientists need to test this to see if this is true or not, but it's interesting all the same.

What have female hormones gut to do with it?

- Your gut microbiome can recycle some parts from oestrogen to be used again
- Men and women tend to have slight differences in their gut microbiome
- Oestrogen helps your brain to uptake glucose, its primary fuel
- Sex hormone levels can influence your mood, how well you think, food cravings and more
- Your gut microbiome may influence how you experience symptoms during menopause

5. The Male Gut-Brain Connection

Men have a different gut microbiome to women. It's these sex-based differences that may explain how some symptoms or diseases are more common in men than in women, and vice versa. This might not only be relevant to gut diseases but also some autoimmune and brain diseases and conditions. For example, what types of gut bacteria you have has been suggested to be either protective or harmful depending on your sex for conditions like depression and chronic fatigue syndrome.[1,2]

Testosterone and male fertility

Both the gut microbiome and male sex hormones like testosterone have the ability to affect each other. Feeding older, male mice probiotic yoghurt gave them bigger balls, they grew more hair and their levels of testosterone were raised to levels similar to those of their youthful counterparts.[3] When male mice – how to put this lightly – had their balls chopped off, their gut microbiome shifted to being more similar to the microbiome of female mice.[4] More recently the gut microbiome is thought to be able to trespass into men's balls and potentially regulate how much sperm is produced.[5] Transplanting the gut microbiome from fibre-fed healthy mice to sick mice doubled their sperm count and boosted their sperm swimming power, a sign of healthy egg-seeking sperm, by 20-fold.[6] There's a testicular microbiome, too, containing a diverse range of bacteria[7] that helps to support a healthy reproductive system.

Sex

During sex between a man and a woman, there's a fair amount of exchanging of fluids – allowing for the transfer of both testicular and vaginal microbiomes between partners, causing short-term changes to the resident microbiome. There's a larger transfer from the vaginal microbiome than from the testicular (and urethra) microbiome.[8] The vaginal microbiome is fairly resistant to change, but a man's urethra microbiome can be reshaped, with some types of bacteria from the vaginal microbiome remaining.[9] As can be expected, not using protection during sex leads to the most transfer of microbes.

Does sexual preference make a difference to your gut microbiome? It seems so, but we don't yet know why. Men who have sex with men are more likely to have a more diverse gut microbiome than men who have sex with women.[10] But that could be due to many factors, like diet and lifestyle habits, and more.

What have male hormones gut to do with it?

- A man's gut microbiome can influence their levels of testosterone and vice versa
- It's thought that the gut microbiome may be able to influence how many sperm are produced and how healthy they are
- During sex between a man and woman there's an exchange of microbes between the vaginal microbiome and the microbiome from the urethra and testes (balls)
- Men who have sex with men tend to have a more diverse gut microbiome, but we don't know why this is yet and could be related to differences in lifestyle and eating habits

6. The Diverse Gut-Brain – ADHD, Autism and Neurodiversity

Just like our microbes, our brains aren't one-size-fits-all. We all experience and interact with the world in different ways, thinking differently, learning differently and behaving differently. Could it be that this neurodiversity is in part thanks to our microbes?

Scientists who followed a group of babies from birth to twenty years old found striking differences in the gut microbiomes of the babies that later developed neurodevelopmental diagnoses like Attention Deficit Hyperactivity Disorder (ADHD), autism and intellectual disabilities. Their early microbiomes were different depending on their diagnosis too, but there were also common themes like having less 'good' gut bacteria.[1]

ADHD

There's no single simple test to diagnose ADHD. The symptoms can usually be grouped into two types of behaviours, including difficulty concentrating and focusing, with a short attention span, and impulsiveness and hyperactivity, like being unable to sit still and acting without thinking. Five per cent of adults and over 7 per cent of children have ADHD, and often also other differences, like autism. In the past few years there's been increasing interest in the gut-brain connection in ADHD, particularly as gut issues, like constipation, are common. Mice studies have suggested that the microbiome might be related to some of the behavioural differences in both ADHD and autism.[2] Transplanting the microbiome from people with ADHD into mice resulted in changes to the mice's behaviour, brain structure and function. People with ADHD also have a different make-up of their gut bacteria than those without.[3] We don't know if ADHD is partly caused by the gut microbiome, but it does highlight that the microbiome might be relevant in ADHD.

Autism

Autism is a life-long condition that can affect how people interact with others, and can vary widely from person to person depending on strengths, needs and challenges. The biggest struggle for many autistic people is communicating and interacting with other people; this can range from not speaking at all to not understanding some facial expressions. There can also be repetitive movements, sensitivity to light and noises, and anxiety.

Might the microbiome be involved in autism? Like in those with ADHD, autistic people are more likely to have gut problems, like constipation and diarrhoea. Children with autism have different microbiomes too.[4] It could be, though, that this is because of picky eating, which is common in autism. While we know the microbiome is involved in the brain and behaviour, whether the microbiome is a factor in why someone is autistic is still up for debate for now. There are hints this might be the case and with time the gut may provide some answers.

What's neurodiversity gut to do with it?

- Both ADHD and autism tend to have different microbiomes and gut issues
- Transplanting the microbiome of people with ADHD into mice changed the mice's behaviour
- For those who are autistic, the differences in gut microbiome could be more related to being picky eaters and the influence that diet has on the gut microbiome
- Is there a role of the microbiome in neurodiversity? We need more research before we know

PART TWO – THE GUT-BRAIN HANGOVER

7. Starving Gut Bacteria

The microbe extinction

We have an unseen crisis. We are drastically losing the diversity of our gut microbes – our closest and oldest allies. Our gut bacteria are disappearing. Tribal cultures that have lifestyles that are similar to our ancestors' have a far greater diversity of gut bacteria than we do. The modern way that we live and eat doesn't make a happy gut microbiome. The Hadza people in northern Tanzania are one of the last hunter-gatherer tribes in Africa. They don't mass farm cattle or sheep; instead they hunt for their food and forage for a wide diversity of edible plants. They eat more than enough fibre, spend a lot of time in nature and are very active. For anthropologists and now microbiologists, they are a modern link to a way of living that has long been lost for most of us. Compared to the microbiomes of the Hadza tribes, we've lost over 124 types of bacteria – vanished from our guts.[1]

A progressively depleted and disrupted microbiome makes it easier for the 'bad' bacteria to dominate. Scientists think that our depleted and disrupted microbiomes could partly explain the accelerated rise of asthma, allergies, intolerances, autoimmune conditions and inflammation-related brain diseases in the last century.

What you eat is one of the most powerful tools you can use to change your gut microbiome. For better, or for worse. And what your gut bacteria need above all else is fibre. In your home you likely have a fridge and cupboards that are stocked with food, so that when you're hungry, you have something to eat or cook close at hand. Your gut bacteria, though, can't pop to the shops to pick up more groceries when they're running low. They rely on you to deliver the food they need to survive and flourish.

If they don't get enough of the fibre-rich food they need, they start to die, or in a bid for survival, start to chew the furniture. That's you. There are two layers of slimy mucus lubricating your insides and coating the gut barrier lining of your intestines. The outer layer is home to many of your gut bacteria. The inner layer is bacteria-free – your body's first line of defence against the murky matter in your gut, a protective barrier continuously renewed by the hour by your gut's skin cells. Fibre-starved bacteria can chew through this inner lining of mucus to reach your skin cells, triggering your immune system into red alert. Danger, your body says! Your gut barrier lining can become inflamed, damaged, and susceptible to 'bad' bacteria leaking from your gut into your circulation.

Fibre-famished

We are in a fibre crisis. We need at least 30g of fibre a day for health, if not more, yet most of us are barely scratching the surface. At best we're reaching just over half of what we need, averaging 15g in the US and 18g in the UK – that's less than the recommended amount for a five-year-old.

This fibre gap has detrimental consequences for your community of gut bacteria and beyond. Most of the health benefits from fibre have been attributed to feeding your gut bacteria, and the metabolites they produce. After all, we can't break down fibre without them. And this connection between fibre and your health is powerful – it's linked to a 30 per cent lower risk of death[2] and lowers your odds for many diseases too, like heart disease, stroke, bowel cancer and type II diabetes. Fibre is the closest thing we have to a superfood. By not eating enough fibre your gut bacteria aren't able to produce those powerful short-chain fatty acids that fight excess inflammation, provide energy to many of your cells and exert their influence across your body, from managing your blood-sugar levels to your mood. Without enough fibre you're more likely to be constipated, and to feel sluggish and tired.

On ultra-processed foods

Minutes tick past fast in our busy lives, and there are always too many things to do. I don't know about you, but there will always be a part of me that wishes I had my own vegetable garden. For most of us, it's far more practical to dash to the supermarket each week, filling our trolleys with sustenance for the days ahead. Two rows of fresh produce in a huge supermarket followed by rows and rows of items in packets. That's not necessarily a bad thing. Packaged food like canned beans, dried pastas and tinned tomatoes give us variety all year round, help to limit food waste and can often be more or just as nutritious as their fresh counterparts. And what a time saver too. Jars of artichokes, olives and pickled onions, and rices, quinoa and buckwheat bagged up and ready to go. Each row contains hundreds of foods, so many to try. A treasure trove of new taste experiences. But then, suddenly, there's a wall of just one type of food. Advertising splashed over boxes of slightly different yet similar sugar-sweetened cereals, with jumping tigers, monkeys and bold colours. Another whole aisle of every flavour of crisps, then multiple types of biscuits, and then a wall of fizzy drinks. Ever realised that the supermarkets purposely place eggs at the back of the supermarket so that you have to walk past and through all the aisles, in the hope that you'll be tempted to buy more? And the products with the biggest profit margin? Ultra-processed foods. Cheap to make, with a long shelf life – but here's the kicker – they're often low in fibre and other nutrients. Though, delicious – yes.

These foods are fine in small amounts but the problem is that we're eating so many of them. And this means we're eating less fibre and fewer nutrients for our health and gut bacteria. Ultra-processed foods account for nearly 60 per cent of the foods we eat in the UK.[3] I have mixed feelings about classifying foods as 'ultra-processed', as there are flaws in how foods are classified this way – I prefer to look more at how nutrient dense a food is instead – but it's the trendy term of the day so let's stick with it for now.

What is an ultra-processed food?

The ultra-processed food categories* are part of the NOVA classification,[4] designed by researchers to look at the overall diets of big groups of people. It wasn't, though, designed to help you know what to put in your shopping basket. Not all ultra-processed foods are made equal health-wise either.† For the most part, though, 'ultra-processed' is another term to group foods that are mostly less nutrient dense, and higher in salt, sugar and fat – which if you have too much too often, aren't great for your health.

Ultra-processed foods tend to be mass-marketed, have a long shelf life, a long list of ingredients, and are wrapped in packaging. If they contain additives, these additives aren't there to only help preserve the food – they are added to make the food tastier.

Ultra-processed food examples: Fizzy soft drinks, sweet or salty packaged snacks, cookies, biscuits, cakes, sweetened breakfast cereals, sausages, burgers, hot dogs, bread (made in a factory).

---

* Officially there are four NOVA categories: ultra-processed foods, processed foods, processed culinary ingredients, and unprocessed or minimally processed foods. I have excluded the 'processed culinary ingredients' group here as far fewer foods fall into this category and tend to be eaten in smaller amounts, e.g. butter, extra-virgin olive oil and honey.

† Studies have found that some foods that fall in the ultra-processed category are linked to either better or borderline effects on health, like ultra-processed breads and cereal products.[5,6] A lot of the evidence for the negative health effects of ultra-processed foods seems to be driven by sugar-sweetened drinks and highly processed meat products.

Processed foods

It can be hard to tell if a food is ultra-processed or simply processed. Processed foods are usually foods that have been preserved through canning, smoking, curing, pickling and cooking to give them a longer shelf life. They tend to keep their original identity (e.g. tinned tomatoes still look like tomatoes). Processing food allows us to have variety in our diets. They tend to be more nutrient dense than ultra-processed foods. Food processing can also make some food healthier for us, like the antioxidant lycopene is higher in tinned tomatoes compared to fresh ones.

Processed food examples: Tinned tomatoes, tinned tuna, jarred artichokes, freshly made unpackaged breads (home-made or in a bakery) and cheeses.

Minimally processed or unprocessed

This is an easier one. Minimally processed means the edible parts of fruits, vegetables, grains and meat that haven't been altered much, if at all, by industrial processing. They might be ground into flour or steamed or fermented. Having lots of minimally processed foods is great for your health.

Low-processed food examples: Fresh, frozen, cooked or dried fruits, vegetables and grains, beans and legumes, sweet potatoes and potatoes, pasteurised milk, plain fruit juice, herbs and spices, yoghurt, tea and coffee.

Tastiness in disguise

Many ultra-processed foods contain additives like emulsifiers and sweeteners. Emulsifiers help to bind foods together that won't normally mix, like water and oil. They're also used to give you a smooth, rich mouthfeel or to keep a food's softness, like in bread. Emulsifiers can be natural or man-made ingredients. Some come from soybeans and seaweed, and others are copycats, manufactured in a lab. All the additives on the market in the UK, US and the EU have been tested for safety even at high doses. Most of the safety studies, though, have been on mice, focusing on whether emulsifiers are able to damage our genes and potentially cause cancer, and not on their potential impact on gut bacteria. You mostly don't absorb additives and so they pass through to your lower large intestine where they're likely to interact with your gut microbiome. Of twenty emulsifiers investigated by scientists, modelled in fake human guts, only two synthetic emulsifiers, carboxymethylcellulose (E466) and polysorbate 80, profoundly impacted gut bacteria leading to inflammation, though many of the others were still found to have a harmful effect but on a smaller scale.[7] Luckily, these two emulsifiers are rarely used, with E466 found in only 1.4% and polysorbate 80 in 0.06% of 6,642 emulsifier-containing foods surveyed in the UK in 2023.[8] Other commonly used emulsifiers we don't know enough about yet, or don't appear to be harmful, like the most common emulsifier, lecithin. In short, it's likely that if you're only occasionally eating foods that contain emulsifiers you're unlikely to be doing any harm to your gut microbiome, particularly if you're eating plenty of nutrient-dense, fibre-rich foods like fruit, vegetables and whole grains. At the end of the day, it seems it's the type, dose and frequency that matters most – with eating a lot of emulsifiers linked to inflammation in a study of 588 people over a year.[9]

Over sugared

Our brains are wired to seek out pleasure. To cavemen, the richness of fat and the sweetness of sugar signalled nutrients and energy. How to encourage us to eat more of it for our survival? Make it enjoyable, make it rewarding. Now, though, it can mean the opposite. Foods that are high in sugar and fat tend to be less nutrient dense, so while you get a heady sense of joy from eating it you're not getting the nutrition with it. Sugar is all in the dose. It's recommended to eat no more than 30g of free sugars a day (see Chapter 17 for more detail), yet in the UK we are eating double this amount, and triple in the US, mostly from sugary foods and drinks. When you eat sugar most of it is absorbed in your small intestine before it even reaches your gut microbiome in your large intestine. But if you eat too much sugar it can overflow into your lower intestine and encourage 'bad' bacteria to thrive. Not a problem occasionally; your gut bacteria are pretty resilient. But if your day-to-day diet is made up of mostly sugary foods and little fibre-rich fruit, veg, whole grains and the like, then this could contribute to an unhappy gut microbiome.

Does sugar feed unhappiness and anxiety? Eating too much added sugar is linked to worse mental health. People who eat more than 67 grams of added sugar a day have a 23 per cent greater chance of developing a mental health disorder after five years than those who eat less than 40g a day.[10]

Too sweet to be true?

Artificial sweeteners make food and drinks taste sweet without the added calories or the blood-sugar response you'd get from sugar. How good are they for your health, though? There's plenty of unwarranted fearmongering around artificial sweeteners. No, they don't give you cancer, but it's now believed that artificial sweeteners are not as inert for your gut microbiome as we originally thought, though like emulsifiers it likely matters what type of sweetener and how much, rather than making sweeping statements across the board. Neither sucralose[11] nor saccharin,[12] for example, affect your gut microbiome. Some are linked to changes in your microbiome that affect your blood-sugar levels, though this effect seems to be highly individual and can vary from person to person.[13] Should we switch back to sugar over artificial sweeteners? Not yet – particularly if sweet foods make up a large proportion of your diet, or you have bad blood sugar control like in type II diabetes.

Who's the real culprit?

Ultra-processed food is really another way of saying food that is less nutrient dense – it just happens to be the new trendy way to say it. Not eating enough nutrient-dense foods is responsible for more deaths worldwide than any other risk factor,[14] and is linked to many diseases.

Your brain and gut need a variety of nutrients, not just fibre. A study of over 230 prisoners provided the perfect setting to showcase how our brain needs nutrition to function well. Prison food is known to be bog-standard fare, decidedly not fine-dining and sadly often lacking in complete nutrition. In the study prisoners were randomised into two groups: one group took a daily multi-vitamin and a tasteless omega-3 supplement, and the other a placebo for a minimum of two weeks. Those who took the placebo – nothing changed. Those who took the supplements, however, had dramatically less antisocial behaviour, with over 25 per cent fewer offences.[15] Supplements, though, contain only a handful of nutrients – a tiny fraction of the 26,000 biochemicals found in food.[16]

What've bacteria gut to do with it?

- Your gut bacteria rely heavily on fibre – yet we're eating way too little of it
- Not eating enough fibre has detrimental consequences on your gut microbiome and your health
- We're eating too many foods that are less nutrient-dense, depriving your gut bacteria of the fibre they love and many nutrients your body needs to thrive
- Some emulsifiers and sweeteners may have a negative impact on your gut bacteria but those are often only present in a few foods
- Eating emulsifiers and sweeteners doesn't seem to be a problem for now if you're eating plenty of nutrient-dense foods too

8. A Sanitised Gut Isn't a Happy One

Clean in the wrong way and disconnected from nature

We live in a microbial world. And at the same time, we're obsessed with cleanliness. There's no doubt that sanitation and hygiene are crucial to health and well-being. This cleanliness has given us clean drinking water, kept disease-spreading rodents out of our homes and prevented the spread of dangerous bacteria through hand-washing and good personal hygiene. It's also far more pleasant too. Gone are the days of the Middle Ages when we bathed once a year and revelled in our own stink. To start with, hygiene was about attractiveness. Mostly thanks to Britain being invaded by the Vikings, who quickly stole the hearts of British women thanks to their weekly baths, trimmed beards and combed hair. They must have smelt like roses in comparison. It wasn't until 1867 that we realised how revolutionary a sterile environment could be for health and disease, when the surgeon Joseph Lister published a scientific article on the importance of handwashing and killing germs during surgery. Before, you could die from a simple operation. Lister's advice revolutionised medi-cal care – patients survived, recovering well and fast – and sterilisation became common practice.

Have we gone too far with our anti-germ obsession? We've tarred all bacteria with the same brush, assuming that they are all bad and harmful. While infectious diseases caused by harmful bacteria have declined, there's also been a rapid increase in auto-immune diseases where the immune system malfunctions and mistakenly attacks healthy cells, tissues and organs – and the gut microbiome plays a crucial role in developing and regulating a healthy immune system.

There's a theory that our distaste for dirt and our sparklingly clean homes, in tandem with our increasingly sedentary and urban lifestyles, mean we don't come into contact with enough different types of 'good' bacteria that we need for our gut micro-biome. We're separated from nature, the microbe-rich soil, the fresh outside air and the multitude of animals that coexist on this planet alongside us. We need to be exposed to these microbes. They help to populate our gut microbiome. They stay on or visit for a few days and pass on through. They help to train our immune system to recognise the 'good' guys from the 'bad'. Our immune system relies on its own personal Interpol, the inter-national criminal police organisation that keeps tabs on known wrongdoers. It helps our immune system to identify and cata-logue who's the harmful pathogen vs the common civilian and to recognise them if and when they appear again to launch an appropriate counter-response.

Antibiotics against bacteria

Antibiotics are one of the most important medical discoveries ever. In just over 100 years they've changed the face of modern medicine and added over 20 years to our lifespan.[1] They've saved the lives of millions of people around the world. Antibiotics are used to treat or prevent some types of bacterial infections, and work by killing or preventing the growth of harmful bacteria. They're prescribed when the infection is too strong for the immune system to overcome. For a long time, scientists only focused on the harmful bacteria and didn't think much of the others. When you swallow an antibiotic, it enters your gut and is digested and absorbed into your body in the same way that nutrients are absorbed from food. From there it circulates around your body to reach the infected area. However, it's entering via your gut, and one of the side effects of antibiotics is that they significantly affect the bacteria in your gut too; if they're broad-spectrum antibiotics, it can be akin to a mass extinction event. It can take months for them to recover, often long after the course of antibiotics is finished.

If you have a bacterial infection and you're prescribed antibiotics by a healthcare professional, then you should take them. By not taking them, the bacterial infection could be more harmful to you and your gut microbiome. What we all need to be careful of, though, is the detrimental effect on your gut microbiome of excessive antibiotic use and particularly unnecessary antibiotics – for example, antibiotics don't work for viral infections like most common coughs. In the first five years of life this is particularly critical as a fragile window of the developing

microbiome, and babies or children exposed to excessive antibiotics during this time may experience long-term problems with
a higher risk of asthma, allergies and autoimmune diseases, and
are more likely to have anxiety or depression later in life.[2,3] As
adults, long-term use of antibiotics in mid-life is also linked to
poorer memory, thinking speed and concentration even seven
years later.[4]

Need to take antibiotics? Here's what to do

Your gut microbiome can take six months to recover and
even then, that recovery may not be complete[5] but it
should for the most part be back to business and not too
much worse off. What can you do to best protect your
microbiome?

Probiotics might not be the answer: Probiotics are
types of bacteria that have been shown to have a specific
health effect, and are often available as a supplement or
drink. Various studies have shown that taking probiotics
with antibiotics can have a mild benefit, for example in preventing antibiotic-induced diarrhoea. Sometimes, though,
probiotic supplements can be harmful. A study found that
taking probiotics after a course of antibiotics slowed the
speed at which the gut microbiome recovered, possibly
outweighing the other potential benefits.[6] This might,
however, be down to the type of probiotic used and we
need more research to know for sure.

Fibre, fibre, fibre: What you eat influences the make-up
of your microbiome. Instead of taking probiotics in the

months following a course of antibiotics you may want to be more gut-centric in what you eat and do. Fibre in particular has been shown to protect the microbiome before, during and after antibiotics.[7]

In the future: The most rapid recovery after antibiotics could be from a faecal microbiota transplant (FMT) of your own poo. Study participants who did this found that the differences in their microbiome disappeared in as little as a day.[8] It's important to note that this is still an experimental and evolving procedure and is not recommended outside of the supervision of a gastroenterologist.

Microbes and the environment

Climate change is significantly disrupting the environment that microbes live in, from soil to water to the air we breathe. We're constantly interacting with our microbe-rich environment; everything we touch, there's a transfer of microbes back and forth. More flooding and intense rainfall may leave us with more bacterial gut infections by contaminating the water supply. There are also other stressors to our gut microbiome, like breathing in air pollution. Air pollution has been shown to change the make-up of the gut microbiome to produce dangerous metabolites, disrupting the protective gut barrier lining and triggering excess inflammation. Air pollution can also have serious effects on how your brain works, and is linked to behavioural changes, mental health issues and neurodegenerative diseases.[9]

What've sanitised bacteria gut to do with it?

- We're losing the diversity of our gut bacteria with potentially drastic health consequences
- We're spending less time outside in microbe-rich environments, like in nature
- Excessive and unnecessary antibiotics kill off many gut bacteria and can take six months or more to recover
- Climate change and pollution both negatively impact the gut microbiome too

9. In a Lonely Body, Lonely . . . Gut?

Are we getting lonelier? How many friends we have and how social we are has steadily declined over the past two decades.[1] And this is a problem for your gut microbiome, because we also get new bacteria from those we interact and live with – sharing bacteria back and forth when we hug, shake hands and kiss. In 1990, only 3 per cent of people in a US survey said they felt lonely often. Fast-forward to 2023 and 17 per cent of adults in the US reported they felt lonely a lot, though thankfully less than during the COVID-19 pandemic.[2] The shift to online working hasn't particularly helped – though it does get the laundry done during the week rather than at the weekend. Those who are lonely tend to have lower diversity of gut bacteria, often linked with poor health.[3] Being socially isolated isn't good for your brain either; it increases your risk of dementia by 50 per cent[4] and you're more likely to experience depression and anxiety. Loneliness has serious health consequences.

Some scientists think that certain gut bacteria may have evolved ways to encourage their human 'hosts' to be more social to expand their bacterial empire from person to person.[5]

Socialising releases a powerful neuropeptide called oxytocin, often called the cuddle or love hormone, helping you feel relaxed, extroverted and at ease with others. From studies in animals, certain gut bacteria are thought to be involved in the release of oxytocin, possibly influencing how much you like being around other people. Human studies have even found links between gut bacteria and personality traits like how conscientious you are and how much empathy you have.[6]

By interacting with others, you're not only interacting with those people but also with their trillions of microbes too. If you think how many times you touch your face or mouth, or pick up food to eat with your hands, you're constantly introducing new bacteria from outside into your mouth, and potentially your gut. Bacteria inhabit virtually every part of your body, inside and out. They're constantly being shared with those you're in contact with, to such an extent that your gut microbiome is more similar to that of those you live with, than those you're related to.[7] It seems we share more than a roof over our heads, or pints of milk in the fridge. The longer you live with someone, the more similar your gut microbiome can grow to be. The more you kiss someone the more alike are the types of bacteria you both have in your mouths, called your oral microbiome. Kissing for ten seconds or longer can transfer 80 million bacteria,[8] both 'good' and 'bad'. While some bacteria pass through like transient visitors, like in the gut, others can comfortably set up home on the tongue's surface for long-term colonisation. In the true academic vein of making anything related to intimacy sound slightly awkward, researchers proposed 'that the first kiss serves as a useful mate-assessment function' by being able to taste (or not) certain 'compatible' chemicals in the other's saliva, some of which are produced by the tongue's bacterial community.[9] Maybe in the future, instead of swiping through dating apps for a love match, we'll be asking our bacteria.

What've connection and socialising gut to do with it?

- Loneliness is linked to lower gut microbiome diversity
- Interacting with others helps introduce new bacteria into your gut microbiome
- We're constantly sharing microbes back and forth between one another – through skin contact, kissing and more
- Your gut microbiome is more similar to that of the person you live with than family members; the longer you live with someone the more similar your microbiomes grow to be

10. Gut-Brain Burnout

Stress – that all-too-familiar feeling that seems embedded in our everyday life, though we wish it wasn't. In the largest and most comprehensive UK-wide stress survey commissioned by the Mental Health Foundation in 2018,[1] three quarters of British adults said that they had felt so stressed at some point in the last year that they were completely overwhelmed and unable to cope. When you feel stressed, you can feel it in your whole body – racing heartbeat, muscles tensing, a tightness gripping your chest, grinding teeth and a flip-flopping stomach. It's your brain's survival system kicking in to alert and save you from danger. Your 'fight-or-flight' sympathetic system takes over – directing blood flow away from your gut and digestion to your muscles, ready to run or fight. Pretty useful when you want to avoid being a crocodile's afternoon snack, but when you're working through today's work emails or walking down the street – not so much.

Occasional stress is fine – it actually helps you to perform well at a job interview or when giving a presentation. Your body recovers fast and returns to normal. It's repeated long-term stress that can have drastic effects on your gut microbiome and your health. When your body is constantly humming with stress, like a train repeatedly hurtling down the same track, the station master – the conductor of your body's various processes – struggles to synchronise with the other 'trains', disrupting the usual timetable. Your 'fight-or-flight' sympathetic system remains overly active and your 'rest-and-digest' parasympathetic system, the brake, struggles to bring your body back to its balanced state. For your gut, this makes it harder to digest your food. It affects your gut bacteria and weakens your gut barrier lining, changing which metabolites they produce and how tryptophan is used in your body.[2] And when your body's stress responses are triggered too often and for too long it can alter how your immune system responds – a train can fall off the tracks – triggering excess inflammation that often marks the first stages of health problems and certain diseases. Chronic stress is linked with cancer, type II diabetes and heart disease[3] and can lead to mental health conditions like depression and anxiety disorders.

Burnout check-in

Repeated stress can lead to burnout. Burnout is where you're emotionally exhausted, tired, drained and feel detached with a loss of satisfaction. The more questions below you answer with 'yes' the more you are suffering from burnout and may need to seek support.

- Do you feel tired or drained most of the time? Yes/No
- Do you feel detached and alone? Yes/No
- Do you feel overwhelmed? Have small problems become mammoth? Yes/No

- Do you feel like you're procrastinating and taking longer to get things done? Yes/No
- Do you feel like you're constantly on edge and at breaking point? Yes/No

Stress and your gut-brain connection

Your gut microbiome can help you to handle stress. Your gut bacteria and their metabolites can neutralise stress-related harmful molecules, acting a little like that calming rational friend playing mediator in an argument. But if your microbiome is disrupted it's not able to do this as well, if at all. Again, studies in mice can give us an early window into how stress rapidly affects the gut microbiome. One way to stress out a mouse? You make it sniff cat poo. Mice that are more resilient to stress have different gut microbiomes to mice who don't cope well with stress.[4] When you're stressed often and for long periods of time, the 'good' bacteria can struggle to thrive, and the 'bad' bacteria can start to take over. And the next time you're stressed, it isn't able to help you cope with it as well. And the cycle repeats. A healthy microbiome can recover after a stressful situation but when it becomes disrupted it slowly loses the ability to bounce back, like a piece of elastic that loses its spring.[5] It doesn't matter how well you're eating, if you're stressed often, your gut microbiome just doesn't like it.

Your brain is usually protected by the blood-brain barrier from damaging molecules, but under repeated stress it can become leaky, allowing harmful inflammatory molecules to make their way through.[6] Your hippocampus, the brain's learning and memory centre, is particularly vulnerable. Prolonged high levels of the stress hormone cortisol have been linked to mood disorders and a shrinking hippocampus.[7] Repeated stress can manipulate your neurotransmitters, including your 'happy' hormone serotonin, changing your mood and how well you're able to think. When you're under stress certain parts of your brain are activated that override your usual ability to make rational decisions. It's understandable, then, how chronic stress is related to burnout and cognitive decline[8] and an increased risk of neurodegenerative conditions like Alzheimer's disease.

Stress and emotional eating

Stress can change the way you eat too. I don't know about you, but it certainly makes me immediately want to start scratching around the cupboards and fridge. Although, not everyone wants to dive into a plate of biscuits, with 40 per cent of people eating more and 40 per cent eating less when they're stressed.[9] For those that do get the urge to stress-eat, it's to use food as a way to soothe uncomfortable emotions. When you're stressed your rising cortisol levels are thought to affect certain neurons, making them more sensitive to tasty foods and triggering the motivation to eat, even without feeling physically hungry.

Stress can make eating well for your gut microbiome hard. When in 2018 the UK government surveyed over 4,600 people, nearly half said that they ate too much or ate less healthily because of stress.[10] We don't talk enough about how stress and emotions can drive food choices. Those who often feel lonely tend to have more brain activity in parts of the brain linked to food cravings, with dampened activity in other parts related to self-control.[11]

Unhappy mind, unhappy gut

Depression: While the cause of depression is complex and can be different from person to person, studies, mostly in animals, are illuminating how the microbiome may impact certain features of some types of depression, like inflammation and stress.[12] As with many other disorders and diseases of the brain, people with depression tend to have a different microbiome, with lower diversity and more pro-inflammatory 'bad' bacteria. They also tend to have lower levels of certain bacteria that are involved in producing your 'I like it, do it again' neurotransmitter dopamine.[13] Scientists have even transferred depressive symptoms from humans to rats by transplanting the microbiome of human donors with depression into rats, changing their behaviour.[14] Certain gut bacteria can also change how well antidepressants work – some types can help to make antidepressants work better, while others do the opposite.[15]

Anxiety: There's a strong link between anxiety and gut symptoms; for some people stress and anxiety can make them urgently need to dash to the loo. There are also microbiome differences in those with anxiety compared to people without. Anxiety traits have also been transplanted between mice by switching the microbiome of different mice, with the anxious and timid mice becoming bolder and more outgoing and vice versa.[16] Studies that have fed participants prebiotic fibres have shown changes in anxiety symptoms, particularly for those with a more anxious personality type.[17]

Irritable bowel syndrome: Irritable bowel syndrome (IBS) is a disorder of gut-brain interactions – related to how your gut, microbiome and brain communicate with each other. It's a collection of gut symptoms, including recurring abdominal pain and diarrhoea or constipation (or both). There's a clear link between the gut and the brain in IBS. Stress often triggers symptoms; 38 per cent of people with IBS have anxiety, and over 27 per cent have depression – double the rates in those without IBS.[18] There's an altered make-up of their gut microbiome, and some probiotics can help to ease certain symptoms. Non-diet strategies targeting the brain, like gut-directed hypnotherapy and yoga, have also been shown to be just as effective for managing IBS symptoms as dietary treatment using the low FODMAP diet.[19] Dietary changes for people with IBS can also improve their mental health, with a Mediterranean diet improving both gut and psychological symptoms.[20]

Psychobiotics: A lot of the evidence that really kick-started scientific excitement about the connection between the gut microbiome and the brain is from research on probiotic supplements – so-called psychobiotics. Now, more and more trials are being done in humans. While not all psychobiotics have had a consistent effect, there have been many studies that have shown they can have anti-anxiety and antidepressant properties, clearly highlighting the gut-brain connection. Other psychobiotic studies have highlighted the role of the gut microbiome in brain function and performance – for example, treating mice with antibiotics, killing many of their gut bacteria, slowed down their brains' ability to make new brain cells, yet it sped up again when they were given probiotics. For more on probiotics, see the FAQs.

What've stress and mood gut to do with it?

- Your body is able to adapt under short-term stress. Occasional stress isn't harmful and can help you perform better
- Your gut microbiome is particularly sensitive to long-term stress – stress changes the make-up of your gut microbiome while a healthy gut microbiome can help you handle stress
- Stress can change your eating behaviours too, making some people overeat and choose less healthy foods; that makes eating to support your gut microbiome more difficult
- People with anxiety or depression have a different gut microbiome than those without

11. Gut-Brain Power

Gut thinking

Could targeting your gut microbiome be a route to thinking better and faster? It's an exciting and powerful thought. A number of studies have linked cognitive performance to the gut microbiome,[1] in particular to your learning and memory. The first insights into how your gut bacteria may influence your brainpower were from mice bred without a gut microbiome – they had memory problems and lower levels of neurons in their hippocampus, the area of the brain that looks after memory and learning. Other mice infected with 'bad' bacteria struggled with their memory under stress, but this was reversed when they were given probiotics.[2] There have been mixed results from probiotic studies in humans on brain performance, with some showing to be helpful, others having no effect and, worryingly, some making brain performance worse[3] – highlighting that there's plenty we still don't know about how to harness these bacteria in supplement form, and that it's important to consider what type of bacteria is used.

It's not only probiotics that can influence your brainpower – prebiotics have also shown potential. For example, taking a prebiotic supplement improved the memory of older adults in just a few months, seeing them perform better on tests usually used to catch early stages of Alzheimer's disease.[4]

Some of these cognitive benefits are thought to be due to the gut microbiome's influence over the immune system – aiding in dampening excess inflammation which can slow down or damage your brain in the long term. When we look at mice studies again, being fed a low-fibre high-fat diet caused the mice's microbiome to become imbalanced and their gut barrier lining weakened, allowing 'bad' bacteria to travel where they shouldn't – up the vagus nerve and directly into the brain. These mice had higher levels of neuro-inflammation, which is known to be a starting sign of many neurological conditions, with cognitive problems often being early warning signs. Yet when the researchers swapped the mice back onto healthy kibble, their gut barrier lining repaired, the translocation of bacteria stopped and the inflammation in their brains reversed.[5]

Ageing gut-brain

As you age, your gut and your brain start to gradually slow a little in their performance – a sign of a long life well lived, and a natural part of getting into your twilight years. The lining of your gut and your blood-brain barrier can weaken, and they're not as efficient at getting the good stuff in or keeping the bad stuff out. You slowly lose the diversity of your gut bacteria, too, as you age. And as you get older, your immune cells stay on duty longer than they should and can start to malfunction, attacking the neurons in both your gut and your brain, which can lead to inflammation.

Transplanting the microbiome of young mice into older adult mice reversed their age-related cognitive decline.[6] It's studies like this that highlight just how much the gut microbiome likely directly affects your brain throughout life, even though we need more research in humans.

Does Alzheimer's disease begin in the gut?

There's growing interest in targeting the gut microbiome to potentially prevent or even treat Alzheimer's disease. There's a familiar gut-brain pattern where some gut disorders are more likely to happen together with Alzheimer's disease. You're six times more likely to develop Alzheimer's disease if you have inflammatory bowel disease, and twice as likely to develop it if you have gastritis, a condition where your stomach lining becomes inflamed.[7] Those with Alzheimer's disease tend to have a more disrupted gut microbiome with lower diversity of bacteria, the perfect environment for opportunistic harmful bacteria to thrive. These changes have been linked to toxic metabolites, pro-inflammatory molecules and lower amounts of our favourite helpful short-chain fatty acids.[8] When researchers transplanted the microbiome of people with Alzheimer's disease into healthy rats, the rat's brains became inflamed, they performed worse in memory tests and had fewer neurons growing in their hippocampus.[9]

What about Parkinson's disease?

Over the last three decades Parkinson's disease has become the fastest-rising brain disease worldwide.[10] It's an age-related disorder that causes parts of the brain to deteriorate, particularly the substantia nigra, which controls movement. There's early but convincing evidence that Parkinson's disease begins in the gut and not the brain. Gut problems like constipation, cramping and bloating can surface years, even decades, before typical symptoms of Parkinson's disease appear. The microbiomes of those with Parkinson's disease are also different from those of healthy people. They produce fewer beneficial short-chain fatty acids and more inflammatory metabolites, and their gut barrier linings tend to be leaky.[11] Scientists have uncovered the presence of the misfolding protein α-synuclein in the neurons in the gut in early stages of Parkinson's disease.[12] When α-synuclein was injected into the guts of mice, it spread up the vagus nerve to the brain, where it selectively killed dopamine-producing neurons (dopamine is closely involved in helping you move your body).

While it's still early days, with most of the evidence to date based on mice, it seems that your gut microbiome is far more intimately tied to your brain health and cognitive function than we previously thought. Parkinson's disease and Alzheimer's disease can both begin to develop decades before, and the key may be to make healthy changes early to potentially lower your risk. What you eat can make a large difference to how your brain performs now and to protect your brain health over time. After all, protecting cognitive function isn't just about delaying or lowering the risk of neurodegenerative diseases, it's also linked to academic achievement, career success, your mood and brainpower – how well you think and remember right now. In essence, feeling like you're on top of your game and knocking it out of the park. And who doesn't want that?

What's gut-brain power gut to do with it?

- An imbalanced gut microbiome can trigger a cascade of events that could damage how well you think
- The microbiome might be involved in both Alzheimer's disease and Parkinson's disease
- Healthy eating is linked to better cognitive function and lower risk of neurodegenerative brain diseases like Alzheimer's disease and Parkinson's disease

What's next in store for your gut?

OK, now it's crunch time! Part Three will describe *how* you can feel happier, think better and make your gut bacteria proud. Part Four is your framework to rewire your brain to a gut-brain mindset before, drum roll please, Part Five – the Genius Gut Method – your ten hacks to feeling your absolute best. At the back of the book, you'll find all the tools you'll need to put these steps into action, including fibre tables, trackers, and more (including the FAQs). But before we dive in there's just one more thing I want to highlight first, right at the beginning of the next section.

PART THREE – THE GUT-BRAIN SOLUTION

12. Broccoli Isn't the New Prozac

Broccoli isn't the new Prozac. Food isn't medicine. There, I've said it.

It might be a shock for you to hear that. It's the exact opposite of what's said by many social media influencers. I do understand that 'food as medicine' is said with good intentions to highlight the powerful effects that food can have on our health. It's simple and snappy, and it does direct our focus towards more healthy and nutrient-dense foods.

Food, though, is not a substitute for medication or treatment. I know this was never the intention but 'food as medicine' lays judgement on an illness as being the fault of someone's diet, overlooking the multiple factors that can contribute to a condition or disease. It can make someone with cancer, or who has depression, think that they got sick because of what they ate. And that if they changed what they ate – they'd be cured.

For some people, what they eat might transform their health and how they feel. But in many cases of illness and disease, diet is just one small part, or may not be a factor at all. The idea that food alone can 'cure' you can burden people experiencing a condition, illness or disease with shame, guilt and stress. It may delay someone seeking treatment or support, thinking that if they had the 'perfect' diet, then they'd be well. Illnesses are complex puzzles, of which food can be only one piece – and the size and importance of that piece can vary widely – or not be relevant at all.

Medicine is:

- **Designed for treatment.** Medicines specifically treat an illness, disease or symptoms.
- **Prescribed in specific doses that have a targeted effect.** Targeted, with precise doses and formulations.
- **Clearly understood to be effective in treating a condition, disease or symptom.** Rigorously tested in clinical trials to meet certain standards of effectiveness.

. . . whereas food:

- **Supports your whole-body well-being and function.** Energy and nutrition contribute to optimal functioning of your body from your gut to your brain. It isn't specific or targeted.
- **Can help with preventing illness and supporting recovery.** This can depend on the disease, condition and how it presents for that person, and is usually part of a holistic approach of which nutrition is one part.

Food and medicine play different roles in keeping you healthy. Just because food isn't medicine, doesn't mean that it can't have a powerful effect on your health. In this book, think of us doing a deep dive together into that one piece of the puzzle – and how big or important that piece is depends on you and your circumstances.

This connection between your gut, your gut microbiome and your brain is brand-new, rapidly developing science. Twenty years ago there weren't any research papers on the gut microbiome, now there are nearly 60,000 – and only more recently has it been connected with the brain. As with most new areas of research, a lot of the early evidence is from cause and effect studies on mice that needs to be translated to humans, or from human observational studies that show patterns but aren't designed to confirm that cause and effect. It's not only far cheaper to study mice to start with but mice studies also allow researchers to look inside the mouse, and to control other factors that can make human studies messy – like where you live, what you eat, how much exercise you've done, and more. Because of this, mice studies help us to identify which bacteria have an effect, and how they do so. As valuable as this research is, mice are not human beings. While the number of human studies in this area are rising fast, many of the insights we have from mice studies still need to be confirmed in tightly controlled human studies. That doesn't mean that we should hide away what we know to date, just because we don't have years of research yet. But it does mean that there will be many questions that still need answers.

13. How to Make Your Gut-Brain Happier

Can what you eat make you happier? Ahh, think of how you feel when you pull a tray of brownies out of the oven and the warm chocolatey aromas flood your kitchen. You're impatient, and before it's fully cooled, you're devouring a thick dark slice. It's heaven. That for sure would make you say yes to the question of if food makes you happier. Food can be a tastebud Moulin Rouge, providing fleeting moments of happiness. Fleeting . . . or so you think. You might be surprised that it's eating more fruits and vegetables, and not necessarily cake, that can make you cheerier in the longer run. The average amount of fruits and vegetables you eat can predict your satisfaction with life and level of happiness.[1] The more you eat, the happier you tend to be. Even adding just one more serving a day of fruit or veg is estimated to have a similar positive effect on your mental well-being as going for a ten-minute walk every day for a week[2] – even small, simple changes can benefit your mood over time.

Does this seem a bit far-fetched and strange? Maybe it's because we've only ever thought about food and nutrition in terms of warding off potential future diseases and living longer. What we haven't thought about is how health can make you feel *today*. Your mood, energy levels, and how well you think. How you feel *right now*.

Of course, we can't be happy all the time, nothing is constant and emotions naturally shift and change. But we're now seeing that what you eat, and your gut microbiome, are more closely involved in your mental well-being than was ever thought possible. Rather than completely cancelling out feeling grumpy or rubbish, or sad and teary, what you eat seems to lift up your baseline happiness and act as a helping hand to guide you back when your mood runs off course. The food you eat affects you in two ways: first from the nutrients and energy you absorb in your small intestine, which directly affects your body. And then through your gut bacteria, where any undigested food passes through to your lower large intestine for them to feed on. And now we have exciting early science hinting at how your gut bacteria are involved in your mood, with certain gut bacteria linked to feeling more positive emotions – like happiness, joy, gratitude and contentment.[3]

Here's an overview and recap of the behind-the-scenes actions of your gut bacteria:*

Your gut happiness

Your gut bacteria help to manage the levels of your happy hormone serotonin. Most serotonin is produced in your gut, but this gut-made serotonin can't cross your blood-brain barrier to reach your brain to influence your mood. Instead, your 'happy'

---

* Note that a lot of our understanding of these interactions is from studies on mice – for brevity and simplicity in this section I haven't referred to this in the text directly but have tried to elsewhere. Like any new developing science, research done in mice needs to be confirmed in humans.

serotonin needs to be made in your brain. Tryptophan is an amino acid found in protein-rich foods and is needed to make serotonin. Tryptophan is small enough to cross your blood-brain barrier to your brain, and your gut bacteria help your brain to get enough of the tryptophan it needs to make serotonin on site. Tryptophan is also used for many different processes in your body, and not just making serotonin. Your gut bacteria can influence how much or little tryptophan gets used for what process. Imbalances in how tryptophan is used have been seen in depression, irritable bowel syndrome (IBS) and neurological diseases.[4]

Tinkering with what you want to eat

The make-up of your gut bacteria can influence how much or how little you're motivated to eat a food through your levels of the 'I like it, do it again' neurotransmitter dopamine.[5,6] When dopamine release is lowered, it can make you less motivated to eat that food, and vice versa – a rush of dopamine makes you more likely to crave and seek out certain foods. While 50 per cent of your dopamine is made in your gut, like gut-made serotonin, this can't cross your blood-brain barrier to your brain. For dopamine to be made in your brain, it needs the amino acid tyrosine. Your gut bacteria help to supply your brain with enough tyrosine to make dopamine on site in the brain.[7]

Re-grouping your emotions back to a higher baseline

Your gut bacteria appear to act a little like tiny grounding hooks for strong feelings – helping you to return to baseline more easily. A 2023 study by Harvard University linked certain gut bacteria with having more positive feelings and to being better able to self-regulate emotions, while those who suppressed how they felt had a lower diversity of gut bacteria.[8] Your amygdala, the emotional centre of your brain, is particularly sensitive to changes in your gut microbiome.[9] Eating a certain type of fibre – that your gut bacteria especially like to feed on – can also help to shift your focus away from the negative and towards the positive.[10]

Easing stress (or ramping it up . . .)

Stress affects your gut bacteria and weakens your protective gut barrier lining, changing the metabolites they produce and how tryptophan is used by your body.[11] The make-up of your gut microbiome can either ease stress or make it worse. A 'healthy' diverse gut microbiome with plenty of 'good' gut bacteria helps your body to handle stress, acting like mini stress buffers. An imbalanced gut microbiome, though, can tip the scales the other way and make stress worse – your gut bacteria aren't as well able to help you handle the resulting stress. How much stress is too much? In mice, two weeks of stress was enough to significantly change their gut microbiome and make them more anxious.[12] It's not all doom and gloom, though; certain types of probiotic sup-plements have been shown to help lower stress.

Dampening down excess inflammation

Excess inflammation is linked to many conditions, diseases and disorders – from some cases of depression to Alzheimer's dis-ease and more. An imbalanced gut microbiome can weaken the gut barrier lining, allowing compounds and bacteria to 'leak' through into your body that shouldn't be there – and can trigger an inflammatory response. On the other hand, a 'healthy' diverse gut microbiome helps to keep your gut barrier lining strong, and produces helpful metabolites, working hand-in-hand with your immune system, to maintain a healthy balanced state that's crucial to your overall health.

Thinking well

A healthier diet is linked to a larger hippocampus – the learning and memory part of your brain that affects how well you think.[13] While certain bacteria are related to better brainpower, on the flip side, 'bad' pro-inflammatory gut bacteria are more commonly found in those who aren't able to think as well.[14] Probiotic and prebiotic studies that impact the gut microbiome have helped to improve people's performance on memory tests, and their attention and focus.

Anxious or calm

There's a strong connection between anxiety and the gut – if you have gut issues, you're more susceptible to feeling low and anxious and vice versa. A number of studies have shown that changing your gut microbiome through what you eat can help with anxiety.[15] While anxiety can be due to many different factors, oxytocin, the warm fuzzy cuddle hormone, can influence how strongly you experience it. Oxytocin helps to make the amygdala, your brain's emotional centre, react less strongly to triggers of anxiety and fear.[16] Your gut bacteria can communicate with your brain through your vagus nerve to influence how much oxytocin is produced and released.[17] Differences in the make-up of your gut bacteria have also been linked to personality traits like how sociable you are.

Feeling full and satisfied

Your gut bacteria depend on you eating to get their own meal. They can shape the action of your gut hunger and fullness hormones, signalling to your brain that you're ready to start or stop eating. As your gut bacteria feed on fibre they produce short-chain fatty acids which can encourage gut fullness hormones to be released. They can also influence food cravings, and possibly even how you taste food too.[18]

Are we microbial zombies?

Rather than zombies manipulated by microbial mind control, it seems more realistic that we've learnt to make use of our gut bacteria and the metabolites they produce, just as much as they make use of us. We've evolved to rely on our gut bacteria,[19] finding ways to make use of them and their waste products – one bacteria's trash is another man's treasure.

Gut food

One of the biggest influences on your gut bacteria is what you eat. And with food you get a double whammy for your brain health – you get the direct effect of nutrients absorbed into your bloodstream from your small intestine, and the impact of what you eat on your gut bacteria when food reaches your lower intestine, helping them produce helpful metabolites for your health. If we're talking about food and mood, then we can't bypass the landmark study that really put the gut-brain connection on the map, even if they didn't have enough funding at the time to take microbiome samples. It's a study called the SMILES trial, and it was the first randomised control trial using food as a treatment strategy for depression.*

The SMILES trial was run in Melbourne, Australia, in 2017, led by Professor Felice Jacka, a leader in the field of nutritional psychiatry. Her research team enrolled 67 people with depression into the SMILES trial for 12 weeks. Half of the participants were guided by a dietitian to eat a Mediterranean diet (a way of eating consistently shown to alter your gut microbiome), while the other half of the control group only had social support – someone to chat to about their lives and hobbies.

What is the Mediterranean diet?

The Mediterranean diet is one of the most studied dietary patterns. It's a style of eating that focuses on fruits and vegetables, whole grains, beans and legumes, nuts and seeds, extra-virgin olive oil, oily fish and lean meats like chicken and turkey. It provides a lot of fibre, and other compounds for your gut bacteria. While it's called the Mediterranean diet, it's really an example of any diet, from any country, that contains a wide variety of plants, fish and lean meat.

---

* Note that depression is a highly complex mental health condition, the causes of which can be very different from one person to the next, requiring an individualised approach to treatment.

At the end of the study, the results were in. And the research team nearly fell off their chairs – they were so surprised by the results! A third of those with depression who changed what they ate weren't clinically classified as depressed any more. The more closely they followed a Mediterranean diet, the more their symptoms improved.[20] This study placed food firmly on the map when it comes to mood. Since then, many studies have followed and we now have consistent evidence that a healthy, balanced diet can significantly help with mood and anxiety.[21] And brainpower too – the Mediterranean diet is also linked with being able to think better,[22] with a lower risk of cognitive decline and dementia.[23] The 10 Genius Gut hacks are specially developed to help you eat in this way.

Fibre me up

What you eat can change how you feel – your energy, your mood and your well-being. If there was just one thing, one change you could make to what you eat that has the biggest impact on the health of your gut and gut microbiome – it's to eat more fibre, the roughage from plant foods (a key feature of the Mediterranean diet). Every 5g of fibre you eat is related to a 5 per cent lower likelihood of depression.[24] People who eat more fibre tend to perform far better in cognitive tests, like on memory and problem-solving.[25] The added bonus? Foods that are high in fibre tend to be really nutrient dense, meaning plenty of bioactive compounds for your gut and brain health and overall well-being too. Fibre is essential for a healthy gut and a thriving gut microbiome, and certain types of fibre have been shown to support your mood and how well you think. We'll explore these different types later on – but before we get into the weeds, the most important thing is working towards getting 'enough' overall and reaching that recommended 30g of fibre a day.

What does an extra 5g of fibre look like?

Food	Quantity	Fibre (g)
Mixed nuts	2 handfuls	5.1
Pear	1 large	4.9
Raspberries	½ cup	5
Baked beans	¼ can	5.1
Red kidney beans	5 tbsp	5.1
Peas	4 tbsp	5.6
Edamame beans	½ cup	4.2
Brussels sprouts	8 sprouts	5.3
Broccoli	4 spears	5
Green/brown lentils	5 tbsp	5.5
Whole-wheat pasta	medium portion	5
Bran flakes	small portion	5.4
Porridge oats	1 cup	6.2
Bulgur wheat	½ cup	4.7
Rye crispbread	3 pieces	6

Food	Quantity	Fibre (g)
Flaxseeds	2 tbsp	5
Chia seeds	1½ tbsp	6
70–85 per cent dark chocolate	½ bar	5.5

What does 30g of fibre look like?

Thirty grams of fibre a day can seem intimidating. But you don't have to live on buddha bowls alone to reach it. In fact, I think you'll be pleasantly surprised by how easy and enjoyable it is by the time you're done with this book. And even if you already eat plenty of salads, that doesn't necessarily mean you're hitting 30g of fibre a day either.

Here is an example of a balanced daily menu which will provide you with at least 30g of fibre, and it's all about making certain swaps and add-ins. Please note that everyone needs different amounts of food, so while I've put the measures in here so that you can see how much makes up what amount of fibre, this is very much a guide and not prescriptive of the amount you 'should' eat, and you may find yourself needing to eat more or less.

Food Name	Measure	Fibre (g)
Breakfast – Overnight oats		
Porridge oats	35g	2.7
Kefir	200ml	0
Mixed nuts	half a handful (15g)	1.3
Chia seeds	1 teaspoon	2.6
Carrot	½ grated carrot	1.3
Apple	½ grated apple	1.0
Blueberries	100g	1.5
Cinnamon	½ teaspoon	0.6
Honey	1 teaspoon	0
	Meal Total	10.4
Lunch – Tuscan white bean, kale and tomato pasta		
Wholemeal pasta	60g	5.3
Cannellini beans	60g	3.9
Tinned tomatoes	½ can or 200g	1.6
Kale	1 cup	0.7
Garlic	1 clove	0
Mozzarella	½ ball	0
	Meal Total	11.5

Food Name	Measure	Fibre (g)
Snack		
Apple	1	2.1
Dark Chocolate (85% Cocoa)	2 squares (30g)	3.3
	Meal Total	5.4
Dinner – Salmon with herby yoghurt, green beans, peas and new potatoes		
Salmon	1 fillet	0
Greek yoghurt	2 tablespoons	0.0
Lemon juice	1 teaspoon	0.0
Mixed herbs (e.g. dill, mint and basil)	1 tablespoon	0.0
Green beans	60g	2.5
Peas	60g	3.3
New potatoes	3 potatoes	2.3
	Meal Total	8.1
	Day Total:	35.4

Try to aim for at least 8–10g of fibre each meal. But don't worry – I'm not going to leave you high and dry – we're going to make this easy and simple, you and me together. A key focus of many of the 10 Genius Gut hacks is to help you reach your 30g of fibre a day without even realising it. Simple, practical strategies that don't take up headspace to improve your gut microbiome and your gut-brain connection.

What about psychobiotics?

There are exciting probiotic studies showing how certain types of bacteria can help to ease anxiety and stress, improve memory and mood, and help anti-depressants to work more effectively. These studies have highlighted the power of the gut-brain connection and have accelerated interest in this area of research. I think it's important to share that probiotic supplements are not tightly regulated like medications are. That means that a lot of probiotic products currently on the market can be fairly dubious in their claims and quality.

Like all supplements, they're 'supplemental' – as in 'as well as' rather than 'instead of' – changes to your diet and alongside (rather than replacing) medication. Probiotics are generally safe to take, and if you want to try a probiotic then you can – though if you are on medication, have a weak immune system, are pregnant or a young child, please check with your doctor first. What I suggest is trying them for eight weeks, and if you feel better, then great! But if you don't, spend your money elsewhere. And what you eat still matters when it comes to the overall health of your gut microbiome. For more on psychobiotics, see page 300 and the FAQs.

14. Your Gut-Brain BFFs

What you eat is one of the biggest influences on your gut microbiome – but there are other factors too. Let's look at some of the ingredients you need to keep your gut and brain healthy and happy:

- A healthy, balanced diet
- Not drinking too much alcohol
- Managing stress
- Exercise
- Not sitting too much during the day
- Sleeping well
- Regular social connection
- Nature and natural light

At its heart this is a book about food, but it would be wrong of me to leave out or gloss over the importance of these other factors too. I won't cover them all, but I do want to highlight some of them, and how they help to support your gut, your gut micro-biome and your mind. Think of them as part of your box of tricks for feeling great.

Moving your body

Any way of moving your body that gets your heart rate up counts as exercise – and your gut, immune system and brain love it. Exercising is linked to a more diverse gut microbiome, helping your 'good' gut bacteria to grow and produce those special short-chain fatty acids – no matter if you've never done much exercise before or you're a seasoned athlete. Exercise can also have profound effects on your mental well-being too, it's as helpful for your mood as taking certain antidepressants[1] – they both tend to work through similar pathways in your brain.[2]

Exercise increases the blood flow to your gut and your brain, providing fresh oxygen and nutrients. For your gut microbiome this acts a bit like an interior designer giving their home, your gut, freshly painted walls, arranging the furniture nicely and puffing the cushions. It helps your gut to work well, moving food through efficiently, maintaining the health of your gut barrier lining, and your gut bacteria thrive accordingly. This extra blood flow to your brain also helps you to immediately feel sharper and more on the ball and can last for at least two hours afterwards.[3] Every time you move your body in a way that raises your heartbeat, your neurotransmitter equivalent of a multi-coloured kids' ball pool is released into your brain – dopamine, serotonin, norepinephrine and acetylcholine.

You might have realised by now that your gut bacteria can be busy bodies. Research in mice has shown that their gut bacteria influenced how motivated they were to exercise. Mice bred without a gut microbiome weren't particularly bothered about running around their enclosure – and in particular their dopamine reward pathway didn't light up, no 'I like it, I want to do it again'. Mice with a gut microbiome, though, were perfectly happy to exercise. Their gut bacteria produced metabolites called fatty acid amides that kick-started the brain's production of the rewarding 'I like it, do it again' dopamine, making them want to run.[4]

We know that all movement that raises your heartbeat is great for your gut and brain, but coordinative exercise seems to particularly stand out above the rest for your long-term thinking ability.[5] Coordinative exercise is basically what it says on the tin; it involves coordination, like for dancing, yoga and gymnastics, but also team or group sports like tennis, netball, football and hockey. It's more complex than sitting on a machine in the gym repeating the same motions, so it makes your brain work harder. Group and interactive sports have the added gut-brain benefit of social interaction too. Exercise where you're engaging your mind at the same time as you move your body has been shown to be great for how well you think and can help maintain brain function in people with Alzheimer's disease.[6] This could be as simple as going for a walk with a friend and chatting as you're moving. Think of your brain like a muscle – working out helps it to get stronger and perform better.

The best exercise for you is one that you enjoy and can stick to. That's it. Find a way of moving your body that you like and can be consistent with, starting small if you need to and building up from there. No gym membership? No matter. Try yoga, tennis or a dance class. Exercise is not punishment – enjoy it and make it fun. Find something that you can stick to for at least two to three months; this seems to be the watershed moment when most people tend to drop out of exercise programmes. Those who can make it past that mark are more likely to carry on for at least six more months.[7] Luckily, though, you don't need to commit to long workout sessions unless you want to – with a workout of 30 minutes equally effective for your mood and anxiety levels as an hour or more.[8] Any movement is better than no movement – even five minutes of dancing can boost your mood and lift your energy levels.[9]

Sleep for the brain

Sleep is crucially important for your health, yet most of us aren't getting enough of it. Not getting enough hours, and not getting enough good-quality deep sleep. Even when we get the chance to sleep more, there's this perception that sleeping in is being lazy, while sleep deprivation is glorified like a badge of honour. Which is a complete contradiction. During sleep your brain recharges itself, it recovers and repairs – sleep is essential not only for your brain to perform well but for your decision-making too. Bad sleep drains how well your prefrontal cortex works – you're tired and more likely to reach for something sweet and comforting[10] and you feel hungrier as well.[11]

How does a bad night's sleep make you feel?

If you don't sleep well – how do you feel? Does your mood change?

_____

_____

How much energy do you have?

_____

_____

Do you feel like it changes how you eat? And how hungry you are?

_____

_____

Do you find it harder to eat healthily or to make positive changes to your health when you haven't slept well?

_____

_____

Is improving your gut microbiome a new target for better sleep? The make-up of your gut bacteria is closely related to how well you sleep – the better quality your sleep the more likely you are to have a diverse gut microbiome and more 'good' gut bacteria.[12] In mice that had their microbiome depleted by broad-spectrum antibiotics, this affected how long and well they slept. Your gut bacteria like routine as much as your body clock does – going to bed and waking up at regular times helps both your sleep and your gut bacteria. Varying the time you go to bed or wake up by 90 minutes is linked to differences in 'bad' gut bacteria and poor health compared to those who have a regular sleep schedule.[13] Your gut bacteria also seem to be early birds – going to sleep earlier is related to a more diverse gut microbiome.[14]

Social bacteria

Your gut bacteria appreciate interactions with others – many of the new bacteria introduced into your gut aren't only from food but from the air around you, from touching surfaces and other people. While your mother's microbiome has a particularly strong link with yours in early life, as you get older that overlap diminishes but doesn't vanish. Even in your eighties you more than likely have some bacteria types still in common with your mum.[17] You share bacteria as a child with your father too – at four years old you share a similar number of types of bacteria with your dad as you do with your mum.[18] This sharing of gut bacteria often happens when you live with someone, and as adults the longer you live with someone[19] – even if you're not in a romantic relationship – the more you share gut bacteria.

How connected we are to others matters for our happiness too. The longest happiness study in the world has been running for decades – since 1938.[20] Every two years the participants are asked detailed questions about their lives, with one consistent finding above all else related to happiness, health and living longer – good relationships. Just one quality conversation with a friend, ideally in person but on the phone or online can help too, can make a positive difference to your mood.[21] Hugs don't only feel good but also help with your health as well – protecting you against stress and infection and suffering less severe symptoms if you get ill.[22] That's the power of connection.

One of the strongest predictors of well-being is the quality of your friendships.[23] When you talk to a friend your blood pressure lowers, stress eases and feel-good endorphins are released. It's quality over quantity that counts the most though. Having just three or more good friendships is related to significantly better life satisfaction.[24] Even interacting with vague acquaintances or strangers can still give us a mental health boost.[25] I used to live in a part of London that had a tiny little fruit stall tucked right outside the station, so I'd pass it at least once a day. The stallholder was one of those warm, cheeky Londoners, and we'd always exchange a word or two and have a laugh as I walked by. Sometimes it's the small things in life that can add a bit of sparkle to the day – for both you and your gut bacteria. In whatever shape or form, we and our microbes thrive on connection.

Microbiome forest

Simply being outside in nature, even if it's just for ten minutes, is related to better mental well-being.[26] Being outside is also an opportunity for your gut bacteria too. One teaspoon of soil contains more microbes than there are humans in the world, and they're hugely important for soil health. A small study had a group of adults rubbing their hands in a bucketful of soil for twenty seconds three times a day, and this simple action increased their diversity of gut bacteria in only two weeks.[27] Turns out all those mud pies children make are very likely great for their gut bacteria. And if you have a garden or a nearby park, spending more time in it is a great way to support your gut microbiome.

15. How to Make an Unhappy Gut Happy

Your brain and your gut are directly and powerfully linked – so much so that just the thought of eating can make your stomach start to produce stomach acid ready for digestion. If you're stressed or upset, this can affect how well your gut works. This can go the other way too. Gut issues can send signals to your brain that there's something wrong. If gut issues are unresolved this could be contributing to you feeling low or anxious. Fifty per cent of people who have ongoing gut problems either became anxious first, and then developed gut issues within 12 years, while the other 50 per cent developed gut problems first and then experienced mood changes or mental distress.[1]

Do you struggle with constipation, diarrhoea or bloating? Make an unhappy gut a happy one by trying some of these changes. I'd always recommend seeing a dietitian or registered nutritionist who can give you personalised advice if your symptoms aren't resolving. You can ask your doctor if they can refer you to one, or see someone privately.

Helping you 'go' when you're constipated

Has your internal plumbing slowed down, and you're finding that it's taking your body a sweet while to 'go'? Do you have hard, lump-like poos? Or do you struggle to get everything out? Constipation is not something you should just ignore and brush under the carpet. It can cause stomach pain, nausea and fatigue. And it also affects your gut microbiome and brain. People who 'go' less often have less 'good' gut bacteria, and more 'bad' pro-inflammatory bacteria, and worse cognition too, equivalent to three years of ageing compared to those who poo once a day.[2]

Poo position with the poo stool

We didn't evolve to sit on a porcelain throne, we evolved to squat, knees up, with a straight, direct passage for your poo to travel down. When you sit on the loo, that passage isn't so straight any more. Your rectum is the final part of your gut; it's a short muscular tube that controls how you 'go', but when you're sitting down on the loo, it can get kinked – choking your exit. If you have constipation, this can make it harder for your poo to vacate the premises. To straighten out the kink and relax the muscles you can raise your knees so that they are higher than your hips by placing your feet on a stool and leaning forward slightly.

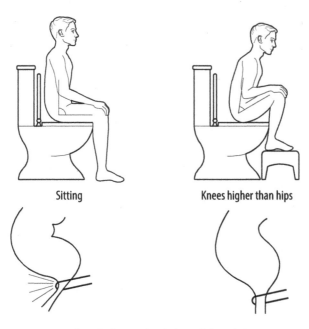

Sitting   Knees higher than hips

Figure 5. How you sit on the loo can help you 'go'

Don't ignore the urge to 'go'

As soon as you feel the need to 'go' – don't ignore it. Suppressing this urge can make it harder to 'go' as you're disrupting your body's natural coordinated process, and if you do this often over time your body can struggle to do its business.

What to eat to help you 'go'

What you eat plays an important role in managing constipation. Eating more fibre can help, as it's good at holding water, keeping your poo soft and easier to pass. As fibre absorbs water, you also then usually need to drink more water and fluids, otherwise you can end up feeling bunged up still. It's worth being aware, though, that for some people with severe constipation too much fibre can make their constipation worse. If you have constipation, you can try one of these:

- Two kiwis a day.[3] Kiwis are high in particular types of fibre that hold water and make your poo softer, making it easier to go.
- Four to five prunes (50g) twice a day.[4] Prunes contain sorbitol, a type of sugar alcohol found in certain fruits, which can also draw in water, helping to soften your poo.

If you need another helping hand, then psyllium is a type of fibre supplement that you can buy from most pharmacies and take with water. It forms a gel in your gut that helps to soften your poo, making it easier to 'go'.

Regular mealtimes

A change in your routine or skipping meals can make it more difficult for a smooth and easy exit. Eating meals at regular times is crucial for managing constipation, as it helps your body to remember what's meant to happen when. This is because eating activates your intestines to move more. It's particularly important to eat something for breakfast as a similar effect also happens when you change from lying down to standing. Together these both help you to move waste through and out of your body.[5]

Try probiotics

Probiotics science is complex and still in its early stages. While you don't need a probiotic to generally support your gut microbiome, certain types can help to ease specific symptoms. Specific probiotics can help to speed up gut transit time by half a day and help to soften your poo so it's easier to 'go'[6] and can also help with bloating.[7] A few examples of probiotic bacteria to look out for are types of *Bifidobacterium animalis lactis,*[8] like *B. lactis* Bi-07[9] or *B. lactis* DN-173010.[10]

Beat the bloating

It's totally normal to have some bloating, especially after meals. If it's making you feel particularly uncomfortable why not give some of these a try:

- **Smaller amounts of food more often:** Large meals can over-load your digestive system making your bloating worse. Instead, try having smaller meals more often (like smaller main meals with a morning and afternoon snack) to help your gut digest food efficiently and ease bloating.
- **Peppermint oil and tea:** Peppermint oil capsules contain a high concentration of menthol, found in smaller amounts in peppermint tea. Menthol helps to relax your stomach muscles and can make pain-sensing muscle fibres less sensitive to discomfort.[11]
- **Avoid swallowing too much gas:** Swallowing air by eating or drinking too quickly, or drinking fizzy drinks, can contrib-ute to bloating. Try to sip drinks rather than gulping and put your knife and fork back onto your plate between each mouthful to slow how quickly you eat.
- **Avoid tight clothing around your stomach:** This can put pressure around your stomach, making bloating worse and more

uncomfortable. Looser clothing helps your stomach to expand and contract naturally while you're digesting so you're less likely to feel bloated.

- **Gentle movement:** Going for a walk after you've eaten a meal can help your digestion to move food through your gut, and can help you feel less bloated.

If you think you have an intolerance, allergy or condition that's causing your bloating then please see a healthcare professional. See FAQs for more information on intolerances and more.

Got the runs?

If you have diarrhoea then make sure you stay hydrated as you can lose a lot of water, and if needed take some rehydration sachets.

- **Smaller amounts of food more often:** Like with bloating, large meals can overload a sensitive digestive system, making your diarrhoea worse. Try spreading out your meals by having three smaller main meals with snacks in the morning and afternoon.
- **Avoid coffee and alcohol:** Coffee can increase your urge to 'go', so can worsen your diarrhoea. Large amounts of alcohol encourage your intestines to release water, and speed up how quickly food moves through your gut.
- **Avoid spicy and greasy foods:** Greasy foods can make your diarrhoea worse as your body finds it harder to break down the high load of fats. Spicy foods contain capsaicin which can irritate your gut lining and can have a laxative effect.

- **Avoid sugar-free chewing gum:** The sweetness is usually replaced with the sugar alcohol sorbitol, which can make your diarrhoea worse.
- **Try a probiotic:** If you have the runs from an upset stomach, *Saccharomyces boulardii* CNCM I-745 has been shown to help to improve diarrhoea from a viral infection within a few days.[12]

PART FOUR – EATING FOR YOUR GUT-BRAIN

16. A New Way of Eating

One mindset shift changed everything for me – that a perfect diet doesn't exist. Letting go of the pressure to eat flawlessly and having a balanced approach towards food – without the guilt and stress – is a true gut-brain mindset.

In this section you'll find the guiding principles behind great gut health. Yet there's nothing about broccoli or fermented foods (yet). On the surface it might not seem relevant to gut health at all – and you might be tempted to skip right on past. I hope you don't, because the next few pages are the key to making healthy eating work for you, and are the foundations for the 10 gut-brain hacks. It's a gut-brain mindset, because we can't just talk about only the gut, it's a two-way relationship. We also need to think about what's going on in your head too – how your thoughts and beliefs around food shape how you feel and what you eat.

Many of these strategies come from behavioural science and an approach called intuitive eating – where by eating intuitively you don't ruminate about what you've eaten, you eat foods based on both what you enjoy the taste of and how they make you feel afterwards, and are guided by how much or how little to eat based on the hunger and fullness signals of your body. It's directly teaching you to listen to your gut, and to be kind to your brain. This approach is particularly connected to better mental well-being – less anxiety and low mood, feeling better about yourself and your body and less stress.[1,2]

Why eat this way?

Well, for quite a few reasons . . .

- It makes eating more gut-friendly foods easier and you're more likely to keep it up too[3]
- It helps you to focus on the positives – *adding in* more gut-friendly foods instead of cutting foods out
- You'll feel less of the stress and anxiety that your gut bacteria don't like
- It takes away some of the mental load that drains your energy
- No food is off limits
- (And it's far more enjoyable!)

No such thing as perfect

'Don't eat that! It's bad for your gut!,' you heard . . .

'Ten foods to never eat for your gut bacteria,' the article says . . . What a load of gut BS.

I'm not a fan of food rules – often they're hurting your gut health rather than helping it. These rules usually involve cutting out or avoiding certain foods and create a lot of food anxiety, which is counter-productive for your gut bacteria. It makes life more stressful than it needs to be, it restricts the variety your gut bacteria thrive off, and cutting out food groups can make your digestion worse.

Gut health food rules can also put all the emphasis on eating just for your gut microbiome and not the nutritional needs of the rest of your body too. If you only focus on feeding your gut bacteria, then might you be missing out on enough protein for your muscles? Or Vitamin B12 for your brain? These nutrients might not directly impact your gut bacteria like fibre does, but they help with the overall health of your body and therefore the home of your gut bacteria.

Classing foods as 'bad' or 'good' is overly simplistic. We're living in a time when certain foods are called 'poison', 'as nutritious as cardboard', 'toxic' and 'worse for you than smoking'. It's dramatic, catchy – designed to draw you in, for you to pay attention. As a scientist it's not always easy to share nuance when your sentences are often chopped into little sound bites, and you don't get to see an article or its headline before it's put out into the world. Other times, it is just as someone has said it. The higher the number of clicks usually means either one of two things: 1) it's a complete myth; 2) it's a gross dramatisation of the science. Some foods are simply more nutrient dense than others. Some of those that contain less nutrition might give you a healthy dose of joy. Absolutely nothing is going to happen to your health or your gut microbiome if you occasionally eat a less healthy (as in lower in nutrients) food. Nutrition might seem like it's ever changing, because those are the articles and video clips that grab the attention. But really – it hasn't changed much. But it turns out that telling people that we're just not eating enough fruit, veggies, whole grains, and other plant foods isn't a sexy 'new' message and so doesn't get the airtime that the BS does.

Try this instead:

- 'This tastes great! I like it, and that's OK.'
- 'I eat flexibly, it's about overall balance.'
- 'I'm going to eat this, enjoy it and move on.'
- 'One meal or day of eating doesn't dictate my health.'

I understand why we like food rules – it's an easy way to say, do this, don't do that. And we like simplicity and order. The problem with food rules is that they try to make nutrition very black and white, do or die – you 'succeed' if you do them, and you 'fail' when you break them. Which, inevitably, you will, because you are a human being and not a robot. Thankfully.

Be flexible, just like your gut bacteria. You don't make or break your gut health in one meal, or even a couple of days or the occasional week. You co-evolved with your gut microbiome and as your prehistoric ancestors only had occasional access to food – maybe it was meat one day, and berries another – your gut bacteria also learnt to be highly adaptive to what you eat. Your gut bacteria, though, are also pretty resilient, they are big-picture thinkers, and don't sweat the small stuff. If you eat three meals a day, across the year that's 1,095 meals. If 219 of those aren't particularly gut friendly across the year, then that won't matter for your gut health, you're still having nutritious balanced meals 80 per cent of the time.

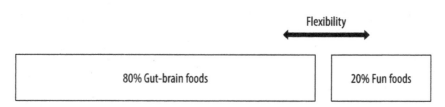

Figure 6. Being flexible and finding your balance

I want you to think of any nutrition advice, including what is between these pages, as a framework that you can apply most days – but it doesn't have to be every day. You might be going out for dinner with friends at your local Italian restaurant, and you shouldn't bypass your favourite spaghetti bolognese. On other days, you might not have had a moment to yourself, you're tired and stressed, and having a takeaway pizza is self-care as much as it is food and nourishment. Or you might simply not feel like eating a salad right now, even if you would another day. By making peace with these, you don't feel like you've 'slipped up'.

We need a balance of foods and nutrients for physical health, and also recognise the joy that food can bring us too. After all, the French have their baguettes, wine, cheese and croissants and they aren't dropping like flies.

Have that piece of cake, enjoy it . . . and move on.

Healthy eating means . . .

- eating foods you enjoy – and not those you don't
- meeting your energy and nutrient needs
- feeding your gut microbiome the foods they love (most of the time)
- a way of eating that you're able to keep up in the long run
- flexibility – there aren't any rules to follow
- not limiting any foods, instead enjoying a variety of them
- enjoying the moments when you eat foods like chocolate, cake and biscuits without the guilt
- not feeling super hungry all the time, but full and energised

What is healthy?

- **Less healthy foods:** Foods that are less nutrient dense and aren't linked to health benefits. These foods are often enjoyable and delicious. Looking at the big picture, they are part of a healthy, balanced diet – eating these foods occasionally doesn't negatively affect your health.
- **More healthy foods:** Foods that are more nutrient dense and are linked to health benefits. These are the foods we want to eat more of, but in a way that is realistic and that we're able to keep up long term.
- **Gut-friendly foods:** These are foods that especially support your gut microbiome to thrive, like fruits, vegetables, whole grains, nuts and seeds, beans and legumes.
- **Food cravings:** A food craving is a strong desire and urge to eat a food and to sometimes eat it past comfortable fullness. You're more likely to crave foods when you're tired, hungry, stressed or feeling down.

Your gut-brain headspace

A bitter aftertaste – the post-meal beat-up:

- 'I ate all those chips – why did I do that?'
- 'I shouldn't have eaten that. I'm such a failure'
- 'Why can't I just control myself?'

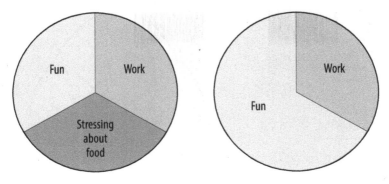

Figure 7. Your daily headspace

Wow, we're not very nice to ourselves sometimes. The self-flagellation of tucking into a bag of crisps on the sofa or grabbing a rare quick Macca's on the drive home. Paying penance by spending extra-long at the gym or being super careful with what you eat the next day. These thoughts can dominate your mental headspace and make you feel miserable. If you break down how much time you spend thinking about different elements of your life, how much time do you spend stressing about food or your body?

What if you just ate that doughnut and moved on? In one study, participants were given a doughnut each. Some were reassured by researchers not to feel guilty or be hard on themselves about eating it, and these participants not only felt better about eating the doughnut but also ate less at their next meal, compared to the group who beat themselves up about eating the doughnut.[4]

Peek into the backstage of your food choices

Most of us know that we need to eat more fruits and veggies, so why don't we do it? It's not because you're bad or lazy or have no willpower. What you eat is often an expression of how you're

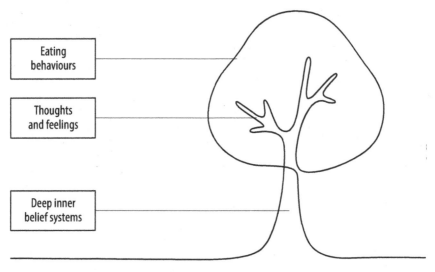

Figure 8. Your food choices

feeling, hiding what's underneath. Food can comfort you after a hard day when you're stressed or feeling down. And that's OK. It's when food is the main or only source of comfort when you're feeling stressed, sad or down, that it can make eating more gut-friendly foods incredibly hard.

I like to think about food choices as a tree. The leaves are your eating behaviours, the visible actions you take like comfort-eating on the sofa after work. You can see the leaves, but they conceal the deeper layers underneath.

Leaf: Comfort-eating chocolate

Branch: Feeling stressed, tired and hungry (Why might this be? Difficult time at work? Relationship?)

Trunk: Viewing chocolate as a 'bad' food to be avoided. Feeling guilty and ashamed for not being 'in control'

You can't see the branches, which are your thoughts, feelings, and your mood.

The branches connect to the tree trunk, embodying your deeper inner belief systems around food and your body, your memories and your associations. This is why it can be extremely hard to make simple changes for your health – because it's not actually that simple at all, particularly if there's an emotional need pushing you the opposite way. Other times you can have the most 'perfect' leaves and think you're doing everything right, but you struggle with how you feel and your beliefs about yourself – the branches and the tree trunk – and so you still feel sad and unhappy. The health of the whole tree matters – and that's what makes you feel truly great. Learning what might be a pattern behind some of the food choices you make can be helpful, especially if it's the only coping mechanism you have when life throws you a curveball.

Cutting out sugar only leads to cravings

Often, cravings are kick-started by feeling hungry, tired or stressed. Cutting out and avoiding the foods you crave only makes the cravings worse.[5] It's kind of like being told not to think about pink elephants. Now pink elephants are all you can think about! There are multiple studies that show that cutting out foods isn't the answer. One study shows this well – they found that women who cut out chocolate had more intense cravings and ate nearly double the amount of chocolate when given it than those who hadn't cut it out.[6]

In the moment of craving, try this:

- **Check in with how you're feeling:** Are you tired, stressed, hungry? Would calling a friend help? If you're hungry, would having a more substantial meal help? Or could you have the food you're craving but bulk out your plate with maybe some nuts, veggie sticks, hummus and cut-up fruit?
- **If you're not hungry, wait ten minutes to reground yourself:** That anticipatory surge of 'ooh, I like it' dopamine is powerful but short and may pass after ten minutes. Move to another room that isn't the kitchen or where you'd usually eat. Going for a brisk, short walk can also help to ease cravings.[7]
- **Hasn't passed? Have it, enjoy it, be present – and move on!** Health is more than just nutrients. Slow down and savour it – how does it taste? Is it smooth or crunchy? Sweet or salty? It's hard to make a change in the moment. Instead, you can try the long-haul craving strategy that'll help for next time.

The long-haul craving strategy

Try to incorporate the food you tend to get the most cravings for into your week more regularly. This takes the edge off how tantalising and 'forbidden' it is. Pair it with more nutrient-dense, satisfying foods – like fruit, nuts and seeds, or hummus and rye crackers – it's a win-win. You get your favourite food, *and* you feel satisfied and great too.

Tools for gut-brain kindness

Gut-brain kindness doesn't have to be a big sweeping gesture. Finding small and consistent ways to practise compassion towards yourself can start the process. Remember – you, your brain and your body – you're on the same team.

- **Approach negative thoughts with kindness and curiosity:** Please don't beat yourself up for negative thoughts; that never did anyone any good. Be kind and curious about why you might think this and where they come from.
- **Rewrite the thought:** Is the thought even true? Rewrite it in a compassionate way.
- **Imagine you're talking to a friend:** Try to take yourself out of the situation and think about it objectively, as if a friend had shared this thought with you. What would you say to them? We're often much better at being kind to others than we are to ourselves.
- **Find a mantra that works for you:** This could be something like:

   'I'm making peace with myself. It's human not to be perfect and that's OK.'
   'Food is more than just nutrients. I enjoyed this and it felt good.'
   'Being healthy is including all foods, it's part of a healthy balance.'

17. Sugar, Baby

Sugar isn't toxic. It's not a poison. You can eat sugar and be healthy. It's not one or the other.

The problem with sugar is not that we're eating it at all – it's that many of us are having too much of it. The reason we get worried about sugar intake is that most sugary foods that contain added or free sugars aren't nutrient dense, and so you're likely not eating enough gut-friendly foods if you're eating a lot of them. These sugary foods are also an easy source of energy – and it's consistently eating more energy than your body needs, whether it's because of sugar or not, that is related to health problems. This is why there's a recommended upper level of 30g of free sugars a day – about seven sugar cubes. Yet British men on average are eating 56g of free sugars a day, and women 44g; for men that's nearly double the recommended amount. That might seem disheartening, but that also doesn't mean you can't ever have anything sugary at all. I want to highlight here – that's seven sugar cubes or 30g-worth of occasional sugary wiggle room.

Why some sugar isn't as bad as you think it is:

- **It provides energy**
- **Your body is built to handle it:** Your body releases insulin, which helps you to manage the rise in blood-sugar

levels, so if you do have the occasional spike your body is equipped to bring your blood-sugar levels back down.

- **It makes food taste good!**

Do added or free sugars affect your gut microbiome? If you're eating a moderate amount of added or free sugars, most of it won't reach your gut bacteria anyway – over 95 per cent of simple sugars are absorbed in the small intestine. If you regularly eat a lot of added or free sugars, though, they can overflow into your large intestine, where your gut bacteria live, lowering the diversity of gut bacteria and encouraging the growth of 'bad' bacteria.[1]

It's the wrapper that matters

Not all sugars are made equal. Many foods naturally contain sugar, like fruit, milk and grains. These sugars, however, are 'wrapped' inside the cells of the food, acting like an obstacle course for your gut during digestion, slowing down the release of sugar into your bloodstream. They also contain a wide variety of other healthy nutrients and bioactive compounds. Sometimes, though, the sugars become 'free' of the cells and are rapidly absorbed – called free sugars. It's regularly eating too many of these free sugars (taking you over your energy needs) that is related to an increased risk of heart disease and other health problems. So it's eating too much added or free sugars that we need to be careful of, and not 'wrapped' sugar naturally found in foods like fruit, milk and whole grains. Free sugars are found in table sugar, honey and syrup, which are usually added to other foods. Fruit juice also contains free sugars, as the juicing process removes the fibre that was part of the cell walls of the fruit. This is why it's recommended to drink no more than 150ml of 100 per cent fruit juice a day, that's a small glass or just over half a regular one. It does still count as one of your fruit and veg a day as it contains many vitamins and minerals – there's plenty of evidence that a little bit of 100 per cent fruit juice is good for your health,[2] so don't feel like you can't have it if you like it.

The big sugar lies

- **'Natural sugar is better'**

Agave syrup, coconut sugar, maple syrup and honey are often touted as being 'better' for you than table sugar. But they are all pretty much the same thing, with very minimal nutritional differences between them. So while they may contain some additional vitamins and minerals they're not in large enough quantities to make a difference to your health.

- **'Fruit is bad for you'**

While fruit contains sugar, that sugar is slowly released and comes with lots of other healthy nutrients and compounds. It's a complete myth that you should avoid eating fruit. Fruits are just as important as vegetables in supporting the diversity of your gut bacteria, and helping them make short-chain fatty acids. You can enjoy fruit whole or blended into a smoothie, which keeps the fibre.

- **'Sweeteners cause cancer'**

Sweeteners provide a sweet taste without providing the body with any sugar, so they can help you manage your blood-sugar levels if you're diabetic. There's been a lot of

---

scaremongering around sweeteners – particularly based on mice studies that link sweeteners to cancer and changes in their gut microbiome. These mice studies often don't use realistic doses of sweeteners though – extensive studies in humans have found no link between sweeteners and cancer,[3] and no detrimental effect on the gut microbiome or its production of short-chain fatty acids in humans.[4]

What foods do most of our free sugars come from?

In the UK, most of the free sugars we eat are from certain foods. We eat:

- 25 per cent from biscuits, buns, cakes, breakfast cereals and other cereal foods
- 26 per cent from table sugar, sweets, jams and sweet spreads
- 15 per cent from sugary soft drinks
- 10 per cent from alcoholic drinks
- 6 per cent from fruit juice

On the next page there's a list of typical snack foods and drinks, with their equivalent amounts of free sugars. It's often the sugary drinks that can easily take you over your 30g threshold a day. But I hope you can also see that occasionally having a few biscuits or a croissant can be just as much part of a varied healthy and balanced diet. Every food you eat doesn't have to be nutrient dense. Cutting out all sugary foods is more likely to lead to overeating, guilt, shame and feeling pretty rubbish about yourself.

Food/Drink	Amount	Free sugars (g)
Coca-Cola	330ml	39
Red Bull	250ml	28
Cool Blue Gatorade	500ml	20
Magnum ice cream	1 Magnum	20
Lucozade	380ml	17
Fruit juice	150ml (small glass)	16
Margarita cocktail	150ml (small glass)	14
Cider	330ml	14
Gin and tonic	250ml	13
Tonic water	250ml	12
Sprite	330ml	11
Milk chocolate bar	2–4 chunks (20g)	11
Vanilla ice cream	1 scoop	10
Fruit yoghurt	1 pot	10
70 per cent cocoa dark chocolate	2–4 chunks (20g)	6
1 tsp of sugar	5g	5
1 tsp of honey	7g	5
Digestives	2 biscuits	5
Cornflakes	1 bowl (60g)	5
Vitamin-enriched water	500ml	4
Croissant	1 croissant	4

Food/Drink	Standard portion size	Free sugars (g)
Oreo	1 biscuit	4
Rich Tea biscuit	2 biscuits	3
Tomato sauce	1 tsp	2
BBQ sauce	1 tsp	2

Is it normal to want something sweet after a meal?

It's perfectly normal to want a little sweet hit after a meal. Growing up, my brothers and I used to call it our separate pudding stomach (I'm sure we weren't the only ones) because even though we felt full, suddenly we'd want something sweet to round it all off.

This is called sensory specific satiety where, as you finish your meal your enjoyment of it declines but your tastebuds are still sensitive to other new flavours, like something sweet. The reason we think this happens is due to evolution. Preferring something sweet after a meal was an advantage to your ancestors – to help them squeeze in extra nutrition and energy that would mean they were more likely to survive. Wanting something sweet was likely because sweetness signalled a quick source of energy. If this speaks to you, then see Hack 7: Join the Dark Side.

18. In Tune With Your Body

Your brain relies heavily on a sugar called glucose for energy. It's a vital fuel that allows each part of your brain to carry out its functions. When your blood-sugar levels lower it signals to your brain that you need more energy, turning on your hunger to encourage you to eat. Ever noticed when you're super hungry it's like there's a compass needle drawing you towards food? Snacks mysteriously call out to you, and you crave a burger or a greasy take-out over a salad? The further your blood-sugar levels fall the hungrier you get, and your brain starts to manipulate your decisions for its own means – get more energy.

Glucose

Glucose is a type of sugar that is crucial for fuelling your brain. It's your brain's main source of energy, helping your cognition, your concentration and the overall performance of your mind. You get glucose directly, or from converting other types of sugars, from carbohydrate-rich foods like whole grains, bread, pasta, rice and fruits and vegetables, dairy, table sugar and sugar-sweetened foods.

Even though your brain takes up 2 per cent of your body weight, it uses up 20 per cent of your energy needs and it's particularly sensitive when you're running low on fuel, and especially your prefrontal cortex. Your prefrontal cortex is the CEO of your brain – it's the mastermind, the key decision maker, the strategic planner, and oversees many functions involved in how you think, what you do and your emotions.

Think of your prefrontal cortex as a battery, charged by the food you eat, but also by sleep, exercise and easing stress. When your battery runs low you struggle to concentrate or make clear decisions, your mood plummets and you feel tired and irritable. And feeling hangry, it's a thing. When you're hungry, you feel more annoyed than you would if you weren't hungry – because your depleted prefrontal cortex struggles to regulate your emotions. Married couples given voodoo dolls to represent their partners were told to stick pins in them each night, depending on how peed off with them they were that day. And those who had lower blood-glucose levels stuck in significantly more pins![1]

Feeling hungry can change your food choices too. When you shift from the early rumblings of hunger to starving hungry the activity in your brain shifts from your practical decision-making prefrontal cortex to the parts of your brain related to reward[2] – you get a stronger urge to eat and your brain manipulates what kind of foods you want to eat too. It wants energy, and fast. Foods that are higher in energy? Foods that tend to be high in sugar or fat, and happen to be less nutrient dense. The ones that taste great! More than fine now and again, but by only eating when you're ravenously hungry, it can skew the balance of what you want to eat and make eating enough gut-friendly foods harder.

Your gut bacteria are closely intertwined with your hunger and appetite. Hormones produced in your gut signal to your brain whether you're hungry or full. When your gut bacteria feed on fibre, the metabolites they produce can help to stimulate your fullness hormones – making you feel full and satisfied. Short-chain fatty acids butyrate and propionate particularly encourage the release of GLP-1, the satiety hormone that's now being used as a weight-loss injection in a concentrated form.

Do you ever feel hungrier on some days than others?

Your energy needs aren't regulated across one day where your body 'resets' and you start the next day afresh. Your body can self-correct its energy needs by increasing or decreasing your hunger signals even two to three days after a day of over- or under-eating.[3]

What does it feel like when you're hungry? What physical sensations are there?_____

What's your mood?_____

Energy levels? _____

Focus and concentration?_____

Listen to your hunger and fullness

Your gut is trying to get you to listen and respond to your hunger and fullness signals.

You might think that you're pretty in tune with your own hunger and satiety signals, but in a world that promotes one restrictive way of eating after another, many of us have consciously or subconsciously taught ourselves to ignore feeling hungry. The classic one I see time and time again is when people say, 'I'm just not hungry at breakfast', then steadfastly ignore their stomachs' rumbling louder and louder throughout the morning, and then have an energy crash in the afternoon. Instead, start eating much closer to the earlier signs of hunger like your stomach feeling a sense of emptiness, and maybe the very early gurgles of stomach rumbling. Hunger can also be feeling empty, tired and moody. When you finish eating there should be a sense of satisfaction and fullness. You can use the hunger and fullness scale below to help you reconnect with when and how much to eat.

Hunger and fullness scale

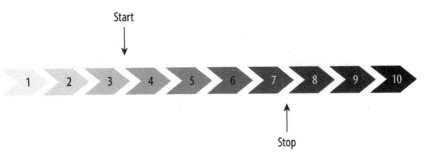

Figure 9. Learn to listen to your gut

Hunger and fullness scale

1. Starving, ravenous – feeling dizzy, faint, shaking
2. Extremely hungry – loud rumbling stomach, deep hunger ache, moody
3. Hungry – some stomach rumbles, sense of emptiness
4. Some slight hunger – could eat something
5. Neutral
6. Slight feeling of satisfaction, but not complete
7. Sensation of stomach fullness, feeling relaxed, satisfied
8. Stomach feels overstretched, a little uncomfortable
9. Feeling stuffed, overfull and uncomfortable
10. Feeling physically sick and overfull, nauseous

A few times in your day take a moment to see which number on the hunger and fullness scale best describes what you're feeling. It doesn't have to be a perfect fit, more like a multiple-choice question where you select the answer most relevant to you in that moment. When you can, you want to start eating at around a 3 or 4. Eating at 1 or 2 is when your brain shifts into survival mode and is more likely to choose those tasty, less nutrient-dense options for immediate fuel. You can also check in when you're eating at the beginning, in the middle and at the end of a meal.

When you're finishing eating, ideally most of the time you want to be landing at around 7. But again, this isn't a hard-and-fast rule, but a tool you can use to kindly and curiously check in with yourself and how you're feeling.

19. Feeling Energised, Feeling Great

I have one friend who practically bounces off the walls because he has so much energy, and he's jokingly encouraged to go for long runs to burn some of it off. He's a lucky outlier though. For the rest of us mere mortals, feeling energised, alert and bouncy tends to be something we have to put a bit of work into.

How you combine foods can help you to have more energy through the day. It can slow down the release of sugar into your bloodstream so that you have a steady energy supply for longer:

- You'll feel more energised
- You'll feel fuller for longer (and so less hungry as quickly)
- It helps you to focus, think well, problem-solve and make decisions
- It lifts your mood and you'll cope with stress better
- You can make gut-friendly choices more easily

Family car vs formula 1

Certain foods are like the Formula 1 cars of energy delivery. When eaten on their own, your blood-sugar levels can surge quickly, delivering energy in short bursts, which is then used up fast. These tend to be foods high in simple carbohydrates like sugar and refined carbohydrates. Great when you're running a marathon and you need a quick boost to keep you going by reaching for a handful of jelly babies. Not so great for every day though – you wouldn't want to drive a Formula 1 car to do your supermarket shop or pick up the kids from school. They're often a thrill of a ride, but that energy is depleted fast, and you can feel tired and hungry quickly if they're eaten on their own.

Formula 1 foods:

- Sweets, candies, white and milk chocolates
- White bread and white pasta
- Desserts, pastries, biscuits and cake
- Sugar-sweetened drinks
- Energy drinks and sports gels

You don't have to get rid of the Formula 1 car altogether though. You can swap out the racing tyres for slower and more reliable road ones. You can add a larger fuel tank, a boot, and some extra seats in the back – and you're ready to rumble. So you don't have to *not* have a Formula 1 car ever, it's how you're adjusting it by adding other foods with it that can help to slow down the release of energy into your bloodstream, keeping you feeling full and energised for longer, and feeling great. Here's the secret.

Feel more energised for longer

Fibre-rich, protein-rich and fat-rich foods slow down the release of sugar into your bloodstream, so that you have a more consistent supply for longer. They act as extra weights to the Formula 1 car to slow it down and tend to contain more nutrients that your body needs. And just like how your converted Formula 1 car is more likely to steal the show when you do a full pimp-my-ride makeover and add in all the new mod cons, rather than only adding some extra seats, it's having a balance of these foods together that best keeps you feeling fuller and energised for longer.

- **Your energy and fullness levels:** If you're on a blood-sugar rollercoaster you're likely to feel tired and sluggish. By eating foods that slow-release energy into your blood-stream, this helps you to keep your energy stable and feel full for longer.
- **Brainpower:** How well your brain works is closely tied to a balanced and consistent supply of glucose. If there are fluctuations in how much fuel is delivered, much like the spluttering engine of a car with a near-empty tank, your brain will struggle to function at its best – you'll find it harder to concentrate or problem-solve.
- **Your mood:** When the amino acid tryptophan reaches the brain a lot of energy is needed to convert it into your happy hormone serotonin and other neurotransmitters. This process relies on glucose to provide the necessary energy for this to happen. If you're on a sugar roller-coaster where your blood-sugar levels repeatedly surge and drop, you're more likely to feel sad or down.[1]

You can slow down the release of sugar into your bloodstream by combining carbohydrates with protein, fat and extra fibre. Again, take this as flexible guidance for most days – it's about balance, remember?

Carbohydrates

Carbohydrates are either simple carbohydrates, like those in sugar, biscuits, cakes, pancakes and pastries, refined white bread and pasta, or complex carbohydrates that have a slower release of energy. Fibre is a type of carbohydrate mostly found in the cell walls of plant foods like vegetables, fruit, beans and legumes, nuts and seeds and whole grains. The more fibre a carbohydrate has the more 'complex' a carbohydrate it is (see page 224 for the fibre:carb ratio).

. . . add fibre

Together with protein and fats, you can add extra fibre to your Formula 1 food (like adding veggies or fruit) and, if you like, you can also swap your Formula 1 food for its high-fibre whole-grain alternatives like rye bread, whole-wheat pasta, or brown rice. Fibre helps to slow down the release of sugar into your bloodstream, and helps you to feel fuller by adding bulk and volume to the food in your gut. Don't forget that your gut bacteria also help you to feel full and satisfied. When your gut bacteria feed on fibre they produce short-chain fatty acids that help to regulate how much or how little your hunger and fullness hormones talk to your brain.

. . . add protein

Protein foods aren't only meat, fish and eggs; legumes, beans, nuts and seeds are also good sources of protein.

Protein is the most satiating nutrient – adding a protein-rich food can slow down the absorption of sugar into your bloodstream and can activate the release of gut-fullness hormones that tell your brain that you're full.[2] Your gut bacteria can break down some of the amino acids into metabolites that can influence the release of these fullness hormones too. Eating protein is vital for maintaining and building muscle mass and supporting your immune system, crucial for healthy ageing and living a long life.

How much protein do you need a day?

Most adults need at least 0.8g of protein per kg of body weight per day.[3] If you're doing resistance exercise to build muscle, then you'll need more protein and 1.2–1.6g of protein per kg of your body weight can help you to maximise muscle gains.

For example, if you weigh 72kg, that's 72 x 0.8 = 58g of protein a day. Try to aim for between 20 and 30g of protein per meal.

A good rule of thumb is making a quarter of your plate full of protein-rich foods or about 20–30g of protein at each main meal to feel fuller and more energised for longer. If you're eating plant-based protein then it'll take up more than a quarter of your plate, as plant protein tends to be lower in protein than animal foods.

For every . . .	Protein (g)	20-30g of protein looks like	Protein (g)
1 beef steak	31	1 beef steak	31
1 chicken breast	31	1 chicken breast	31
1 salmon fillet	31	1 salmon fillet	31
1 cod fillet	21	1 cod fillet	21
¼ block firm tofu	18	⅓ block firm tofu	24
½ can tuna	16	¾ can tuna	24
2 slices bacon	12	4 slices bacon	24
½ can baked beans	11	1 can baked beans	22
½ can red kidney beans	10	1 can red kidney beans	20
glass of milk	9	2½ glasses of milk	22
1 cup quinoa (cooked)	9	2½ cups quinoa	22
½ can chickpeas	9	1½ cans chickpeas	27
1 pork sausage	8	3 sausages	24
½ can green lentils	8	2 cans of green lentils	32
3 tbsp Greek yoghurt	8	8 tbsp Greek yoghurt	21
1 egg	7	3 eggs	21
1 vegetarian sausage	7	3 vegetarian sausages	21
1 glass soy milk	6	3 ½ glasses soy milk	21
1 tbsp cottage cheese	4	6 tbsp cottage cheese	24

. . . add fat

More healthy vs less healthy fats

More healthy fats are found in foods like avocado, extra-virgin olive oil, fatty fish, nuts and seeds – these fats have a positive effect on your health.

Many animal products like bacon, red meat, salamis and butter can be high in fat, particularly a type of less healthy fat called saturated fat, which, if you eat these foods regularly in large amounts, isn't great for the health of your blood vessels and arteries – and consequently for your heart and brain (encased in a web of blood vessels).

Fats also help to slow down how quickly sugar is absorbed into your bloodstream. They do plenty more though. If you want to make the most of your fruit and veg, pair them with some fat – even a little bit can help you to absorb more nutrition, as many bioactive molecules and vitamins are fat-soluble.[4] They also tend to carry flavour molecules really well and add a rich mouthfeel, helping make food taste great.

The high-energy formula

For a satisfying meal that will keep you feeling full and energised for longer, aim for your plate to include carbs, fibre, protein and fats. This will help to slowly release the energy from your meal. Some foods can be high in more than one nutrient, like beans and legumes are high in protein and fibre, nuts are high in fat and fibre (and protein), and oily fish is high in protein and fat. Don't feel like you must always combine every single element – apply it how you feel works best for the meal or snack that you're eating.

Carbs	Fibre foods	Protein foods	Healthier fat-rich foods
Whole grains Formula 1s Potatoes	Vegetables Salad greens Fruit Beans Legumes Kimchi Kraut Nuts and seeds	Tinned tuna Salmon White fish Chicken Turkey Beans Chickpeas Hummus Tofu Seafood Tempeh Cottage cheese Eggs Greek yoghurt Nuts and seeds Nut butter Other meat, fish and dairy	Avocado Extra-virgin olive oil Sesame oil Cheese Nuts and seeds Cottage cheese Greek yoghurt Nut butters Olives Oily fish

High-energy meal examples

Green mixed salad, chickpeas, tinned tuna and yoghurt
tahini dressing

Rye bread, avocado, tomato and egg

Pasta, chicken, bacon, olives, tomatoes and salad

High-energy snack examples

Oat crackers, cottage cheese and kimchi

Banana with nut butter

Dark chocolate, prunes and almonds

Hummus with whole-grain pita

Nuts, apple and cheese

Canned tuna, avocado and rye bread

Greek yoghurt, pear, honey and thyme

Balanced Formula 1s

Chocolate cake, berries and Greek yoghurt

Sweets, nuts and apple

White bread, poached eggs, spinach and avocado

20. Your Tasty Brain

OK, we do have one absolute rule here. Food must taste good. For most people taste is the deciding factor in what to eat, how much to eat and if you're happy to eat that food again. And I don't think that should change. Instead of fighting this, let's use it to make it easier to eat more gut-friendly foods.

Say goodbye to sad limp salads.

No thanks to dry rice cakes with a thin smear of peanut butter.

Adios to watery soups and sticks of celery.

And welcome to so, so much more.

How to make more healthy food taste good

There are two aspects to making any food taste good. Flavour and texture. Let's think about why a burger tastes so mouth-watering. It's got umami and fattiness from the meat, there's sweetness from the bread and fried onions, acidity from the tomato, crunchiness from the lettuce leaves and saltiness from the seasoning.

- **Umami:** Savoury taste that gives depth and complexity. Found in tomatoes, cheese, meat, soy sauce and mushrooms.

- **Sweet:** This could be from fresh or dried fruit, bread croutons, sweet potatoes, Greek yoghurt, honey, a touch of table sugar and more.
- **Salt:** Saltiness can be from seasoning a dish with salt, or adding foods that are salty like feta cheese, anchovies and salted nuts.
- **Fat:** Fat lends more of a creamy mouthfeel to a dish and is a great flavour booster. You can add avocado, extra-virgin olive oil, fatty fish like salmon, trout and mackerel, and nuts and seeds or fermented dairy.
- **Acidity:** Acidity balances fat well, like from the juice of lemons, limes and oranges, vinegars, kefir, or other fermented foods like kimchi and sauerkraut.

These are all taste elements that make a dish well-rounded, satisfying and enjoyable. Whenever a chef is creating a dish, they're always thinking about these flavour principles. A bowl of salad leaves and a few lonely slices of tomato doesn't inspire your tastebuds. Add in some grilled chicken, croutons, feta, toasted pumpkin seeds and broccoli – and what about a green kefir dressing – now that sounds more fun. For you *and* your gut bacteria. More variety for your tastebuds, more different types of gut-friendly foods for your gut microbiome.

The base to every great salad dressing

Remember this ratio – it's the secret to any great dressing. You add one third acidity to two thirds fat, with ½ –1 tsp of something sweet, a pinch of salt and any extra flavourings you like.

Acidity:

Lemon juice

Lime juice

White wine, red wine or sherry vinegar

Apple cider vinegar

Balsamic vinegar

Fat:

Extra-virgin olive oil

Rapeseed oil with a touch of sesame seed oil

Any other oil that is liquid at room temperature

Sweet:

Sugar

Honey

Maple syrup

Saltiness: Season with salt (and pepper).

Extras:

Mustard adds great flavour and also helps to emulsify the mixture so that it doesn't split. You can also add some crushed garlic, herbs and spices for extra flavour. For creaminess add kefir, yoghurt, or blend in some avocado.

Enjoy gut-friendly foods by:

- **Balancing flavours of sweet, salt, fat, acidity and umami.**
- **Dressing it up:** Add a salad dressing or sauce.

- **Creating a texture medley:** There is a reason we say variety is the spice of life. A medley of veggies is going to taste better as the variety of flavours is more fun for your tastebuds.
- **Adding herbs and spices:** Not only super high in nutrition but great for added flavour.
- **Making a salad? Finely chop it!** This can make a huge difference. Chopping up the components means you get a delicious flavour variety at every mouthful, and not just one large lonely salad leaf at a time.

Try these flavour boosters

- Cheese
- Avocado
- Salad dressings
- Herbs
- Lemon juice
- Extra-virgin olive oil
- Toasted nuts
- Seed mix
- Harissa paste
- Roasted garlic
- Croutons
- Spice mixes
- Marinades
- Pesto
- Mustard

- Mayonnaise
- Pomegranate molasses
- Capers
- Olives
- Greek yoghurt
- Soy sauce
- Chutneys
- Pickles
- Tahini sauce
- Anchovies

21. Small Changes Are Successful

There's a recipe to success for making any new change – and one that you can actually keep up over time. No more go big, go home. No more trying to punish yourself as a way of forcing you to do it. Instead, it's making small – and I mean *small* – changes that are easy and enjoyable, that you'll be best able to stick to and keep up over time.

The golden rules of eating in a way you can stick to

- Keep it enjoyable
- Keep the change easy
- Keep calm and carry on

Nail the three points above and you can make any change work for you.

We have the power to rewire our own brains, forming new neural pathways by repeating actions over and over again until it becomes natural and easy.

Keep it enjoyable

It goes without saying that a new habit must be something that you enjoy – you're far more likely to keep it up. If you don't like kimchi, don't eat it – how about kefir instead? If you hate the gym what about a dance class or yoga? Habits that feel like a punishment not only make you feel like rubbish but are so much harder to keep up. So make it easy and fun. And praise yourself too! Give yourself regular pats on the back, tell yourself you're awesome. You've got this, you're doing great. Be your own cheerleader. There is power in believing in yourself and in believing you can do something, it improves your mental well-being[1] and makes it easier for you to achieve it.

Keep the change small, keep it easy

Any change you make needs to be achievable even on days when you're tired, feeling crummy and – let's be really honest with each other – the well of motivation has run to a very slow, tiny trickle. Where we tend to go wrong is when we set a big goal when we feel super motivated right at the beginning. This happens when we make New Year's resolutions; buoyed by the thought of a fresh start anything seems possible. We feel really inspired, and we lay out grand life-changing plans on how we'll completely change and feel like a totally new person. What happens is that motivation naturally diminishes over time, and the harder the new habit you've set for yourself the more difficult it is to do – until you stop and give up.

Professor BJ Fogg from Stanford University uses a fantastic example of how to take tiny steps to make a habit. If you're wanting to start flossing your teeth, then set your goal to floss one tooth. Yes that's right – just one tooth. That small. You might think, well what's the point, that's silly. But when you start making a change, the first thing you want to do is make the starting action a habit, the beginning motion to making the change. It's setting the action of a habit that's the hardest part. Building up and adding more teeth to floss is a natural progression from that. But to start with – you need something so small and so easy that even on days that you just can't compute or you don't have time and there are too many other things going on – you can still floss one

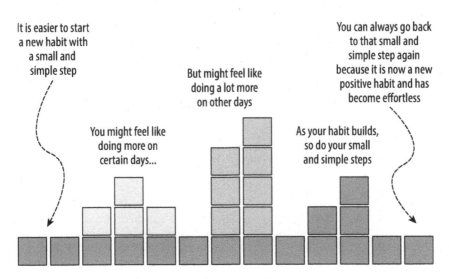

Regular small and simple steps

It is easier to start a new habit with a small and simple step

You might feel like doing more on certain days...

But might feel like doing a lot more on other days

As your habit builds, so do your small and simple steps

You can always go back to that small and simple step again because it is now a new positive habit and has become effortless

Figure 10.   Start with a small change

tooth. Even small changes can have a big impact over time. It might be something as small as adding a nut, seed and wheat-bran mix on top of your breakfast each morning, or taking a piece of fruit in your bag to work each day.

Lower the threshold of what you think 'good enough' is. It needs to be small enough that on a day you're feeling your lowest you feel like, yea I think I still could do that. And then build up from there.

Keep calm and carry on

By starting with a tiny habit and slowly building up to your goal, you've given yourself the flexibility to show up daily in a way that works for you. In stages of your life where you're feeling like you're on top of the world, that's a great time to ramp up towards your end goal. Say a week later, though, you find out some bad news, and at the same time work is extra busy and you have a thousand deadlines to meet – here is the shocker – YES, you can return to a smaller version of the habit. By being flexible you're far more likely to keep to it.

The hacks in this book are meant to be practical. They're meant to be easy. I want you to look at these steps and think:

- 'OK, I can do that!'
- 'Yes, I could start small and work up towards that!'
- 'I can keep this up even on the curveball days when life is the pits.'
- 'I'm struggling today, and that's OK. How can I make this easier for myself?'

Every single hack is designed to make your life easier and better, going straight to the heart of how to feel your absolute best. How to support your gut, your gut microbiome and your brain – for more energy, better mood and putting the z in zest. I have complete faith in you making flexible changes that work for you – particularly now that perfectionism and rigid rules are in the bin.

PART FIVE – THE GENIUS GUT METHOD

Your 10 gut-brain hacks to superpower your second brain

Genius Gut Hack 1: Half Your Plate With Veggies
Genius Gut Hack 2: Go for the Colourful Five
Genius Gut Hack 3: Eat the BGBGs
Genius Gut Hack 4: Opt for a Daily Ferment
Genius Gut Hack 5: Make Early Dinner Your Friend
Genius Gut Hack 6: Oily Fish Twice a Week
Genius Gut Hack 7: Join the Dark Side
Genius Gut Hack 8: Protein- and Fibre-Power Your Breakfast
Genius Gut Hack 9: Zen Out Your Brain, Zen Out Your Gut
Genius Gut Hack 10: Drink Up!

Hack 1: Half Your Plate With Veggies

Most of us need to eat more veg. Do you know how much veg you actually need for your health, though? Like in real terms, if I pulled all the food out of your fridge onto the table in front of you and said let's arrange this into meals, how much of it would be veg?*

I don't want to talk about cups or servings or grams here. It's not often that you have the time and energy to weigh or measure what you eat – if you even want to. Instead, let's keep it simple. There's no magical mystique to this step and if you're looking to bio-hack your metabolism with a special Aztec berry, then this isn't the book you're looking for. What I can confidently guarantee is that this single change is one of the biggest impacts you can have on your gut bacteria and health. Make half your plate veggies. You don't have to cook anything new if you don't want to, you don't have to think hard about how to go

---

* A meta-analysis by Imperial College London estimated that 800g of fruits and veg a day could prevent 7.8 million premature deaths worldwide.[1]

about it. You can simply change the proportion of veg that you already have on your plate to a generous half, or add in some new types. That's it. Eyeball the amount and go.

Filling half your plate with veg is like getting dressed for the day. Your fruit and veg are your everyday clothes – whether you're in your well-worn trackies or spruced up to go out for dinner. Fancy-smancy nutrition hacks (if they're legit) are more like accessorising with a belt or a hat. No matter how great your styling is, you don't leave the house without at least your underwear on. Accessories are just that, nice embellishments but not essential. Get the clothes on first, and then you can add the rest if you want to.

Eating more veg doesn't have to be a chore. Veggies are exciting and delicious and they absolutely have main character energy. This is not signing your tastebuds away to a lifetime of mouth-sadness. This is throwing a party for them. It's always baffled me how we tend to think of meat as the only star of the show at any given meal. If I were to hand out Oscars to food it would be to charred cabbage slathered in tahini dressing, crunchy hazelnut-dusted garlic green beans and honey-roasted spiced carrots. Veggies are bright, colourful, packed with flavour and textures. The possibilities with veggies are endless.

If you like, feel free to add some fruit in there too – they're equally good for you. Fruit could make up half your plate at breakfast, or add it into your lunch or dinner – they make a delicious balance to salty cheese or crunchy nuts in salads, for example. Or if you prefer your fruit separate to your veg, have a bowl of chopped fruit for afterwards.

Why make half your plate veg (or fruit)?
For your gut bacteria

You're in a partnership with your gut bacteria, and I'm here to act as your relationship counsellor. Sometimes you just need someone else to point out 'the thing', the elephant in the room, even if you kind of knew it already. Fruit and veg contain the double whammy of fibre and polyphenols, a group of antioxidants that act as rocket fuel for your gut bacteria (more on polyphenols soon). They're nutrient powerhouses packed with vitamins, minerals and plant biochemicals that are vital for your gut and your brain. Not only that, but the bacteria naturally present on fruits and vegetables make their way to your gut and contribute to your diversity of gut bacteria[2] (did you know an apple alone contains 100 million microbes?[3]).

To feel your absolute best

Fruit and veg can make you happier too. A study of people who upped their fruits and veg were not only happier than the group who didn't change what they ate, but also happier than they'd been before the study too – in only eight weeks.[4] Psychologists have been able to predict how happy someone is purely based on how much fruit and veg they'd eaten the day before.[5]

To boost your brainpower

Eating more fruit and vegetables supports optimal brain function because many of the various nutrients and bioactive compounds they contain are crucial for your brain health. You don't have to go from zero to hero either, as even starting small has powerful benefits. Having two or more servings of veggies a day – so not even a huge amount – is linked to having the cognitive age of someone five years younger as you get older.[6] Consistency matters too. Those who eat veggies daily are 56 per cent less likely to have cognitive problems later in life than those who rarely or never eat them.[7]

Fresh or frozen?

The frozen aisle is your secret weapon for those days when your fridge is empty and you haven't got the time or energy to go to the shops. There are so many different types of frozen fruits and vegetables available these days – peruse the frozen aisle next time you're at the supermarket and see what's on offer. Frozen fruit and veg are usually frozen straight after picking, locking in their nutrition – making them just as nutritious a choice as fresh, and often cheaper too.

Is organic better for you?

Choosing to eat organic food is a personal decision, especially considering that it usually costs more. While some studies suggest that organic foods have slightly more nutrients, it's unclear if this difference is enough to affect your health.[8] Most pesticides used on non-organic produce are regulated and present in minuscule amounts unlikely to harm humans. However, research on the impact of pesticides on the gut microbiome is ongoing, and there are some early findings in mice that some pesticides could be harmful to their gut bacteria,[9] but we don't know how this affects us as humans. Pesticides do not cancel or limit the powerful benefits of non-organic fruit or veg. Ultimately, whether you choose organic or non-organic depends on you and your circumstances, and one isn't necessarily better than the other – particularly if buying only organic limits your variety or the amount of fruit or veg you eat because of the cost.

Make half your plate veggies by:

- **Upping the amount of veg that you would normally have:** This is a great starting point to ease you into eating more veg, by shifting the amount that you usually put on your plate. If you're short on time you could also make a weekly roasting tray of veggies to help you add more on to your plate – you can add them into salads, curries or whizz them up into a tapenade.
- **Bulking up the amount by adding other veg too:** We've been doing veg wrong for too long – they shouldn't be bland and boring. By getting creative and having a variety of veg it's not only going to be more interesting for your tastebuds but will also provide a variety of fibre and polyphenols for your gut bacteria too. Roast veg with spices, chop-shred-and-dress your salads, dollop ricotta on top or sprinkle with nuts . . . the opportunities are endless.

- **Adding more veggies to stews and sauces:** Remember that you can add more veg into dishes and they don't have to just be as a side. When you make your base of onion and garlic, why not add some carrot and celery too? You could swap out half the meat in a bolognese for lentils, or add some extra veg like mushrooms, tomatoes and spinach into stews and sauces.
- **Having a veggie starter like a salad, veg sticks and hummus, or soup:** If you're making half your plate veggies for your main meal but struggling to finish them, then this could be the solution for you. Researchers found that by having a veggie starter, the participants ate nearly a quarter more veg than they did when just having them with their main meal.[10]
- **Mashing or pureeing your veg:** Many veg work well as mashes or purees, like cauliflower, white beans, carrots and sweet potatoes.
- **Adding a veggie dip:** I always keep some shop-bought hummus and guacamole in my fridge that not only count as an extra load of veggies but also as a condiment of sorts.
- **Stocking up on long-lasting veg:** Stir-fry frozen veg or add to soups, stews and pasta sauces. Vacuum-packed beetroot is also useful to have in the fridge as it lasts a long time, doesn't need cooking and can be eaten hot or cold. Root veggies, cabbages and squashes also have a longer life than other veggies.
- **Not knocking leftovers:** Make at least one extra portion when you cook. And that will either roll over into a whole new dish or can be added as a side to your next meal.

Do potatoes count as a vegetable?

White potatoes, yams, plantains and cassava are vegetables but they tend to be excluded or limited from many 'eat more veggies' guidelines. This is because they aren't as dense in nutrition and they tend to be associated more with other starchy foods, like grains. They still contribute valuable nutrients, though, and while they don't technically count towards your veg intake we shouldn't dismiss them altogether. I feel potatoes have been unfairly maligned for too long and seem to stir up strong opinions – I once knew someone so adamant they're bad for your health that their reaction to any mention of potatoes' positive qualities was jokingly dubbed 'potato-gate'.

In defence of potatoes:

- **Potatoes help you to feel full:** Of 100 foods, boiled potatoes had the highest satiety index score,[11] meaning they are more likely to help you feel full and satisfied for longer. Though sadly the same can't be said for mash and fried potatoes, despite how delicious they are.

- **Keep their skin on for extra fibre:** While potatoes aren't a high-fibre food, because we eat so many of them they have the potential to still make a significant contribution to our fibre intake – particularly if you keep the skins on – doubling the amount of fibre. You can do this with other veg too, like sweet potatoes, carrots and parsnips, and some fruit, like kiwis.

- **Reheat and eat for your gut bacteria:** Potatoes are high in resistant starch, which your gut bacteria particularly likes. Cooling cooked potatoes can triple their resistant starch content – making leftovers not only less hassle but potentially even better for your gut bacteria too.[12]

Put It into Practice . . .

I will . . .

_____

_____

e.g.

- make double the amount of veggies when I cook so I have extra left over to have at my next meal
- eat a salad starter twice a week on Wednesday and Friday evenings
- stock my freezer with frozen peas and spinach

So I can . . .

_____

[your Genius Gut goal]
e.g. make my plate half veggies (or fruit)

So that . . .

_____

[your Genius Gut 'why']
e.g. I feel my absolute best!

What's veg gut to do with it?

- Eating plenty of vegetables is important for both your gut bacteria and your brain health
- Make half your plate from vegetables (or fruit) at breakfast, lunch and dinner
- You can increase the amount of veggies you usually have or add in some new veg
- Having a veggie starter can help you to eat 25 per cent more veg than if you only had it with a main meal
- Keep the skins on root veggies and certain fruits like kiwis for extra fibre

Hack 2: Go for the Colourful Five

Variety really is the spice of life – particularly for your gut micro-biome. Lots of different types of gut bacteria – a more diverse gut microbiome – is linked to good health and, for those with certain gut bacteria, with better emotional well-being.[1] The more different types of bacteria you have, the more different types of metabolites they can produce – and there's around 50,000 of them.[2]

A diverse microbiome:

- Helps to make your microbiome more resilient against being disrupted
- Protects you from 'bad' bacteria by blocking their growth[3]
- Is better able to produce vitamins and beneficial metab-olites for your health and mood
- Keeps your gut barrier lining healthy and strong – preventing it becoming weak and leaky
- Supports your immune system to function at its best

What helps with your diversity of gut bacteria? Food! A variety of colourful gut-friendly foods. Eating a wide variety of gut-friendly foods supports your different types of gut bacteria to thrive because, like us, your gut bacteria have their own taste preferences too. Some of your gut bacteria like a particular type of fibre or polyphenol, and others another. A little like how I love mushrooms and maybe you think they're slimy and disgusting and would prefer to avoid them like the plague.

What counts as a plant?

Fruit, vegetables, beans and legumes, nuts and seeds, whole grains, spices and herbs are all plants.

An easy way to think about how to provide your gut bacteria with a range of different menu items is to think about plant shape and colour – the shape of broccoli versus a tomato, and the colour of black beans to the sunshine yellow of a mango.

Variety of shapes

The shape of a plant (let's just use veg as an example here for ease) is mostly down to different fibre types and how those fibres are arranged. The long, skinny carrot contains different types of fibre or different arrangements of fibre to the umbrella of a mushroom, yet broccoli and cauliflower tend to be more similar.

Fibre makes up a large part of the cell walls of plants, providing structural support that is a large factor in their shape and texture.

Eating different shapes and textures of plants, from a round juicy tomato to a banana, provides your gut bacteria with a variety of fibre types – a smorgasbord feast. Even parts of the same plant can be different, like the bulb of a beetroot compared to its leaves and stalks. You don't have to get too specific with this one, but it's an easy way to think about variety.

While fibre in general is great for your gut microbiome, there are certain types of fibre that are extra special for your gut bacteria.[4] There aren't particular shapes you can look out for, but there's a list on the following page of which foods contain them. These fibres are called prebiotic fibres, because they particularly help your 'good' gut bacteria to grow and thrive, and have been shown through scientific studies to give a specific health benefit.

Eating plenty of prebiotic fibres not only increases your 'good' bacteria, but helps you to:*

- Feel fuller (buh-bye, hunger!)
- Crave sweet and salty food less[5, 6]
- Be more emotionally grounded – helping you to recognise, understand and manage your emotions[7]
- Shift your attention from the negative to the positive[8]
- Be less stressed[9]
- Feel less anxious[10]
- Think well and remember more in later life[11]

Fascinating, right? It's like your gut bacteria saying, 'hey – scratch our back, we'll scratch yours'.

---

* Some of this evidence is based on prebiotic fibre supplements. See page 300 on how to download a free list of probiotics and prebiotics for stress, cognition and mood.

Prebiotics

A prebiotic is a substance that feeds specific 'good' bacteria in your gut, helping your health. Some prebiotics are fibres, and others are not. Confirmed prebiotics include the fibres fructo-oligosaccharides (FOS), inulin, and galacto-oligosaccharides (GOS). There are also candidate prebiotics like resistant starch, pectin, polyphenols and omega-3s. Add some of the foods below to your shopping list, but remember that your gut bacteria love a range of different plants, so even if a plant isn't on this list, it's still great to include.

Top prebiotic containing foods:

- Chicory root
- Jerusalem artichoke
- Garlic
- Leeks
- Onions
- Beans
- Asparagus

Polyphenols

Polyphenols are a powerful group of molecules found in all plant foods. There are more than 8,000 different polyphenols, yet you can only absorb 5–10 per cent of polyphenols by yourself. The other 90–95 per cent land in your large intestine and onto the kitchen table of your gut bacteria. Most of the powerful health effects of polyphenols can be attributed to your gut bacteria breaking them down into beneficial metabolites. Like certain types of fibre, polyphenols have a prebiotic-like effect, particularly helping your 'good' gut bacteria to grow. There are also many compounds that are similar to polyphenols, let's call them polyphenol's 'cousins', that have a slightly different chemical make-up and are thought to influence your gut bacteria too, but are less studied.

In short, polyphenols:

- Support a healthy gut and a diverse gut microbiome
- Help your 'good' gut bacteria to grow and produce helpful metabolites

Some polyphenol metabolites function as antioxidants – molecules that act like protective Power Rangers against inflammation and damage. Your brain is particularly sensitive to trouble, with damage to your brain's cells associated with ageing and increased risk of brain diseases. A lot of this potential for trouble the brain can bring upon itself. Like a car, your brain uses a lot of energy even at rest, let alone when you're awake and multi-tasking to the max. And like any vehicle, your brain can also produce waste 'exhaust fumes' which need to be cleared away so that they don't build up. Antioxidants come to the rescue and neutralise them, helping to keep your brain fit and healthy.

What foods contain polyphenols?

High amounts of polyphenols are found in plant foods like veggies, fruit, whole grains, beans and legumes, nuts and seeds, and herbs and spices. They're also found in many drinks that are derived from plants, like coffee and tea (See Hack 10, Drink Up!). Polyphenols and their cousins give many plant foods their colour – with different colours often due to different types.

Extra-virgin olive oil

Extra-virgin olive oil tastes great and contains more polyphenols than most other oils. Contrary to popular belief, it's also completely fine to cook with too. Cooking veggies in a fat like extra-virgin olive oil can help you to absorb fat-soluble vitamins and other bioactive compounds. How to choose the best olive oil? The European Food Safety Authority (EFSA) introduced a health claim based on extra-virgin olive oil containing 25mg/100g of some specific types of polyphenols (not total polyphenol count) that you'll find displayed as an EFSA label on bottles. Only 10 per cent of extra-virgin olive oils on the market today meet this health claim.[12]

The simplest way to get a variety of polyphenols in your diet is to think of colour. Polyphenols and their cousins give many plant foods their colour – the red to tomatoes, the green to spinach and the purple to aubergines. Different types make different pig-

The colourful five	Example foods
Purple	Blueberries, aubergine, red grapes, purple plums, blackberries, red cabbage
Red	Tomatoes, strawberries, raspberries, cherries, red peppers
Orange/Yellow	Carrots, sweet potato, citrus fruits, mangoes, butternut squash
Green	Broccoli, kale, spinach, peas, green beans, courgette, herbs
White/pale yellow	Potatoes, cauliflower, garlic, lychees, bananas

ments. This is where those age-old messages of 'eat the rainbow' really start to make complete sense, lavishing your plate with vibrant purples, sunbursts of yellow, ruddy reds and deep greens.

These pigment compounds seem to particularly give your brain a little mental high five. People who eat two pieces of citrus fruit a day, rich in flavones, are less likely to be depressed than if they'd only had an orange or grapefruit once a week.[13] Carotenoids, present in carrots, sweet potato and squash, can significantly improve your brain's performance – like your memory, attention span and how quickly and well you think and problem-solve.[14] Berries and dark-green veg are also particularly high in polyphenols and polyphenol-like compounds, and are covered in the next chapter.

Colourful five days

Try for a range of colours across your day and your week, for a variety of polyphenols, their cousins and other important nutrients too.

Day of the week	Purple	Red	Orange/ yellow	Green	Pale yellow/ white
Monday					
Tuesday					
Wednesday					
Thursday					
Friday					
Saturday					
Sunday					

Which foods contain the most polyphenols?

While there isn't a recommended threshold for polyphenols yet, in the UK most adults eat only 600–1000mg of polyphenols a day – getting more polyphenols from tea, coffee and chocolate than from any other food group, including fruit or veg.[15] And yet many of the best sources of polyphenols are from herbs, spices, beans, berries and nuts. Eating more plants means not only providing your gut bacteria with more fibre, but more polyphenols too.

In the table below you'll see the top polyphenol-rich foods, including spices, herbs, beans, dark chocolate and nuts. Usually, the darker the fruit or vegetable – or the more vibrant the colour – the more polyphenols and similar compounds it contains. So black beans and red adzuki beans contain more polyphenols than white beans. Herbs and spices particularly dominate this list as they are very nutrient dense. Drying herbs concentrates the nutrients – but it's important to remember how much you're realistically able to eat in one sitting. It's highly unlikely you're going to be adding 100g worth of herbs or spices to your meals, that's about two and half jars! In fact, I'm going to say please don't do that for the sake of your tastebuds alone. Though I do encourage you to try and include herbs and spices as often as possible where you can – even one dose of spices can influence your gut bacteria.[16]

Top 15 polyphenol-rich herbs and spices	Total polyphenol mg/100g
Cloves	16,048
Cinnamon	9,700
Dried marjoram	9,306
Dried spearmint	6,575
Dried basil	4,318
Dried oregano	3,117
Dried sage	2,920
Caraway seeds	2,913
Dried rosemary	2,519
Dried camomile	2,483
Dried coriander	2,260
Dried fenugreek	2,250
Turmeric powder	2,117
Cumin seeds	2,038
Nutmeg	1,905

Top 30 polyphenol-rich foods	Total polyphenols mg/100g
Adzuki beans	8,970
Cocoa powder	5,624
Black beans	4,846
Lentils	3,697
Capers	3,600
Chestnuts	2,757
Black elderberries	1,950
Dark chocolate	1,860
Walnuts	1,575
Pistachios	1,420
Red Swiss chard leaves	1,320
Pecan nuts	1,284
Prunes	1,195
Globe artichokes	1,142
Raisins	1,065
Broad beans	1,039
Dried figs	960
Blackcurrants	821
Buckwheat whole grain flour	791
Wheat	696
Hazelnuts	672
Wild blueberries	656

Top 30 polyphenol-rich foods	Total polyphenols mg/100g
Blackberries	569
Blueberries	550
Dried dates	485
Gooseberries	470
Red cabbage	451
Redcurrants	448
Plums	410
Peanuts	406

Why I'm not the biggest fan of 'eat 30 plants a week for a diverse microbiome'

If you're interested in gut health, you may have heard the advice to eat 30 different plants a week for a diverse gut microbiome, based on findings from a large US study in 2018.[17] Some people find this target particularly useful. And if that's you – that's great! Personally though, there are a few reasons why I don't typically recommend '30 plants a week'. Around the time the study came out I was researching the gut microbiome at King's College London, and was particularly interested in plant diversity – how many different types of plants you eat, like vegetables, fruit, beans and legumes, whole grains, nuts and seeds, herbs and spices. The study's analysis on plant diversity was only one small part of what the researchers looked at, so I emailed the lead author for some extra detail on how they collected the data and did the analysis. I found out the following – directly copied and pasted from his response.

The participants were asked one question:

'In an average week, how many different plant species do you eat? e.g. If you consume a can of soup that contains carrots, potatoes and onion, you can count this as three different plants; if you consume multi-grain bread, each different grain counts as a plant.'

How the researchers arrived at '30 plants' was by comparing the microbiome of those who ate 10 plants or less in a week to people who ate 30 plants or more in a week. That to me, based on the example above, seems to be more of a comparison of people who eat any plants in the week at all, versus those who don't. All of a sudden, too, in the context of how the study describes what can count as 'one plant' – aka, a smidge – 30 plants doesn't actually seem that much. According to the study, the spice mix in your KFC chicken bucket counts as 11 plants. It's one single study, and not a very rigorous one at that either. The results are based on one survey question, and not on carefully collected dietary data. It's very much not the 'new five a day' which is based on a large body of evidence.

That doesn't mean we shouldn't think about plant diversity – it makes sense that eating a diverse diet is one of the best things you can do to support your gut bacteria. But it needn't be stressful. What I want to avoid for you is the feeling of panic that you must buy a thousand different types of fruit and veg that'll inevitably end up rotting in the back of your fridge because you already ate that one on Monday. That you don't need to do any mental logistics, religiously noting down and cross-referencing every plant you've eaten that week, because if you're anything like me you don't remember what you ate yesterday let alone four days ago. Now that might resonate with you, or it might not at all. If you find having a target of 30 plants a week helpful, and each of those servings is a normal amount (aka smidges don't count), then truly – that's fantastic and I'm more than pleased. But if you don't, know that that's OK too. I prefer to think about getting a variety of colours and textures into my day instead.

Make it easy

Set yourself up for diversity success with these diversity hacks. When you're shopping, choose the 'medley' options when you can – so swap cannellini beans for mixed beans, raspberries for fruits of the forest, and one type of lettuce for mixed bags of salad greens. Have fun with different foods too: try a new food like freekeh or bulgar wheat. It's amazing what you can find these days in the freezer section as well; the humble pea, for so long the solitary pop of colour among a sea of frozen beige, is now joined by a riot of different fruits and veg and even frozen chopped herbs, garlic and ginger, which can save a lot of time and effort.

Shopping for diversity hacks

Fresh:
- Mixed bags of stir-fry veg
- Mixed bags of salad leaves
- Shop with rainbow in mind – white veg, purple/red veg, orange veg, green veg
- Garlic puree
- Ginger puree

Frozen:
- Frozen forest fruits
- Mixed frozen vegetables
- Any other frozen veg and fruit
- Sliced rye bread (you can toast straight from the freezer too)

Store cupboard:
- Mixed bags of nuts and seeds
- Cans of mixed beans
- Lentils
- Mixed grains
- Pickles, e.g. onions, capers, gherkins
- Jarred vegetables, e.g. artichokes, olives, capers, sun-dried tomatoes
- Less common grains, e.g. pearl barley, freekeh, quinoa
- Dried herbs
- Spices

What have colourful plants and fibre types gut to do with it?

- A diverse gut microbiome is linked to better health and
  emotional well-being
- Eating a variety of different plant foods is linked to a
  diverse gut microbiome
- Different types of fibres and different combinations of
  fibres give shape and texture to plant foods

- There are particular types of fibre that help your 'good' gut bacteria to thrive – called prebiotics – and these can influence your mood and stress levels
- The colour of plants often comes from polyphenols and their cousins, that also have a prebiotic-like effect on your gut bacteria
- Try to eat a rainbow of fruit and veg across your day to provide your gut bacteria with a range of fibre and polyphenols – particularly your colourful five

Hack 3 – Eat the BGBGs

This isn't about the 70s band The Bee Gees who sang the massive *Saturday Night Fever* hit 'Staying Alive'. Incidentally, that song has been used to train medical professionals to do lifesaving CPR because it has a similar beat to the human heart, making it an easy rhythm to match chest compressions to. Instead of being the funky movers of the dance floor, these BGBGs are the disco-groovers of your gut-brain connection – and, you have to admit, calling them the BGBGs does make it easier to remember them. Beans, Greens, Berries, Grains (nuts) and seeds. Yes, I had to sneak the nuts in there somehow.

The BGBGs all have different attributes but there are two commonalities that tie them all together – fibre and polyphenols. By eating the BGBGs often, it'll make it easy to reach your 30g of fibre a day – and without you even realising it. You're providing your gut bacteria with the food they need to produce their key brain-signalling molecules between your gut and your brain – short-chain fatty acids. These short-chain fatty acids help keep your gut barrier lining and your blood-brain barrier healthy. They help to lower overactive excess inflammation, fine-tune your neurotransmitters and support your brain's 'nanny' proteins that care for your brain cells.[1] Most of

SHOPPING LIST

☐ *Black beans*
☐ *Blueberries*
☐ *Milled flaxseed*
☐ *Wheat bran*
☐ *Spinach*
☐ *Rye bread*
☐
☐
☐
☐

Figure 11. Add BGBGs to your weekly shop

the studies on the benefits of these foods for the brain have looked at conditions like depression or diseases like Alzheimer's disease, although these findings are still relevant for all of us – helping how well you think, supporting your mood, and protecting your brain health.

The way I like to frame the BGBGs is as 'most days' foods. They're there on your weekly shopping list along with your other mainstay essentials of eggs, milk, and the rest of your routine staples. So if you have a shopping list that you write or maybe you keep on your phone, go add them now as you're reading this to help you remember.

Most days beans

The magical tooting fruits. Though technically they aren't a fruit, they're a seed. Of all the areas in the world where people live the longest and healthiest, called the Blue Zones, it's beans that are one of the common defining features across every cuisine from Mexico, to Italy, to Japan. Eating beans every day is one of the biggest dietary predictors of living a long life – even if you only eat a small amount.[2] They're also high in fibre, polyphenols and plant protein and contain potassium, magnesium and folate – nutrients that are important for the proper functioning of your body, including your brain.

They have some of the highest protective dietary effects against thinking or memory problems later in life, with three

Bean	Fibre (g) per 100g (cooked)
Pinto beans	9
Black beans	8.7
Split peas	8.3
Lentils	7.9
Chickpeas	7.6
Mung beans	7.6
Kidney beans	7.4
Adzuki bean	7
Butter beans	7
Cowpeas	6.5

servings of beans a week linked to a 38 per cent lower risk of cognitive decline.[3]

Luckily for us, beans also happen to be delicious – they've got that carby comforting texture that isn't too far off potato or pasta, like pillowy white beans, or they add a nutty texture like lentils. Many of them are particularly high in polyphenols – with adzuki and black beans getting an extra special mention. Only to add to the party for your gut bacteria, they're higher in fibre than fruits and vegetables too. It's this high fibre content that give beans their 'tooty' nature. We've all heard the children's rhyme 'beans, beans, good for your heart, the more you eat, the more you fart,' but it wasn't until my grandmother brought it to my attention that I discovered there's a second part too: 'The more you fart, the better you feel, so we have beans at every meal!'

While you don't have to have beans at every meal or every day (you don't *have* to do *anything*), I do want to encourage you to think of beans as more of a food you enjoy often rather than on a random occasion. They're incredibly versatile, cheap and have a long shelf life. Adding in half a can of chickpeas to a salad or stew, or whizzing them up as a hummus, can give you an easy fibre boost, as well as keeping you feeling fuller and more satisfied for longer. Beans are particularly high in the prebiotic fibre galacto-oligosaccharides that feed your 'good' gut bacteria. Simply adding one cup of beans a day, without making any other changes, can help your gut microbiome diversity and your 'good' gut bacteria, producing more helpful metabolites and lowering excess inflammation.[4]

Over time your gut gets more used to eating beans so the

extra toots and bloating should settle down as your gut bacteria adjust. A bit like when you get a shiny new car and it's very exciting to drive to start with, but then you get used to it because you're using it all the time – it's the same for your gut bacteria.

If you're struggling with bloating and feeling gassy look at Chapter 15, 'How to Make an Unhappy Gut Happy'. You can also try the following:

- Start small, even if that's half a tablespoon of beans to begin with
- Go slow – slowly increase the amount you eat, listening to your body. If you have any stomach pains or issues then you might be increasing it too fast
- Buy tinned or jarred beans or lentils rather than dried, and rinse them as it helps them to be more digestible if you have gut issues

We're having a bean renaissance, with every chef, food TikTokker, Instagrammer and keen home cook worth their salt waxing lyrical about the delicious comforting textures and flavours of beans. No longer are beans only baked beans on toast, we're now enjoying them in salads, stews, pasta dishes, risottos and more. If you can afford to splash out on the posher jarred variety, then I do think it's worth it for flavour alone, particularly as beans can easily be the star of a dish. Tinned beans can do just as well, though, and are more affordable, or you can cook your own. Most dried beans need to be soaked in water overnight before boiling, but red lentils don't – you can add them straight into most dishes but they work particularly well in stews and soups.

Should you avoid beans because of . . . lectins?

Beans are especially rich in lectins – a type of protein that gives the pseudo-wellness brigade the heebie-jeebies. Lectins are produced by all plants as a natural defence against pests, their own built-in bodyguards, and they're particularly high in beans, lentils and whole grains. When they're eaten in their active state, they can cause not-so-nice side effects and interfere with the absorption of minerals like calcium and iron. That sounds dramatic right? Luckily for us, though, we don't eat lectins in their active state – we don't eat beans or whole grains raw. Lectins are water-soluble so they leach out into water if they are soaked or boiled, and the heat of cooking deactivates them. The irony of all this fear-mongering around lectins is that we have multiple studies in large populations that clearly show how good these foods are for us, with beans and whole grains consistently linked with lower rates of heart disease, type II diabetes and other diseases. And of course, they're great for your gut too.

Bean	Total polyphenols (g/100g)
Adzuki beans	8,970
Black beans	4,846
Lentils	3,697
Broad beans	1,039
White beans	208
Pigeon peas	186

Split peas	141
Runner beans	109
Butter beans	96

Daily greens

Dark-green leafy vegetables are some of the most nutritionally packed veggies there are. In one 2014 study that ranked the nutrient density of 41 plant foods, the top 15 were all dark-green leafy veggies with watercress, Chinese cabbage, chard, beet greens and spinach scooping the highest spots.[5] They also contain a specific sugar called sulfoquinovose that particularly supports your 'good' gut bacteria. As the bacteria feed on sulfoquinovose they release a by-product that certain types of 'bad' bacteria don't like.[6]

Despite this, you'll be surprised that even though dark-green leafy veggies are some of the highest-fibre vegetables, they're lower in fibre than some other BGBG foods – like wheat bran, rye bread, beans, and most nuts and seeds. Which is a complete contradiction to what we think is high fibre – we tend to think of

Dark-green leafy veg	Fibre (g) per 100g
Kale	4.1
Collard greens	4
Beet greens	3.7
Cooked spinach	3.7
Dandelion greens	3.5

big bowls of salad, chomping for hours on lettuce perhaps (incidentally, lettuce only contains 1.8g fibre per 100g). No shade on lettuce but this is where the BGBGs come in to their own – they're fibre-smart, giving you that extra fibre boost without you even noticing. You need a range of foods to hit your fibre target, and the BGBGs are here to help.

Dark green leafy veg are not only high in polyphenol-like compounds, but also folate, a B vitamin crucial for neurotransmitters like your happy serotonin and 'I like it, do it again' dopamine. This likely partly explains why dark-green leafy veggies are linked to lower odds of depression.[7] Just over half a cup of cooked dark-green leafy vegetables (or one and a half cups uncooked) a day is related to having the cognitive abilities of a brain 11 years younger in later life.[8] Popeye really should have had a giant muscly brain rather than flexing his biceps.

Green leafy veg:

- Spinach
- Kale
- Collard greens
- Lettuce
- Rocket
- Watercress
- Bok choy
- Beet greens
- Swiss chard

Eat more green leafy veg by . . .

- Adding them to an omelette
- Stir-frying with garlic, ginger and soy sauce
- Adding to smoothies
- Putting them in a sandwich or wrap
- Making a big green salad
- Adding to stews, soups and pastas
- Making a green kale pesto or whizzing into dressings

Daily berries

The little studs of seeds are berries' secret to how they're higher in fibre than many other fruits, and their dark vibrant colours are a clear display of how packed they are with polyphenols and their related compounds – in particular anthocyanins and flavanols, known for their anti-inflammatory and antioxidant properties.

Berries	Fibre (g) per 100g
Raspberries	6.5
Blackberries	5.3
Dried cranberries	5.3
Blueberries	2.7
Cherries	2.5
Strawberries	2.1

Berries help to increase your 'good' gut bacteria, particularly those that produce short chain fatty acids.[9]

They might put you in a feel-good mood, and possibly help you think better too. The metabolites from fibre and polyphenols not only have anti-inflammatory effects but they also improve blood flow to your brain, with the influx of blood-rich oxygen and nutrients acting like a battery charger for your executive and emotional control circuits. Two cups of strawberries a day for three months improved study participants' memory and they

Berries	Polyphenol (mg/100g)
Black elderberries	1,950
Blackcurrants	821
Wild blueberries	656
Lingonberries	652
Blackberries	570
Blueberries	550
Bilberries	525
Gooseberries	470
Redcurrants	448
Cranberries	315
Strawberries	289
Black grapes	185
Red raspberries	155
Green grapes	122

made decisions faster.[10] In another trial, just two hours after a wild blueberry drink both children and young adults rated their mood as significantly better compared to those who had a similar-tasting placebo drink.[11]

Wild blueberries seem to get the most polyphenol airtime but look how the humble blackcurrant that your grandma likely made into jam pips it to the post on the polyphenol count. It's a great example that you don't need to fork out a lot of money for the latest 'hot' trend if you don't want to, with many everyday versions being just as good for you and far cheaper.

Eat more berries . . .

- Have berries for breakfast with kefir, nuts and seeds
- Add to smoothies, or freeze into ice lollies
- Add as a hint of sweetness and different texture to savoury salads
- Have them as a snack with cheese
- Have as a dessert with Greek yoghurt and toasted walnuts
- Buy frozen berries and keep in the freezer to enjoy all year around (and they're often cheaper, too)

Daily grains

If you're going to reach your 30g of fibre a day, it'll be a lot easier with whole grains. They're high in fibre, polyphenols and many other nutrients which help you to feel your absolute best. Whole grains help your 'good' bacteria to grow and to make more short-chain fatty acids.[12] They're also a great source of energy for your brain as whole grains contain complex carbohydrates. Whole grains are what they say on the tin – they contain the whole grain. Whereas foods made with refined flour, like white breads and pastas, that aren't whole grain, have lost some of their fibre during the milling process. Eating whole grains is linked to better mood, less anxiety, lower likelihood of depression[13] and maintaining better brain function over time.[14]

If you cook extra grains for another day, you're also saving on time and hassle. Grains contain starch, and when they are cooked and then cooled, like with leftovers, the shape of the starch molecule changes, turning some of the starch into another form called resistant starch. Starch is usually absorbed in the small intestine, but resistant starch bypasses into your lower intestine

Grains	Fibre (g) per 100g
Wheat bran	44.5
Oat bran	16.1
Barley flakes	16
Rye flakes	15
Rye crackers	14.3
Rye flour	14
Oatcakes	10.4
Popcorn	10.1
Oats	10
Pumpernickel bread	9.6

to your gut bacteria. Resistant starch acts very similarly to fibre, feeding your 'good' gut bacteria and helping them to produce more short-chain fatty acids. Even if you reheat left-over grains, you still get this benefit. If you store your fresh bread in the freezer (you can toast directly from frozen) the cooling process can also increase the amount of resistant starch available.[15]

If you're making half your plate veggies or fruit at most meals, an easy way to think about how many whole grains to eat is to make them take up a quarter of your plate. Simple swaps can also make a big difference to how much fibre you eat, such as swapping white bread for a higher-fibre one like rye bread, your white pasta for brown whole-wheat pasta, or going for a mixed or wild rice rather than white. There are many different types of whole grains out there, try some new ones that you haven't had before – maybe pearl barley, freekeh or bulgar wheat and see how you like them.

The most useful way to tell if a cereal, bread, pasta, bar or snack is a gut-friendly food is not to necessarily rely on whether it calls itself 'whole grain' or 'high-fibre' on the packet. That's because in Europe a food only needs to be 51 per cent whole grain to be able to claim it's a 'whole grain', in the UK it's at least 8g of whole grains per serving, and in the US it needs to be 20 per cent per serving. So not all whole-grain products are necessarily made equal. Instead, let's look at both its fibre content and how much total carbohydrate it contains. It involves a little maths – but once you get the hang of it, it can save you a lot of hassle between trying to figure out which food to choose between your two favourite cereals.

Look at the back of the pack at where it gives the nutrition information either 'per portion' or 'per 100g'. You can use the ratio between total carbohydrates and fibre to help you decide which one to choose. You're looking for at least 1g of fibre to 10g of total carbohydrate. An easy way to calculate this is by adding a 'zero' on the end of the fibre amount, and seeing if that number is higher or lower than the total carbohydrate. If the fibre is the same value or higher, you're onto a fibre-rich winner relative to it's carb content.

For bread to meet this ratio, it usually needs to contain seeds and be made with whole-wheat flour or rye flour (which is particularly high in fibre). Does it matter if your bread is ultra-processed, aka bought in a shop? It seems not. A study that looked at sub-groups of ultra-processed foods found that ultra-processed bread was linked with being protective against diseases despite being ultra-processed,[16] likely because of its fibre content. That's why I think there's more for us to understand about ultra-processed foods, and that maybe this one big umbrella term isn't actually that helpful. Particularly when we don't all have the luxury to get fresh bread from a bakery or to make our own.

For oats, you can choose rolled oats, steel-cut oats or oat groats as they contain more fibre than ground oats, where some of the fibre is lost through processing. Different types of bran like wheat bran, oat bran and barley flakes are also especially high in fibre – and can be great to add into a mix with nuts and seeds to sprinkle onto your breakfast in the morning.

Nuts and seeds

Last but certainly not least are nuts and seeds. I keep a jar of mixed nuts and seeds by the kettle; it's my go-to snack with a

Nuts and seeds	Typical portion size	Portion (g)	Fibre (g)
Peanuts	1 handful	30	2.4
Almonds	1 handful	30	4.8
Walnuts	1 handful	30	2
Cashews	1 handful	30	1.3
Pistachios	1 handful	30	2.2
Pecans	1 handful	30	2.9
Brazil nuts	1 handful	30	1.9
Sunflower seeds	1 tbsp	10	0.86
Pumpkin seeds	1 tbsp	12	1
Sesame seeds	1 tbsp	11	1.6
Chia seeds	1 tbsp	10	3.9
Flaxseeds	1 tbsp	9	2.5

cup of tea, but they're also great on top of kefir and berries in the morning for breakfast, or quickly toasted to generously sprinkle over salads or roasted veggies. In fact, I'm hard pressed to think what nuts and seeds can't be added to – suiting both sweet and savoury. Nuts fully deserve their prime spot for both your gut and brain health. Nuts aren't only high in fibre and polyphenols but also healthy fats too – encouraging the growth of 'good' gut bacteria[17] as well as acting to protect your heart and blood vessels across your body, including your brain. Eating a handful of mixed nuts a day for as little as four weeks can support your gut microbiome and help you think quicker and better.[18]

The BGBGs counter

This BGBGs counter is an easy checklist that you can refer to most days – in a way that works for you.

Most days							
Food	Mon (✓)	Tues (✓)	Weds (✓)	Thurs (✓)	Fri (✓)	Sat (✓)	Sun (✓)
Berries (Daily)	☐	☐	☐	☐	☐	☐	☐
Beans (3–4+ a week)	☐	☐	☐	☐	☐	☐	☐
Dark-green leafy veg (Daily)	☐	☐	☐	☐	☐	☐	☐
Whole grains (¼ plate)	☐☐☐	☐☐☐	☐☐☐	☐☐☐	☐☐☐	☐☐☐	☐☐☐
Nuts and seeds (Daily)	☐	☐	☐	☐	☐	☐	☐

Put It into Practice . . .

I will . . .

_____

_____

e.g.

- Add the BGBGs to my weekly shopping list
- Put nuts and seeds in a jar by the kettle
- Have berries when I feel like a sweet hit after lunch
- Add beans to my dinners on Tuesday, Thursday and Friday this week
- Check the fibre-to-carb ratio to find a high-fibre bread
- Buy some spinach and kale to make green smoothies

So I can . . .

_____

[your Genius Gut goal]

e.g. eat my BGBGs most days

So that . . .

_____

[your Genius Gut 'why']

e.g. I will feel more balanced and energised!

What have BGBGs gut to do with it?

- BGBGs are beans, greens, berries, grains, nuts and seeds and are particularly great for your gut microbiome and brain health

- Beans are higher in fibre than fruits and vegetables, and are rich in polyphenols
- When choosing grain products like bread, cereals and pasta – look for one with at least 1g of fibre to 10g of total carbohydrate (see the back of the pack)
- Berries, dark-green veggies, nuts and seeds are also high in fibre, polyphenols and other healthy compounds that look after both your gut bacteria and your brain

Hack 4 – Opt for a Daily Ferment

Fermented foods are foods that have been transformed by safe, friendly bacteria and yeast into something uniquely other. Sourdough rises, and jars of kimchi and kraut start bursting with bubbles – almost like magic. The bacteria and yeast feed on the starches and sugars in the foods, changing them – how they look, their nutrition and their flavour. These aren't the microbes that grow a fuzzy mould carpet on a past-its-sell-by-date cream cheese at the back of the fridge. These bacteria and yeast are not only safe to eat but are often good for you too.

Bacteria and yeast naturally coat raw foods and are present in the air all around us. They're everywhere – we just can't see them. Much of this fermentation action is down to a type of common bacteria called lactic acid bacteria that produce lactic acid and a little alcohol as a by-product of feeding on the starches and sugars in a food. Lactic acid helps to preserve the food by changing its acidity, preventing it from spoiling, and is why ferments often have a mild tangy, almost vinegar-like taste. In the past, fermentation was used as a way of preserving food before we had fridges. While ferments might seem to be the latest hot trend, they are having more of a comeback – we've been eating them for thousands of years.

During the human race's time on earth scientists think that our brain has tripled in size while our guts have shrunk by 40 per cent. For a long time, this brain growth and gut shrinkage were thought to be because we discovered fire and cooking – making less work for our gut and more easy energy for our brain. But there's a far more likely explanation. Fermentation.[1]

Like cooking, fermentation can make nutrients easier to absorb. Like cooking, fermentation makes it easier for your gut to digest your food and keeps it safe to eat for longer. However, prehistoric cooking relied on certain tools, wood, and know-how to make a fire. And that was likely beyond our capabilities at the time. Whereas fermentation can happen naturally everywhere and at any time, all that was needed was to store food away, perhaps in a cool dry cave – and fresh food either ferments or spoils.

How can you spot a fermented food?

You can ferment almost any food. Funnily enough we eat a load of fermented foods without even knowing it, from fresh crusty bread, a glass of red wine, olives, and creamy stinky cheese. Fermented foods fall into two main groups: fermented foods that are 'alive' where the microbes that fermented the food are still living when you eat it, and foods that have been fermented but the microbes have died – usually due to the heat from cooking, pasteurisation or canning. A good rule of thumb is if it's alive, you'll find it in the fridge section of the supermarket and not the other aisles. If you keep a live fermented food out of the fridge too long, like kombucha or kimchi, the on-going fermentation speeds up at room temperature and if it's jarred or bottled it'll be at risk of exploding after a few days or weeks from all the pressure build-up from the gasses released.

There are other foods that aren't fermented but sometimes get confused with ferments, like vinegar-soaked pickles. While vinegar is a fermented food, foods preserved in vinegar aren't fermented so they aren't seen as fermented foods themselves. While vinegar pickles don't offer as many gut-health benefits as fermented pickles, vinegar – and particularly polyphenol-rich vinegar (typically dark-coloured vinegar) – does support your gut

Live ferments	Dead ferments	Not a ferment
Sauerkraut	Sourdough	Vinegar pickles
Kefir	Pasteurised yoghurt	Jams, jellies and chutneys
Live yoghurt	Shelf-stable ferments	Smoked meat and fish
Miso	Ready-made tempeh	Tinned foods
Unpasteurised cheeses	products	Dried fruit and veg
Pasteurised cheeses	Tempeh	
(but far less)	Jarred or tinned olives	
Kombucha	Wine, beer, spirits	
Kimchi	Soy sauce	
Fermented veg	Coffee	
Cottage cheese	Cocoa	
Fresh olives	Pasteurised vinegar	
Kvass	Fish sauce	
Natto		
Fermented salamis		
Unpasteurised vinegar		

bacteria[2] (another reason to get behind salad dressings!). To add to the confusion, some foods like sauerkraut can be either pickled or fermented, so something to be conscious of if you're specifically looking for a live one – pick the one in the fridge section.

Live fermented foods provide new bacteria to your gut, helping your gut microbiome to become more diverse.[3] Though we shouldn't completely mourn the death of live microbes killed off in cooked or pasteurised ferments. Even when the microbes have died, they can still be good for you. While they aren't alive any more their cell walls are still present in the food, and can influence your immune system and contribute to your gut health. And there are other benefits from the fermentation process itself too.

Fermenting superpowers:

- Makes some nutrients more absorbable by breaking down certain molecules that can act like absorption blockers
- Produces helpful metabolites during fermentation
- Makes more of some vitamins, like B vitamins
- Can make certain foods more digestible for people with gluten or lactose intolerances, by breaking down some of the gluten and lactose, e.g. sourdough bread and kefir
- Can help with blood-sugar control compared to their non-fermented version as the bacteria and yeast feed on some of the sugars, lowering the sugar content
- Enhances texture and flavour!

Many fermented foods are partly a microbial collaboration between us and the food. In Korea, if you're thought to make great kimchi you're complimented by being told you have 'son-mat', meaning you have good 'hand-taste'. And many of the bacteria used to ferment cheese today are similar to those found on our skin. A few years ago, the Victoria and Albert Museum in London had a food exhibition, and displayed cheeses (thankfully only to view and not to eat) fermented with bacteria collected from body parts of famous people – bacteria from their belly buttons, armpits, toes and nostrils. It looked like cheese, smelt like cheese – but I'm not sure if anyone was brave enough to see whether they tasted like cheese.

Transient visitors but not residents?

When you eat live ferments, the bacteria in the food have to survive a long journey and harsh terrain through your gut. The Indiana Jones of bacteria can battle through your stomach's swilling sack of acid and the alkaline bile in your small intestine to make it to camp gut microbiome in your lower intestine. Not all make it, but some do.[4]

When these new bacteria get to your large intestine, they don't necessarily receive a hero's welcome. The bacteria already in your gut have worked hard to be part of your gut microbiome. There's only so much food to go around, and they're competitive with each other for food and space. You can imagine that when visitors arrive from 'outside' those bacteria have to work to establish themselves, but most don't succeed. They tend to instead pitch a tent for a few days or so, and then move on through your gut and out into the world again, leaving your body in your poo. It's harsh I know. That doesn't mean that they don't still influence your health while they're there. Think of them as temporary travelling musicians in your orchestra; they might bring a slightly different element to the music of your gut microbiome, but unless you keep topping them up, they pass on through. A few can end up staying, providing they get the food they need to thrive without too much competition.

Are fermented foods probiotic?

Fermented foods are often called probiotic foods – but very few really are. A probiotic is a specific type of bacteria, called a bacterial strain, which has been shown in scientific research to have a health benefit if it's present in a certain amount. The problem is we don't usually know what type of bacteria are present in, say, a bottle of kefir or a jar of kimchi, and whether they're in a large enough quantity to have a particular health effect. That doesn't necessarily mean they aren't doing us any good though.

How many ferments for your gut?

With ferments, even a little and often likely helps. So if you're new to ferments, don't feel like you need to go from zero to hero straight away. If you're already a ferment fan, then you'll be particularly interested in the following study from Stanford University. The researchers found that eating six or more servings* of fermented foods a day increased the participants' diversity of gut bacteria and lowered their levels of inflammation in ten weeks.[5] I get that six servings a day sounds like a lot, though I hope the table below shows that it's perhaps not quite as intimidating as it might seem.

Really, the key is to find a number that works best for you. You can always build up to more. Remember that many studies, including this one, do not investigate what is the 'best' or the 'minimal effect' dose, and instead choose a large quantity that will help them more clearly see a potential effect within the short timeframe of the study. You, though, are here for the long run. For you, ten weeks in your lifetime is nothing, a blink of an eye. That means any amount of ferment, no matter how small, over

Meal	Ferment	Ferment counter
Breakfast	Berries, **live yoghurt**, nuts and seeds, granola	1
Lunch	Tinned tuna, baked potato, green salad, **cottage cheese** and **kraut**	2
Afternoon snack	Apple and **unpasteurised blue cheese** on oat cracker and **fermented pickles**	2
Dinner	Chicken with **kimchi** fried rice and long green beans	1
		6

---

* The study considered a serving size as follows: kombucha, yoghurt, kefir, buttermilk, kvass = 6oz (170g); kimchi, sauerkraut, other fermented veggies = ¼ cup (30–50g); vegetable brine drink = 2oz (50g)

months and years, will more than likely support your gut microbiome and your health. So please find a balance that you enjoy.

Where to buy ferments

Buying ferments can be expensive, though it does save the time and effort of making them. You'll find them in large supermarkets, specialist health food stores, or online deliveries from smaller producers.

Ferment your mood

What about fermented foods when it comes to your mood and how well you think? There's fascinating early evidence around fermented foods and your mind. A study of over 700 people looked at a sub-group who had traits of anxiety. It became clear that those who ate fermented foods were less anxious than those who didn't.[6] Another study found that drinking two glasses of kefir a day for only four weeks changed parts of the brain that handle emotions, and participants were better able to read the emotions of others.[7] Fermented foods seem to help how you think too, with people who eat fermented foods every day tending to maintain healthy brain function for longer in life than those who don't.[8]

Kefir

My introduction to kefir was as a teen, from an artist who'd recently returned from Turkmenistan where she'd spent time with nomadic travellers. She'd grown to like the acidic tang of fermented milk and far ahead of the trend she'd been making kefir herself for years. I'd never heard of fermenting before, and as she handed me a glass part of me prayed I wouldn't be struck down with food poisoning. I gulped it down and was no worse for wear – and fast forward to now it's a routine go-to in my life.

If you're just starting out with fermented foods, try a fermented dairy like live yoghurt or kefir. Yoghurt and kefir have the most evidence to date of all fermented foods for your gut bacteria and your health. Both yoghurt and kefir are fermented using specific types of bacteria, though kefir contains a broader spectrum of bacteria and some types of yeast too. Kefir seems to potentially influence the two-way communication between your gut and your brain. In mice, kefir has been shown to change their gut bacteria, signalling to their brain to release more of the calm neurotransmitter GABA.[9] Drinking kefir daily has also been shown to improve the part of your memory that's involved in remembering faces, names and where you last put your keys.[10]

Fermenting tricks:

- Make your own kefir by buying kefir grains online and adding them to milk. You can also 'backslop' shop-bought kefir to fresh milk to make your own kefir. Far cheaper and saves on plastic bottles too!
- If you can't eat dairy or choose not to, kefir can also be made with coconut milk or water, though they tend to not contain as many types of bacteria as dairy kefir.

Kombucha

Kombucha is a fermented tea that gets a lot of airtime but surprisingly there are very few studies on its health effects, and none on the gut microbiome of humans. One thing to be fairly cautious of is that commercial kombuchas can be high in added sugar to make them more palatable. That's because a lot of sugar is added to the tea to help feed the yeast and bacteria, and if the kombucha isn't properly fermented it can still be high in sugar. Which is of course fine to enjoy now and again but not under a halo of gut health. A real kombucha will taste quite sour and not that sweet. Some commercial producers also pasteurise their kombucha so that it has a longer shelf-life but that kills the live microbes.

- Check the added sugar, and ideally choose one below 5g per serving
- The label should say raw or unpasteurised to make sure you're getting live microbes
- If it's traditionally fermented, you'll sometimes see a little bit of cloudiness forming at the bottom of the bottle from the bacteria and yeast

Cheese

Cheese can be made with pasteurised or unpasteurised milk – with unpasteurised milk containing naturally present live bacteria, which are killed during pasteurisation. Even so, most cheeses, even if pasteurised, will contain some bacteria in the final result, as bacteria are added back into the milk to curdle it into curds and whey – and voila – cheese. Depending on the type of bacteria used, the cheese can have different flavours and textures. It's worth noting that foods made with unpasteurised milks also have a higher risk of carrying bad bacteria which could make you sick, so it's not recommended for people who are pregnant, small children or for someone who is unwell or with a weak immune system.

- Choose unpasteurised cheeses if you can, unless you're pregnant, have a weak immune system, are unwell, or are a child, for an extra dose of bacteria. Though if you prefer to choose pasteurised then do so.
- Older cheeses don't necessarily come with higher amounts of live microbes, with Grana Padana, Parmesan and Swiss Gruyère showing no detectable live bacteria when aged past a year[11]

Top 10 cheeses containing high levels of microbes	Age
Tilsit	2–4 months
Queso fresco	5 days
Swiss cheese	6 months
Gouda	1 month
Parmigiano Reggiano	2–5 months
Stilton	Within shelf life
Provolone	3–10 months
Pecorino Romano	3–10 months
Muenster	Within shelf life
Mozzarella	Within shelf life
Manchego	5 months

But isn't cheese bad for you?

Cheese contains high levels of saturated fat, which isn't great for the health of your blood vessels, including the ones supplying your brain with nutrients and energy. However, the health effects of dairy seem to be related not just to their components but also to something called their 'food matrix'. No, this isn't the film *The Matrix* with Neo versus Agent Smith, this is a matrix as in how all the molecules in a food are arranged together, kind of like a Tetris game. You can have exactly the same or similar colour and number of blocks but they can fit together differently.

Cheese and butter, even though very similar in nutrients, have different effects on the health of your blood vessels, likely because of their different food matrices, with butter increasing your 'bad' cholesterol more than cheese.[12] The live bacteria present due to the fermentation of cheese also help to prevent some of the impact of the saturated fat on your cholesterol levels.[13] It's likely all in the dose though – a meta-analysis found that people who ate 40g of cheese a day, about the size of a box of Tic Tacs, tended to have on average a 10 per cent lower risk of heart disease and stroke than those who ate both less or more.[14]

Cheese ideas

- Snack on cheese with fermented veggies on an oatcake or cracker
- Shave or crumble cheese into salads, or on top of veggie dishes
- Blend with yoghurt into dips
- Melt into sauces or whizz soft cheeses into dressings

Kimchi, kraut and other fermented veg

Fermented veggies have the trifecta of gut health: they contain fibre, polyphenols and live microbes, alongside vitamins, minerals and other bioactive compounds. Eating fermented veggies can change the bacteria you have in your gut, with eating fermented veggies, like kimchi, lowering the amount of 'bad' bacteria present and increasing the 'good' types.[15]

- You'll find live ferments in the refrigerated section
- Choose a variety – have fun and enjoy trying new flavours and combinations!
- Keep any utensils clean (no double dipping!) when getting ferments out of their jar so that you don't introduce any possibly pathogenic bacteria into your ferment. The same if you're making your own, make sure your hands are clean.
- If your ferment gets a layer of mould – bin it. Scraping it off only removes the part you can see. One of the biggest disruptors to your microbiome? Food poisoning. Not worth it.

Kimchi, kraut and other fermented veggies
- With cheese and crackers
- Add to a salad
- As a tangy side with meat
- Stir into rice or grains
- On top of avocado toast

Sourdough

Sourdough bread is made without commercial yeast, and instead with a starter culture of flour, yeast and bacteria called the 'mother'. It's this microbial action that helps the bread dough to rise. As sourdough bread is baked in the oven, the live bacteria and yeast are killed off by the cooking heat. That doesn't mean that the sourdough process doesn't still bring a little somethin' somethin' to the party. It's more digestible for those with sensitive guts, as the fermentation breaks down some of the gluten and fructans which can give some people uncomfortable gut symptoms when consumed in large amounts. Some of the nutrition in sourdough is more easily absorbed, as the fermentation process breaks down certain compounds that act as nutrient blockers.

Many supermarkets have copped on to sourdough being a trend and have churned out 'faux-doughs' that aren't made in the traditional slow sourdough way. Some easy tips to make sure yours is the genuine article is to look on the ingredient list on the back of the pack:

- Should only contain flour, water and salt
- Shouldn't be made with commercial yeast
- Shouldn't have a long shelf-life of a few weeks or months

Remember that just because a bread is sourdough, that doesn't mean it's high in fibre. The fibre comes from the type of flour that's used, and whether it contains any seeds or not. Sometimes a commercial regular bread from the shops can contain more fibre, and so can be just as good if not a better choice for your gut bacteria.

How to choose a bread

Here's what I look for when I'm buying bread:

- Is it made with a whole-grain flour or rye flour?

- Does it contain seeds?
- Is it sourdough?
- What's the fibre to carb ratio? (See page 224)
- Does it taste good?

The last question is non-negotiable – there's no point buying a bread you don't like.

Put It into Practice . . .

I will . . .

_____

_____

e.g.

- Buy some fermented veggies to try
- Add kefir to my smoothie in the morning
- Snack on cheese, apple and oatcakes

So I can . . .

_____

      [your Genius Gut goal]
      e.g. eat two/four/six daily ferments

So that . . .

_____

      [your Genius Gut 'why']
      e.g. I will feel like my best self

What have ferments gut to do with it?

- Bacteria and yeast break down starches and sugars during the fermentation process, changing the food's nutrition, flavour and look
- Live ferments contain bacteria that are still living when you eat them, potentially adding new bacteria to your gut microbiome
- Fermented foods that contain bacteria that aren't living any more due to the bacteria being killed off during cooking, pasteurisation or canning still offer many health benefits
- Eating six or more fermented foods a day can increase the diversity of your gut bacteria and lowers excess inflammation, but even a little and often counts

Hack 5 – Make Early Dinner Your Friend

We are creatures of habit more than we realise. Have you ever woken up, glanced at the clock and seen it's a minute before your alarm was due to go off? It might seem spooky but really it's more that your body is a rigorous timekeeper and is fond of a schedule. Even if you don't feel like it's your personality type, your body is very much a Type-A, well-organised and colour-coordinated calendar kind of person. So when you jet off somewhere hot and blissful on holiday in a completely different time zone, your body's nice neat schedule is disrupted and the first night or two you wake at odd times. Human evolution evidently didn't consider the need to adapt to the speed of aeroplane travel. Likely if your body had its way you'd only travel on horseback or foot.

Your body runs on an internal clock tied to the light and dark of day and night. Your eyes feed back to your brain whether it's light or dark, specifically to your hypothalamus, the part of your brain that coordinates your unconscious bodily functions like breathing, heart rate and body temperature. Your body listens to this clock rhythm so that it's prepared for certain functions to take place at particular times. You also have another closely related but different clock that manages your eating routine and works closely together with your main body clock. Your gut microbiome fluctuates in amounts, rising and falling throughout the day in sync with both your eating and body clock. Your gut bacteria help to 'pass on the time' to other organs in your body, like your liver, keeping them up to date on the schedule.[1] Having meals at regular times that are aligned with your body clock's natural rhythms can help to support your gut microbiome.[2]

Eat an early dinner

Your body is biologically wired to digest food and uptake nutrients when you're supposed to be active and awake, and not when you're supposed to be asleep. That doesn't mean that your body doesn't keep digesting while you're asleep, because it does, but it's less efficient at it compared to when you're awake. Eating not too late in the evening gives your body a head start to focus on digestion, which is already slowing down in preparation for rest. Participants in a small but tightly controlled study went to bed at the same time, 11pm, yet half had dinner at 6pm and the other half ate later at 10pm. Those who had dinner earlier had lower levels of the stress hormone cortisol even though the meal was the same.[3] Eating within the hour before bed can also affect how well you sleep too.

Eating window

A fancy way of saying you're aligning your meals with your body clock is called Time-Restricted Eating (TRE). TRE is where you eat within a certain range of hours across the day, particularly giving your body an amount of down-time to rest and digest. TRE is just a technical term for the window of time that you eat food in, your eating window – the time from when you first eat something in the morning, to the last mouthful you eat at the end of the day. So if you had boiled eggs and avocado on toast for breakfast at 9am, and then the last thing you ate was dinner at 7pm, then your feeding window is the time in between – ten hours. An eating window of ten hours is linked to better mood, more energy and less hunger, and better cognitive performance too.[4,5]

What's your eating window?

Work out your eating window by writing in the box below the first and last times you ate in the day, then calculate how many hours are in between.

Time of first meal	Time of last meal	Eating window (difference in time)

TRE is related to:

- Sleeping better at night
- Less likely to feel hungry

- More energy
- Better mood
- Higher diversity of gut bacteria
- Better blood sugar and fat control
- Improved blood pressure

Many of the health benefits from time-restricted eating are likely partly thanks to your gut microbiome. Just like us, your gut bacteria also need enough of a well-earned fasted break overnight, encouraging more different types of gut bacteria and allowing the 'good' bacteria to flourish.[6]

Can you eat or drink outside of your eating window?

It's important to remember these hacks are not hard and fast rules. If you're hungry then be flexible, listen to your body and have something to eat if you need to.

Aim for an eating window of around ten hours. Try to eat your last meal of the day a bit earlier, listen to how you feel, and find an approach that sticks (for the most part). And remember that any health advice is never a hard and fast rule. It's a tool that you can bring into play most of the time when you can, at the best time that works for you. I'm a firm believer that TRE should never get in the way of going out for dinner with friends.

What's meal timing gut to do with it?

- Your eating window is the time from when you first eat something in the morning to the last thing you eat in the day
- Aim for a ten-hour eating window for better mood and more energy

- Your body runs on a body clock and likes routine. Eating at regular times can help with your digestion, so that your body knows that it's time to eat
- Be flexible – listen to your hunger and eat something if you need to, even if it's outside of your eating window
- Don't let TRE get in the way of enjoying dinner out with friends

Hack 6 – Oily Fish Twice a Week

If oily fish is spoken about in relation to your health, it's usually to do with your brain. And with good reason too. What might surprise you is that it's also good for your gut microbiome, even though it doesn't contain any fibre. Fish contain fats called omega-3s that influence your brain and your gut microbiome.

Omega-3s help your gut bacteria to produce more of your helpful short-chain fatty acids.[1] Those who have higher levels of omega-3s in their blood have been shown to have a more diverse gut microbiome and more 'good' bacteria, even if they don't eat much fibre.[2] Surprisingly, fish can also contain a small amount of polyphenols but only because they eat polyphenol-rich algae which can transfer and accumulate in their body.[3]

Let's circle back to your brain and omega-3s though. Your brain is made up of 75 per cent water, but if you were to hang your brain out to dry, 60 per cent of what remains is made up of fat. And one third of this fat is omega-3s, or specifically mostly a type of omega-3 called DHA. Omega-3s are crucial in determining how well your brain functions at all stages in life.

There are three main omega-3s:

- Docosahexaenoic acid (DHA)
- Eicosapentaenoic acid (EPA)
- Alpha-linolenic acid (ALA)

It's DHA that's particularly important for your brain as it makes up part of the membranes of your brain cells, including your neurons. And you need to get it from food to get enough DHA for your brain. Fish is a great source of DHA, however you can find the omega-3 ALA from plant foods like walnuts, flaxseeds and chia seeds. The problem is that ALA converts very poorly to the DHA that your brain particularly needs, so it can be harder to get enough.

Food sources of DHA and EPA	Food sources of ALA*
Animal sources: Fatty fish like salmon, mackerel, sardines, trout, tuna, prawns, sprats, fish roe Plant sources: Algae oil supplement	Plant sources: Flaxseeds, chia seeds, hemp seeds and walnuts

---

* Remember that ALA omega-3s are harder for your body to convert into DHA, happening slowly and producing only small amounts of EPA and DHA.

Eat more fish!

A 2019 meta-analysis of randomised controlled trials found that supplementing 1g or more of omega-3s (DHA and EPA) a day significantly helped ease depressive symptoms.[4] While a supplement isn't the same as a piece of fish, it does suggest that perhaps we should be eating more than the current national guidelines of at least one portion of oily fish a week (that only provides half the amount of omega-3s suggested above). The SMILES trial on food and mood[5] recommended at least two portions of oily fish a week, providing at least 6g of omega-3s – a similar weekly amount to the omega-3 supplements in the meta-analysis on depression.

Top food sources of omega-3s	Omega-3s (g/100g)
Walnuts*	7.5
Mackerel	4.8
Kippers	3.4
Farmed salmon	3.3
Sprats	2.7
Wild salmon	2.6
Sardines	2.5
Herring	1.8
Trout	1.7
Sea bass	1.7

---

* Remember that these contain ALA omega-3s and are harder for your body to convert into DHA, happening slowly and producing only small amounts of EPA and DHA.

Regular fish eaters tend to retain more grey matter in key brain regions like the hippocampus and prefrontal cortex in later life,[6] which is linked with better cognitive function and is considered a positive sign of brain health. Eating more than four portions of fish a week, and not just oily fish (that's double the national guidelines), is linked to a slower age-related decline in memory. And those who eat more fish tend to have memory abilities in later life similar to those four years younger.[7] In fact, researchers that evaluated the lifestyles of nearly 8,000 participants over five to ten years found that eating fish was one of the most important dietary factors in having better mental faculties than your peers[8] – and who secretly doesn't want to be mentally running circles around everyone else?

So let's find your fishy tipple and go for it – be it sushi, fish curry, smoked salmon with scrambled eggs or pulling out all the stops and throwing a whole fish on the summer BBQ stuffed with aromatic herbs and lemon.

Buying fish – choose sustainable

Eighty per cent of the seafood we eat is made up of just five species. With a third of fish now fished beyond sustainable limits, it's important to consider which to buy for the planet and not just health and taste. Supermarket fish are labelled if they are from more sustainable food sources so it's worth checking when you shop – it will either say 'responsibly' or 'sustainably' sourced. Organic fish also tends to have a lower environmental impact too. How sustainable a purchase is can depend on the type of seafood, how they're caught or farmed and where they are fished from. If you're looking for a more sustainable option then you can try some of the following swaps:

Bluefin or yellowfin tuna —> pole- and line-caught skip-jack or albacore tuna

King or tiger prawns —> organic or certified prawns

Wild Atlantic salmon —> Alaskan Pacific salmon, organic or certified farmed salmon or farmed trout

Other sustainable fatty fish options include sardines, mussels, crab, herring, anchovies and mackerel.

If you're shopping at your fishmonger for fish or at a supermarket fish counter you can ask for information on where the fish is from and how it was caught.

DHA omega-3 is nothing without its friends

Fish is not only a great source of protein and omega-3s but also contains B vitamins, choline and iron that are important for brain health and work together with the omega-3 DHA. DHA, like any superstar, need a behind-the-scenes team to make it shine. DHA relies on B vitamins and choline to be able to do its job – it just doesn't work as well without them. This likely explains why there's some frustrating confusion around omega-3 supplements and mood and cognition, with some studies showing an effect, and some nothing.

DHA relies on other nutrients to be able to reach your brain, like B vitamins and choline – because who likes to rock up to a party on their own? Only the very brave – most of us would like

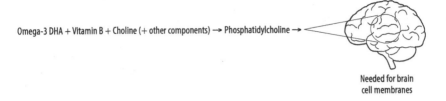

Omega-3 DHA + Vitamin B + Choline (+ other components) → Phosphatidylcholine →

Needed for brain
cell membranes

Figure 12.   DHA needs other compounds before it can be used by your brain

at least a friend or two with us before making an entrance. For DHA to be used by your brain it needs to 'arrive' as another type of fat called phosphatidylcholine where DHA is bound with choline by your B vitamins – and only then can Cinderella go to the ball. It's phosphatidylcholine that is important for the cell membranes of the neurons in your brain and is essential for them to function properly. You can also find choline in meat and eggs, and B vitamins in dark-green leafy veg.

Shopping – the fresher the better

To pick a fresh fish look at how clear the eyes are and how red the gills are. When fish aren't fresh their eyes start to cloud and dry, and the gills dull in colour – they should be a vivid deep red. If you're not sure, or the fish is already cut up into fillets, you can always ask the fishmonger or at the supermarket fish counter which is the freshest catch.

Cooking fish

You know what's so great about fish? That it cooks quickly – you can have a meal ready in under 15 minutes in the oven, or even less in a frying pan. I do remember, though, when I first started learning to cook I was completely terrified of fish and avoided it at all costs for a long time. I was worried about undercooking it so that the insides were still raw. Or worse, overcooking it so it was bone dry and chewy. So if you feel anything close to the same, please take this as a sign to push those fears aside and give it a go.

Cooking in a pan?

This works best for thin fillets of fish like mackerel or sole. If it's a thicker fillet like a cut of salmon then it's easiest to bake it in the oven. When frying a fish, the trick is to pat the fillet with paper towel to get rid of excess moisture, and this helps to prevent sticking. Heat the pan to hot – if you hover your hand over the pan you should be able to feel an intense heat. Only then add in a bit of oil, and your fish. This is the part where you need to be brave and not touch it or poke it for a few minutes, otherwise it'll stick. Breathe! It'll all come good. After a few minutes the sides of the fish will have started to shrivel up and not be translucent any more. That's your cue to flip it. Same again, resist moving it around for a few minutes. It should then be done.

Baking in the oven?

A good rule of thumb for salmon or most fish fillets is about 10–15 minutes at 180 degrees Celsius, though it depends on how thick the fillet is. If you're nervous about overcooking it then the secret to keeping it really juicy and idiot-proof is to make a folded 'bag' out of baking parchment and bake in the oven. In this 'bag' you put your fillet of fish, and some liquid like white wine or just some extra-virgin olive oil with some lemon slices and herbs, whatever you like. Close up the 'bag' and cook in the oven until done. It also makes cleaning up an absolute doddle too.

How to tell it's cooked

The fish shouldn't be translucent any more. You'll see that some of the juices coming through the fish flesh should have just turned white. It should 'flake' easily with a fork. And if in doubt – cut into the fattest part of the fish so that you can see properly for yourself. That's the easiest way to build up confidence until you can tell if it's ready just by looking at it. People care more about how it tastes than it looking like a nice neat fillet anyway!

I don't eat fish – what should I do?

Plant sources of omega-3s like walnuts, flaxseeds and chia seeds contain ALA, which your body struggles to convert to DHA. Some algae, though, do naturally produce DHA and EPA. Algae oil supplements can be a great choice instead of fish or fish oil omega-3 supplements if you're a vegan or vegetarian, if you can't eat fish, choose not to, or simply don't like it. And try to make sure you're eating enough foods high in B vitamins like dark-green leafy veggies, whole grains and beans.

A fishy warning: mercury

Mercury is a natural element, but mostly due to industrial pollution there's too much of it in our oceans. It can be harmful to eat a lot of mercury. Mercury naturally accumulates in fish, and no matter where you find fish in the world there will be a small amount of mercury. Some fish, though, contain more mercury than others – particularly fish that are bigger and have lived longer. This is why if you're pregnant or trying to get pregnant you shouldn't eat shark, swordfish or marlin or have more than four cans of tuna a week as the higher levels of mercury can damage a developing baby's nervous system.

As with most things, it's all in the dose, so it depends on how much you eat and how often. For most of us, eating bigger fish is perfectly safe. If you're worried about mercury you could always aim to eat more smaller types of fish like sardines, anchovies and herring, or seafood like clams, crab and crayfish. Salmon and trout are also usually low in mercury.

Put It into Practice . . .

I will . . .

_____

_____

e.g.

- Stock up the freezer with frozen prawns
- Add trout or sustainable salmon to my weekly shopping list
- Make sure I have tinned tuna and canned sardines in the cupboard ready to go
- Make a prawn and veggie stir-fry tonight

So I can . . .

_____

[your Genius Gut goal]

e.g. eat oily fish twice a week

So that . . .

_____

[your Genius Gut 'why']

e.g. I feel great

What's oily fish gut to do with it?

- Omega-3s are types of fats that support a diverse gut microbiome and are crucial for brain health
- A particular type of omega-3 is called DHA, which makes up part of the cell membranes of your brain's neurons
- Aim to eat at least two portions of oily fish a week
- Try to choose sustainable fish options

Hack 7 – Join the Dark Side

A little bit of what you fancy does you good

Chocolate has to be one of life's greatest pleasures, don't you agree? I'm pretty sure every person in the UK has *that* 2000s M&S TV advert permanently tattooed in their brain, the one with the sensual Nigella-like narration over a slowly oozing chocolate fondant. By acknowledging that you are a human being – and not a robot – and therefore you enjoy, and sometimes crave, something sweet, then a small regular bit of 85 per cent dark chocolate can have your back by giving you that needed hit of satisfying sweetness.

Reasons to be grateful for dark chocolate:

- Dark chocolate is surprisingly high in fibre, containing around 11g fibre per 100g!
- Cocoa powder is particularly rich in polyphenols – the higher the cocoa content of your chocolate the greater the polyphenol content.
- It contains theobromine, meaning 'food of the gods'. Theobromine is from the same family as caffeine but has a smoother 'hit'. It also acts by widening your blood vessels to improve blood flow, getting more oxygen and

nutrient-rich blood to your brain, making you feel more alert and focused.

- Chocolate contains compounds that mimic anandamide, a neurotransmitter that can make you feel blissfully happy, and phenylethylamine that acts like an autotuner to your happy hormones for a feel-good mood.[1]
- It satisfies some of your sweet tooth!

Is it 85 per cent dark chocolate that both your gut and your brain particularly enjoy? One trial found that eating 30g (about two squares) of 85 per cent dark chocolate a day (though sadly not 70 per cent cocoa content) improved participants' mood and their diversity of gut bacteria. The researchers found specific links between mood and certain gut bacteria types – suggesting that some of dark chocolate's mood-boosting effects are influenced by your gut microbiome.[2]

Enjoy your dose of 85 per cent dark chocolate

Really dark chocolate can be quite punchy in flavour – it's very dark and intense. If you find 85 per cent a little hard to handle, have it with some fruit and nuts – they provide extra sweetness and texture, and will also sneak in extra fibre too. It's a win-win for when you're looking for something sweet after a meal, or if you're feeling like a sweet snack in the afternoon.

Try some of the combinations on the next page to get a minimum 5g of fibre.

Food	Quantity (g)	Fibre (g)	Total (g)
85 per cent dark chocolate	30 (2 squares)	3.5	6.6
1 small pear	115	3.1	
85 per cent dark chocolate	30	3.5	5.0
3 medium strawberries	39	1.5	
85 per cent dark chocolate	30	3.5	5.5
10 raspberries	40	2.0	
85 per cent dark chocolate	30	3.5	5.6
1 medium apple	174	2.1	
85 per cent dark chocolate	30	3.5	5.3
3 dried apricots	24	1.8	
85 per cent dark chocolate	30	3.5	6.1
1 handful mixed nuts	30	2.6	
85 per cent dark chocolate	30	3.5	5.1
1 small tangerine	40	0.6	
1 oatcake	11	1.0	
85 per cent dark chocolate	30	3.5	5.6
Almonds (10 whole)	10	1.6	
Raisins (1 tbsp)	18	0.5	
85 per cent dark chocolate	30	3.5	5.1
2 prunes	16	0.8	
Cashew nuts (10 whole)	18	0.8	
85 per cent dark chocolate	30	3.5	5.6
Popcorn (3 handfuls)	15	2.1	

Put It into Practice:

I will . . .

_____

_____

e.g.

- Stock up on 85 per cent dark chocolate
- Pair dark chocolate with some almonds and some fruit
- Enjoy myself!

So I can . . .

_____

      [your Genius Gut goal]

      e.g. satisfy my craving for something sweet

So that . . .

_____

      [your Genius Gut 'why']

      e.g. I feel happier and more balanced

What's dark chocolate gut to do with it?

- Dark chocolate is surprisingly high in fibre, and is a rich source of polyphenols
- Dark chocolate contains compounds that can make you feel good
- 85 per cent dark chocolate can change your gut bacteria that are linked to changes in your mood
- Pair dark chocolate with fruit or nuts after meals when you feel like something sweet, or as a sweet snack that gives you 5g of fibre

Hack 8 – Protein- and Fibre-Power Your Breakfast

I'm a strong believer in breakfast. What gets me frustrated about the whole 'to eat breakfast or not to eat breakfast' debate is it seems to centre only around weight. The jury seems out on that one (and in my own research I found no connection between them).[1] There are many more reasons we should be talking about breakfast. What about your health, your mood, your energy levels and how well you think? And your gut microbiome? That seems to have been missing from the conversation. Let's change that. Skipping breakfast can make you feel more tired, and more anxious.[2] Not only that, it leaves a significant nutritional gap in your day too. So if you're a breakfast skipper who runs on coffee fumes, I hope I can persuade you to pick up breakfast again.

> ### Not feeling hungry in the morning?
> Your body is very adaptive, so if you regularly or always skip breakfast, over time it learns that no food is coming so your hunger signals can switch off. This can work both ways: you

can retrain your body to recognise that you will be having breakfast. It can take a little while for your body to relearn this, so in the meantime you can try these.

Start with something small and light and build up from there:

- Smoothie
- Small bowl of Greek yoghurt or kefir with fruit, nuts and seeds
- Baked egg, spinach and feta muffin
- Peanut butter and banana on toast

Try to eat at the same time each morning: Your body runs on its own internal clock, and it gets used to meals being at certain times. Eating at the same time each morning (when you can) can help ease your body into understanding 'this is a routine – it's time to eat'.

Move your body first: Doing some exercise in the morning can help to 'wake up' your body's metabolism and increase your appetite. This could be going for a walk, doing some stretches or going for a run or work-out class.

Your gut bacteria want to break the fast, too!

Breakfast skippers tend to eat less healthily than those who do eat breakfast,[3] so that's less gut-friendly foods for your gut bacteria. Skipping breakfast makes it that much harder to get enough fibre in your day for your gut microbiome. Consistently across countries, from the UK and US, to Mexico and Australia, those who skip breakfast eat less fibre, vitamins and minerals than breakfast eaters.[4] Many of these nutrients are also important for your brain health too, like B vitamins. Breakfast skippers also tend to snack more, and eat more less healthy foods.

Eating breakfast seems to make us happier. Studies have found that those who eat breakfast every day are the happiest, while those who never eat breakfast had the lowest mood.[5, 6] A meta-analysis of selected studies including over 400,000 participants found that those who skip breakfast had a greater likelihood of depression and were more likely to be stressed – across all age groups.[7]

Let's be honest, between you and me, and the pages of this book. Breakfast is a rush, isn't it? It's an afterthought. It's become a habit of grabbing a quick slice of toast or a bowl of cereal. You're either halfway out the door or sitting down at your desk already. There's so much opportunity to make breakfast more of an occasion, particularly now that I've nudged you – it'll make you feel good and set you up for the rest of the day.

A fibre-rich brekkie for your gut bacteria

The ultimate breakfast combo is to think back to Chapter 19 on how to combine foods to keep you feeling full and energised for longer. Here we're going to focus particularly on adding fibre, and in the next mini section protein, to your breakfast, which will set you up to conquer the day each and every time. Let's start with fibre for your gut bacteria.

To begin . . . make your breakfast gut-friendly:

- **Whole grains:** e.g. whole-grain toast, whole-grain cereal, rolled-oat porridge

- **Fruit:** e.g. berries, tropical fruit, baked apples, pears
- **Vegetables:** e.g. green smoothies, wilted spinach with eggs, grated carrot in bircher muesli, roasted tomatoes
- **Beans and legumes:** e.g. hummus or a beany shakshuka
- **Nuts and seeds:** e.g. sprinkle on sweet or savoury, smear toast with nut butter
- **Fermented foods:** e.g. kefir or yoghurt, veggie ferments to avocado on toast or with some eggs

Adding protein means fewer cravings later

Scientists have found that eating breakfast dramatically eases sweet and savoury cravings later in the day, but it was a protein-rich breakfast that reduced cravings the most for savoury, less nutrient-dense foods.[8,9] The trick is to add in fibre *and* protein to your breakfast. You're feeding your gut bacteria their own breakfast, kick-starting their production of short-chain fatty acids, and at the same time setting yourself up for the day where it'll be easier to eat more gut-friendly foods later too.

Here are your no-brainer breakfast suggestions:

- **20-30g protein:** Keeping you feeling fuller and energised for longer – like eggs, smoked salmon, cottage cheese, Greek yoghurt and nut butter
- **Fibre and polyphenols for your gut bacteria:** Whole grains, veggies, fruit, beans and legumes, nuts and seeds – this could be a whole-grain cereal, seeded rye bread, berries or roasted tomatoes and spinach
- **Some ferments (if you like):** Ferments like kefir, yoghurt, sourdough bread and fermented veggies

When you're making breakfast, think how you can add a vegetable or fruit

You could . . .

- Slice some apple into your porridge
- Add some courgette, spinach and herbs to your scrambled eggs
- Crush some raspberries on top of your peanut butter and jam toast

Nuts, seeds and brans like wheat bran and oat bran are particularly high in fibre too and are great to add to your breakfast.

Remember that you're making changes for most days rather than strict and rigid rules. So you don't have to throw your favourite sugary cereal into the bin, you could enjoy it occasionally or add Greek yoghurt, fruit, nuts and seeds to it for an extra protein and gut-friendly fibre boost.

In the table on the next page you can see three breakfast examples that give you around 10g of fibre and 20g and above of protein. These are guidelines rather than set amounts; you may find you feel like eating a bit more or less depending on your body's hunger and fullness signals that day.

Description	Food	Protein (g)	Fibre (g)
Smoked salmon, avocado and scrambled eggs on pumpernickel toast	1 slice pumpernickel rye bread	3	6.2
	½ avocado	1.3	2.2
	2 eggs	13	0
	Toasted mixed seeds (1 tbsp)	2.7	0.7
Total		20	9.1
Overnight oats	35g oats	4.1	2.7
	Chia seeds (1 tsp)	0.9	1.7
	200ml kefir	7	0
	½ handful of mixed nuts (15g)	4.1	1.3
	½ grated carrot	0	4
	½ grated apple	1	1
	Cinnamon (1 tsp)	0	1.6
	Honey (1 tsp)	0	0
	Blueberries (100g)	0.9	1.5
Total		18	10.4
Cottage cheese, tomato and basil toast	2 slices pumpernickel rye	6	12.4
	Cottage cheese (150g)	15	0
	Basil (5 leaves)	0	0
	1 tomato	0.425	0.85
	Black sesame seeds (1 tsp)	0.7	0.6
Total		22.4	14.3

Savoury breakfast ideas

- Avocado on whole-grain toast with cottage cheese, feta and tomatoes
- Eggs with smoked salmon, spinach and rye bread topped with sauerkraut
- Veggie omelette with pesto, peppers, tomatoes, onions and spinach
- Courgette whole-grain savoury pancakes with Greek yoghurt, tomato salsa and poached eggs
- Tomato, hummus, basil, cottage cheese and toasted seeded whole-grain bread
- Chicken breast with stir-fried greens, avocado, halloumi in a whole-grain wrap or pita

Sweet breakfast ideas

- Quinoa breakfast bowl with toasted almonds, berries and Greek yoghurt
- Bircher muesli with grated apple, grated carrot, cinnamon and kefir
- Whole-grain honey pancakes with Greek yoghurt, mixed fruit and nuts and seeds
- Nutty granola trail mix or whole-grain cereal with berries, Greek yoghurt, nuts and seeds
- Fruit smoothie with tofu and nut butter
- Chia seed pudding with fruit, nuts and seeds

Put It into Practice:

I will . . .

_____

_____

e.g.

- Make a batch of bircher muesli so I have breakfast ready to go in the morning
- Stock up on protein-rich brekkie items like eggs, cottage cheese and Greek yoghurt
- Add veggies or fruit to my breakfast

So I can . . .

_____

      [your Genius Gut goal]

      e.g. eat a protein- and fibre-rich breakfast

So that . . .

_____

      [your Genius Gut 'why']

      e.g. I will have more energy through the day

What's a protein and fibre breakfast gut to do with it?

- Breakfast skippers tend to eat less healthily and eat less fibre than breakfast eaters
- Eating breakfast provides your gut bacteria with fibre, polyphenols and more!
- Having a protein- and fibre-rich breakfast will help you have more energy throughout the day, and you'll have fewer food cravings too

Hack 9 – Zen Out Your Brain, Zen Out Your Gut

Stress has a huge impact on every part of your body, from your brain to your gut and gut bacteria. Stress reduces blood flow to your gut, slowing down or speeding up your digestion. For some people this can lead to being constipated, with slow-moving food causing an accumulation of gas, making you bloated and uncomfortable. Others, though, need to dash to the loo with the runs. Stress can also change how much stomach acid you produce, sometimes causing heartburn. I'd see clients in my nutrition clinic with digestive problems – and a large part of their symptoms were often made worse by stress. Your gut and gut bacteria don't like stress. Your gut bacteria are affected directly by your stress hormone cortisol, and indirectly by the effect that stress has on disrupting both its home, your gut, and your immune system, which also plays a role in shaping your gut microbiome.

Reducing stress through stress management techniques can help your gut bacteria to stay resilient and thrive. A study on mindfulness-based cognitive therapy not only eased the anxiety of anxious participants, but shifted their microbiome to be more similar to that of the healthy controls. The people whose bodies were efficient at using tryptophan, the building block of serotonin, had the biggest improvements – and this was linked to certain gut bacteria.[1] In a different study, older adults with mild memory problems saw their thinking skills improve when they practiced mindfulness. These improvements were connected to changes in their gut bacteria, suggesting that the brain can influence certain gut bacteria types.[2]

Your emotions affect your digestion

In 1822, Dr William Beaumont first showed how emotions can affect your digestion[3] – clearly connecting the gut and the brain – and became the founding father of gastroenterology, the medical speciality of the gut.

For a long time Beaumont was a doctor on the army front line, and many of his experiments were on soldiers seeking treatment. A 19-year-old French-Canadian soldier called Alexis St Martin had been shot in the stomach, and as it healed it formed a permanent opening to his stomach – an inch-wide window into his gut. Beaumont saw St Martin's gut as a prime opportunity to conduct some unique science. He would dangle different foods attached to a string into St Martin's stomach to monitor how quickly they would be broken down by St Martin's stomach juices. This continued over a course of ten years – St Martin was employed by Beaumont as his servant and human guinea pig in exchange for food, a room and a small income. The relationship between them wasn't always smooth sailing – Beaumont found that when St Martin was upset or angry the acidity of his stomach acid wasn't as strong, and his stomach took longer to empty.

De-stress your gut

Are you like me, where you know how good meditating could be for your stress levels but you never seem to end up actually doing it? Even if meditating monks have gut bacteria linked to lower levels of anxiety, depression and heart disease.[4] If so, I have an alternative for you. It's simple, it works from the get-go, it's free, and it doesn't require anything more than counting to four. It's breath control – and it's even more effective than meditation for improving your mood.[5] The effects are immediate, too, just one five-minute session can significantly lower your stress and anxiety.[6] These techniques are effective for managing stress-related gut symptoms, too, by relaxing your second brain, your gut's enteric nervous system.

When you're stressed you tend to breathe quickly and shallowly, breathing in more than you breathe out, speeding up your heart rate – your sympathetic 'fight-or-flight' system takes control. By focusing on your exhales, you slow down your heart rate, making you feel calmer and more relaxed – shifting the balance back towards your 'rest-and-digest' parasympathetic system. In this way something as simple as controlling your breathing for a short period of time can have powerful effects on your mental well-being and therefore your gut and gut bacteria too. The best part about breath control is that it can be done anywhere at any time and with next to no effort. You could be sitting in a plane about to take off, in the middle of a frustrating conversation with a client, or hiding in the bathroom for just a moment's respite from a noisy kid's party. No one need know. There's no dramatic exaggerated humming, no need to have your eyes closed or to stand in a particular pose if you don't want to. There are many different breathing techniques, and while I'm going to share three here, the best type is the one that works best for you, that you feel most comfortable using when and where you need to.

Breathe for your gut
The long sigh

Do you ever catch yourself sighing? It's one of the ways your body naturally responds to tiredness or stress. You can mimic sighing to help calm you and make you feel more grounded. Researchers have found that a daily five-minute breathing technique called cyclical breathing made people happier and less low and anxious than other breathing techniques or meditation.[7] That's some power to something as simple as a sigh!

Inhale, pause briefly, inhale further until your lungs are full – so two deep inhales – then slowly exhale through your mouth until your lungs are fully empty. As you breathe in make sure to breathe in through your nose – this makes small subtle vibrations that can

BREATHE OUT
SLOWLY AND
FULLY

BREATHE
HALF IN

REPEAT FOR
FIVE MINUTES

BREATHE
FULLY IN

Figure 13. The long sigh (Image: Stanford Lifestyle Medicine)

calm activity in the emotional processing parts of your brain.[8] Repeat this for five minutes or until you feel better, aiming for around one breath cycle every 10 seconds if you can[9] (on average at rest we breathe 12 breaths a minute).

Box breathing

Box breathing is a technique often used by the US military as a quick way to return their breathing to a normal rhythm, managing their stress and helping them to stay focused during critical army operations. It's sometimes called square breathing too as you follow a pattern like the shape of a box or square.

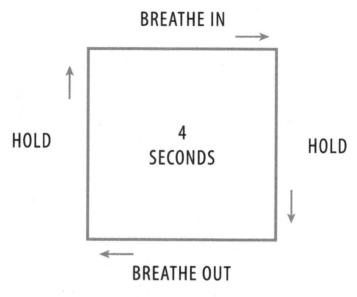

BREATHE IN

HOLD

4
SECONDS

HOLD

BREATHE OUT

Figure 14. Box breathing

- Breathe in through your nose counting to four
- Hold your breath for a count of four
- Breathe out through your mouth counting to four
- Hold your breath for a count of four
- Repeat

If you find counting to four too much, you can try a count of two or three.

4-7-8 breathing

The 4-7-8 breathing technique is based on a yoga breathing method called pranayama. It's also the technique that the TV character Ted Lasso's therapist suggests he uses to help with his panic attacks, and it does help to reduce both stress and anxiety.[10]

- Breathe in for a count of four through your nose
- Hold your breath for a count of seven
- Purposefully exhale from your mouth with a 'whoosh' through pursed lips for a count of eight
- Repeat

This is also often used as a way to calm your body to help you sleep at night, with a good long night's sleep linked to a more diverse gut microbiome.[11]

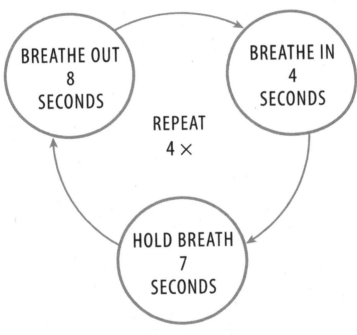

Figure 15. 4-7-8 breathing

Stress mindset

Being able to identify that some stress is good for you – that some stress can help you perform better and focus well – can help stress work for you and not against you. Recognising that some occasional stress isn't harmful can avoid the conundrum of 'oh my god I'm so stressed that I'm stressed'. Remember it's consistent long-term stress that can be damaging, and not feeling stressed now and again.

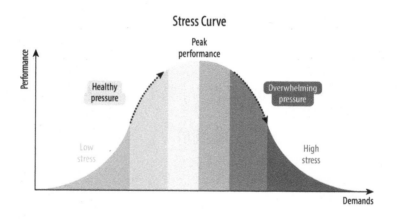

Figure 16.   Remembering that a little stress can be good for you (Image: Derek Hill, Waking Waves)

The positive stress approach

- Stress is natural and can be good for me
- Stress can help me be more resilient
- My body can naturally recover after stress without any harmful side effects
- Stress can help me to perform better and focus well
- Stress helps to challenge me and helps me grow

The negative stress approach

- Stress is always harmful and bad for my health
- I'm stressed that I'm stressed – it's making it worse
- I feel overwhelmed and I'm struggling to cope

Put It into Practice

I will . . .

_____

_____

e.g.

- Practise the long sigh, box breathing or 4-7-8 breathing for five minutes a day
- Try a breathing technique when I'm feeling rushed, stressed, or upset

So I can . . .

_____

[your Genius Gut goal]

e.g. manage my stress

So that . . .

_____

[your Genius Gut 'why']

e.g. I will feel calm throughout the day

What's stress gut to do with it?

- Your gut bacteria don't like stress, and neither does your gut – this can cause uncomfortable gut symptoms for some
- Mindfulness interventions that reduce stress have been shown to ease anxiety and improve cognition, and are linked to changes in gut bacteria
- Breathwork is an easy and effective way of managing stress – and can be used anywhere
- How you view stress matters too (and can avoid the 'I'm so stressed that I'm stressed' conundrum); by viewing some stress as good for you it can help you to manage your stress better

Hack 10 - Drink Up!

Did you know that the recommended eight glasses of water a day is a myth? While it can be a useful benchmark, how much water you need changes day to day depending on the weather – like when you're sweltering in the sun vs cosied up at home in the winter by the fire. It depends on how much exercise you do too, and how much you sweat. Or if you've eaten salty foods, like salted nuts or pizza, which can make you thirstier. On average we drink only half a litre of water a day[1] and over 65 per cent of us are chronically under-hydrated.[2] How can you tell if you're de-hydrated? Your poo is useful in understanding the health of your gut – let me tell you your pee can tell you volumes too. Your thirst signals and the colour of your pee are great ways to tell you how hydrated you are, and if you need to drink more water or other fluids.*

Your pee shouldn't be the colour of concentrated apple juice. That's a sign you need to drink more water or other hydrating fluids. It should be the colour of pale lemonade – close to clear but still pale yellow.

---

* As you age your thirst signals can become less strong, so you might not feel thirsty, and this is where the eight glasses of water (or coffee, tea and other drinks) recommendation can be useful.

WHAT COLOUR IS YOUR PEE?

CLEAR	PALE LEMONADE	DEEP YELLOW	CONCENTRATED APPLE JUICE	DARK BROWN
Drinking too much water or other fluids	Optimal hydration	Mildly dehydrated	Dehydrated	Very dehydrated

Figure 17. Are you dehydrated?

Hydrating your brain

Your brain is made up of 75 per cent water. This might make you think of your brain like an upside-down water canister – but unfortunately you're not actually able to store water like a camel. If you're not drinking enough, your brain is particularly sensitive to even minor changes in hydration levels. Losing just 2 per cent of your body's water can affect how well your brain works.

- Your brain cells shrink! (temporarily)
- You become tired and sleepy
- You can't focus well or concentrate
- You find tasks harder to complete
- Your mood drops[3]

When your body is dehydrated the volume of your blood goes down, causing water to move out of your cells so that they temporarily shrink. This leads to less blood flow to your organs, including your brain, so it has to work harder.[4] Studies have shown that if you feel thirsty, you perform worse.[5] A hormone called vasopressin helps to counteract dehydration by telling your kidneys to reabsorb water back from your pee – and this is what makes your pee darker in colour as it's more concentrated. It's thought that dehydration affects your mood as vasopressin can also influence other neurotransmitters, like your happy hormone serotonin.[6]

If I gave you a glass of water, though, your mood, alertness and concentration would immediately bounce back.[7] Water absorption happens very fast. Within five minutes of drinking a glass of water, you can see changes in the level of water in your cells, peaking at 20 minutes, yet it can take an hour and a quarter for you to completely absorb one glass.

When you wake up

When you sleep you naturally lose water as you breathe out moisture into the air, and to help your body to self-regulate your body temperature. So when you wake up, chances are that you're mildly dehydrated. Start your day with some water – drinking two glasses of water (or 500ml) in the morning has been shown to enhance mood and energy, and improve memory.[8]

Drinking for your gut

Staying hydrated isn't only important for your brain but for your gut and gut microbiome too.

Why hydrate for your gut:

- It helps you to make saliva, kick-starting your digestion
- In your stomach, the liquid gets combined with your stomach juices to make a sloppier mixture, helping you to digest your food
- Certain nutrients dissolve into water, making it easier for your body to absorb them
- It keeps things moving through and softens up your poo, making it easier to 'go'

Your gut microbes particularly like a nice moist poo,[9] giving them a warm and squishy environment to grow and multiply. They also like your poo to be able to move through and not hang around for too long; they'd rather have a nice fresh new meal arrive rather than being stuck with the same food contents to eat. A study found that people who don't drink enough water have distinct differences in their microbiome compared to those who do,[10] and particularly the bacteria that are involved in looking after your gut barrier lining.[11]

Hydration – what counts?

Water is the most hydrating drink. But don't feel like you only have to drink water to be hydrated. Pretty much any drink or liquid food is hydrating. Tea and coffee count towards keeping you hydrated as well as soup and high-water veggies like cucumber and watermelon. Some people say that tea and coffee are dehydrating because they contain a natural stimulant that helps you to feel more alert yet also makes you want to go to the loo sooner as it increases blood flow to your kidneys, so you produce more pee. But because coffee and tea contain enough water, it overrides this mild effect. Alcohol, though, while a liquid, is not hydrating and a significant part of a hangover is due to being dehydrated, so if you have an occasional cheeky tipple, try to drink water alongside it.

Staying hydrated isn't the only thing drinks offer. Many drinks also contain other components that can help to support your gut bacteria. Swapping in some new drink options can be a great easy way to add some extra goodness for your gut microbiome and your brain too! Plenty of drinks are rich in polyphenols or are fermented (see Hack 4 on daily ferments). Coffee, black tea, green tea and red wine are some of the highest polyphenol-containing

Top 10 polyphenol rich drinks	Total polyphenols mg/100ml
Concentrated grapefruit juice	351
Coffee (decaf or caffeinated)	267
Red wine	215
Pomegranate juice	204
Apple juice	142
Black tea	104
Cider	98
Rosé wine	82
Orange juice	72
Green tea	62

drinks (though I'll explain later why alcohol isn't your best go-to for polyphenols).

Tips on staying hydrated

- Keep some water by your bed at night and for the morning when you wake up
- Carry a water bottle in your bag with you and by your desk
- Flavour your water with slices of lemon, crushed basil, and other fruit
- If you drink alcohol, drink a glass of water in between to stay hydrated
- Snack on high-water-containing foods, particularly in the summer when you're more likely to be dehydrated, like watermelon, cucumber and tomatoes
- You don't have to drink tea hot, you can add the bag straight into a glass of iced or room-temperature water and it will infuse with flavour and polyphenols

---

Coffee

I co-authored a scientific paper a few years ago where we found that of all the food and drinks we looked at, coffee was the most strongly related to the gut microbiome. And the more coffee you drank the greater the diversity of your gut bacteria.[12] Within reason, of course! Coffee is particularly high in polyphenols, and let me surprise you – did you know that coffee contains some fibre too? And I don't mean chewing on coffee beans, but actually your morning cuppa can contain up to 1.8g of fibre in a 240ml mug – that's more fibre than orange juice.[13] Now if you're like me you're thinking, 'huh, but orange juice has those little bits in it whereas coffee is a smooth, clear drink', that's because coffee contains a type of fibre that easily dissolves in water so you can't see it.

Compared to espresso or filtered coffee, instant coffee isn't only cheaper but also tends to contain slightly more fibre. Though choose the coffee that you like best, particularly as the fibre difference between them is so small – but isn't it good to know that the cheaper, more low-brow version can land on top sometimes?

For people with anxiety or certain gut symptoms, though, caffeinated coffee is bad news. The caffeine in coffee can mimic anxiety, and it can be hard for your brain to recognise that it's not. Your heart rate can quicken, you may feel restless and less at ease. For those with gut symptoms it can speed up how quickly things move through your gut, making you rush to the loo. So coffee isn't for everyone – and if you suffer with IBS or other gut symptoms, then likely coffee isn't for you. For those of us who get jittery on regular coffee but still love the taste, like me, decaf coffee is an option and still contains some fibre but slightly less than full 'caf'.

If you drink coffee, how much coffee should you have?

Caffiene is the original cognitive enhancer. If you drink coffee, most of the benefits seem to be at around two cups a day. A study of nearly 400,000 people found that having one to two cups of coffee a day was related to better brain health and function, better than having no coffee or drinking decaf. Yet having more than six cups a day was linked to smaller brain volume and 53 per cent greater odds of dementia.[14] So some, but not too much, seems to be the sweet spot. Caffeine can cross the blood-brain barrier and stimulates the release of your 'I like it, do it again' dopamine and your 'fight or flight' alert neurotransmitter norepinephrine, so you feel more awake, focused and energised. But it's not only caffiene that's at play.

The chlorogenic acid polyphenols that are plentiful in your cup of Joe, whether it's caffeinated or decaf, are thought to be the key drivers of many of coffee's benefits, and can help you feel more alert too. Your pot of coffee at home might actually contain the most chlorogenic acids. Roasted ground coffee from the supermarket was found to have the highest content of chlorogenic acids compared to other coffees with around 240mg in one mug of coffee.[15]

The chlorogenic acids in a cup of coffee helps with your:[16]

- **Motor speed:** e.g. how quickly you can text on a phone or type on a keyboard
- **Psychomotor speed:** e.g. tasks where you need both mental and physical coordination, like playing an instrument or operating machinery
- **Executive function:** e.g. how well and quickly you make decisions, plan and adapt – key for juggling life
- **Shifting attention:** e.g. tasks that need you to keep shifting focus, like driving, where you're looking at the road, your mirrors and responding to movement of other cars

Drink your coffee in the morning, not in the afternoon

Let's say you have your morning cup of coffee at 8am and then another halfway through your morning at 11 – a cheeky cappuccino, or whatever your go-to is. It takes your body time to breakdown the caffiene. Twelve hours later, a quarter of it is still swilling around your bloodstream. Right when you're trying to go to sleep. What the caffeine does is block the receptors for your drowsy neurotransmitter adenosine, making you feel more awake, and so harder to fall asleep. For all those people who think they fall asleep fine after a post-dinner espresso, it can also affect how well you sleep – making it harder for you to reach a deep restorative sleep. You wake up bleary eyed and groggy, and . . . yes . . . reach for a coffee. The cycle repeats. Pro tip: if you're having your coffee, have it early in the day, ideally before midday. After that, switch to decaf, which has 97 per cent less caffeine than regular coffee.

Black tea, green tea and matcha

Not everyone likes coffee – and that's completely OK. Only drink coffee if you enjoy it and it makes you feel good. If you're not into coffee, maybe you're someone who's more of a tea drinker. Tea's most abundant polyphenols are catechins. These polyphenols have anti-inflammatory and antioxidant effects that support your immune system – by drinking tea you're 30 per cent less likely to get flu.[17] Great news for tea-loving Brits. Herbal teas and fruit teas also contain polyphenols but in smaller amounts – and can be great ways to flavour water, either hot or cold.

Tea	Polyphenols mg/100g
Black tea	104
Green tea	62
Peppermint tea	31
Fennel tea	23
Chamomile tea	23

If you weighed dry black tea vs coffee grounds, black tea contains more caffeine. But as we use less actual tea to make a cuppa, it ends up that there's less caffeine in your mug of tea than there is in a cup of coffee. Tea also contains an amino acid called L-theanine that fine-tunes the effect of caffeine, relaxing you but not so you feel drowsy – you feel alert without the jittery crash you sometimes get with coffee.[18]

Green tea and black tea are made with the same tea leaves; the difference between black tea and green tea is how the leaves are processed and treated. Matcha is a powder made from green tea leaves, but instead of soaking the tea in water, then extracting the tea, the ground tea leaves are blended in and drunk with the water. Matcha is therefore a more concentrated version of green tea, more nutrient dense, and can contain three times more catechins[19] and more L-theanine, helping you to feel less stressed, and giving you a slight attention and memory boost.[20]

Tea made with matcha also contains fibre, like coffee, but tends to vary in the amount depending on the matcha.[21] While we don't yet have evidence, like we do with coffee, for matcha's effects on your gut microbiome (unfortunately we didn't have data on matcha in the study mentioned in the first line of the section on coffee), based on its nutrition content it's likely as good for your gut bacteria. So choose whichever you enjoy the most. And if you don't like either, that's not a problem – you don't have to drink or eat anything you don't enjoy.

Cheers to red wine

You really don't need me to tell you that alcohol interferes with how well your brain works, making it harder to control your balance, memory and speech. And judgement. I'm sure that's not a new revelation. If drunk in excess* alcohol is consistently linked to being bad for your health. Scientists now think that even a small amount of alcohol isn't good for your gut or your brain.[23] Alcohol can irritate your gut lining, making food move through faster, and changes how your body absorbs fluids. You also pee a lot as alcohol limits the amount of vasopressin that is released, which is why you become dehydrated. I wouldn't suggest starting to drink alcohol for your gut bacteria or your brain, and ideally you wouldn't have any alcohol at all, but if you do drink alcohol, then red wine might be the best choice for your gut bacteria.

The occasional glass of polyphenol-rich red wine is related to a more diverse gut microbiome,[24] though arguably it's still better to get your polyphenols elsewhere, and not from alcohol. Or you could choose an alcohol-free version. Another study showed

---

* UK guidelines recommend no more than six glasses of wine or six pints of beer a week for your health.[22]

that both red wine and non-alcoholic red wine significantly changed the participants' microbiome and were coupled with health benefits like lower blood pressure, blood-fat levels and inflammation.[25] If you do drink, then red wine might be the better choice, though try to have no more than one glass a day.

Put It into Practice:

I will . . .

_____

_____

e.g.

- Put a water glass by my toothbrush to remind me to drink water in the morning
- Add herbal tea bags to a water jug and keep by my desk
- Make a matcha latte or coffee with breakfast

So I can . . .

_____

[your Genius Gut goal]
e.g. stay hydrated and support my gut microbiome
So that . . .

_____

[your Genius Gut 'why']
e.g. I will feel more alert and focused

What's a drink gut to do with it?

- Look for lemonade-coloured pee for optimal hydration
- Drink two glasses of water in the morning for your mood, energy and memory
- Coffee is linked to a more diverse gut microbiome, likely because it's rich in polyphenols and contains some fibre. Though if you have gut symptoms then it can make them worse because of the caffeine content
- If you drink coffee, up to two cups a day seems to be the sweet spot for your health and brainpower
- Tea is a great alternative to coffee for your gut bacteria, if you're not a coffee drinker
- Alcohol dehydrates you, and drinking excessively isn't good for your gut, gut microbiome or brain
- If you are going to drink alcohol, choose an occasional glass of red wine for your gut bacteria

Epilogue – Looking After Your Gut-Brain Connection

My first full-time job was as a chef – on a super-yacht. While most of my friends were hunting for their first jobs in the city, I was sailing around the world. Despite all that, I couldn't understand how my mood was constantly swinging up and down and I felt tired all the time, when I was living this amazing life. I ate a 'perfect' diet, after all. Or what I thought was a 'perfect' diet. I didn't eat meat, downed green powders and fancy supplements like there was no tomorrow – and cake and chocolate were strictly off the menu. Yet on days I was stressed or down, I'd guiltily plough through packets of sweets and Snickers bars, quickly hiding the wrappers in the bin. What I didn't want to acknowledge was that in the name of 'health and wellness', I was subconsciously terrified of feeling too full, drained and exhausted, riding a rollercoaster of anxiety and low mood. Because it wasn't really health and wellness. I wasn't listening to my body at all. And it made me feel awful.

What I needed was a switch to a gut-brain mindset. To eat in a way where I felt strong, energised, focused and happy. I stepped back from my (not-so) 'perfect diet' mentality. I thought about adding in foods for my gut bacteria, and not cutting foods out. I felt happier and more balanced, and I ate all foods, not sweating a little fun deliciousness either. There's a special kind of peace when you can enjoy eating without the emotional load of guilt and self-bashing – and less stress is a win for your gut bacteria too.

I've written this book to give you a clear path on how to feel your absolute best. The recent wave of research into the gut-brain connection clearly shows how interwoven your mental and physical well-being really are. We have plenty of rigorous trials now that highlight how what you eat can change your mood, and we're rapidly understanding the exciting new and developing science of how your gut bacteria are closely involved. The food you eat impacts your brain, both directly, and indirectly through your gut bacteria. And because your gut microbiome is so readily changed by what you eat, it opens up a new chance to improve your whole-body well-being. I want nothing more than for you to read this book and think, 'OK, I can do that.' That you know what to eat for your brain, your gut, and your gut microbiome – to feel great, to feel happy, to have energy and so much more. Because we all need a bit more of that in life. By looking after both your gut and your brain – your gut-brain connection – you're on the path to feeling your absolute best, and I know this is the start of a whole new chapter for you. I can't wait to hear about it.

Free psychobiotic download

Go to www.emilyleeming.com and you can download your probiotic and prebiotic guide for stress, mood and cognition when you subscribe to my free newsletter Second Brain.

APPENDIX – YOUR GUT KIT

The Genius Gut Method Checklist

Food Group	Most days checklist						
	Monday	Tues-day	Wed-nesday	Thurs-day	Friday	Satur-day	Sunday
Whole grains	☐☐☐	☐☐☐	☐☐☐	☐☐☐	☐☐☐	☐☐☐	☐☐☐
5 colour vegetables	☐☐☐	☐☐☐	☐☐☐	☐☐☐	☐☐☐	☐☐☐	☐☐☐
Fruit (2 per day)	☐☐	☐☐	☐☐	☐☐	☐☐	☐☐	☐☐
Berries (1 handful per day)	☐	☐	☐	☐	☐	☐	☐
Nuts (1 handful per day)	☐	☐	☐	☐	☐	☐	☐

Food Group Potential serves	Most days checklist						
	Monday	Tuesday	Wednesday	Thursday	Friday	Saturday	Sunday
Ferments (1–6 per day)	☐☐☐ ☐☐☐	☐☐☐ ☐☐☐	☐☐☐ ☐☐☐	☐☐☐ ☐☐☐	☐☐☐ ☐☐☐	☐☐☐ ☐☐☐	☐☐☐ ☐☐☐
Protein per meal (20–30g)	☐☐☐	☐☐☐	☐☐☐	☐☐☐	☐☐☐	☐☐☐	☐☐☐
Drink plenty of water/tea/ coffee/fluids							
Weekly							
Beans and legumes (3–4 times a week or more)	☐☐☐☐						
Oily fish fillet (2 times per week or more)	☐☐						
85 per cent dark chocolate	☐☐☐☐						
Fun foods!	Find your balance						

Gut Glossary

Archaea

Archaea are types of microbes that are similar, but different, to your gut bacteria. They are less common and less well understood.

Bacteria

Bacteria are a type of microbe that make up most of your gut microbiome. We know more about them than other gut microbes.

Carbohydrates

Fibre, starches and sugars make up carbohydrates. Carbohydrates are found in fruits, vegetables, grains and dairy. Your body uses carbohydrates for energy, and this is particularly important for your energy-hungry brain. Simple carbohydrates like those found in refined grains and sugary foods are digested rapidly and have the potential to dump quick bursts of sugar into your bloodstream. Complex carbohydrates are found in fruits, vegetables and whole grains and are digested more slowly, supplying a slower release of sugar into your bloodstream.

Fats

Like protein and carbohydrates, there are different types of fats that can have different effects on your health. Some are less healthy for your heart while others are protective. You can find the protective fats in foods like avocado, oily fish, nuts and seeds and extra-virgin olive oil. While less healthy fats are found in fatty meats like bacon, steak and sausages. Fats provide essential fatty acids that are critical for your cell membranes, particularly in your brain and nervous system. Certain vitamins, like vitamins A, D and E, are better absorbed with the help of fats.

Fibre

Fibre is found in plant roughage from whole grains, fruits, vegetables, beans, legumes, and nuts and seeds. You can't digest fibre yourself – your body cannot digest or absorb it. Instead, you need your gut microbiome to help break it down. Fibre isn't just one thing either, there are lots of different types of fibre.

Fungi

There are different types of fungi in your microbiome and these include yeasts and moulds. The role of these fungi in your health is less understood compared to what we know about bacteria.

Gut microbes

An abbreviated term to refer to the collection of microorganisms in your gut and includes bacteria, viruses, fungi and archaea.

Gut microbiome

The gut microbiome includes all the microbes that live in your gut, but also their genes, the stuff they produce and their interactions with your body.

Gut microbiota

Your gut microbiota is a collection of microorganisms (or microbes for short) that includes bacteria, viruses, fungi and archaea that live mostly in your lower intestine.

Immune system

The immune system is an intricate network of cells, tissues and organs that work together to defend your body against harmful invaders.

Inflammation

Inflammation happens when your immune system is trying to protect you from harm. It's a natural, helpful reaction that's part of the body's healing response. Inflammation, though, can become harmful long term.

Metabolites

A metabolite is a small molecule produced by your gut microbiome as a by-product of breaking down the food you eat. Metabolites play a crucial role in your health.

Polyphenols

Polyphenols are antioxidant compounds naturally found in plants, like fruits, vegetables, whole grains, beans and legumes, and nuts and seeds. They have a prebiotic-like effect by feeding your 'good' gut bacteria.

Prebiotics

A prebiotic is a substance that feeds specific 'good' bacteria in your gut, helping your health. Prebiotics are often types of fibre, but they can be some other food components too. Prebiotics are found naturally in food or as an added ingredient or supplement.

Probiotics

A probiotic usually refers to a supplement or sometimes a food that contains live bacteria. The definition of a probiotic is a type of microbe that, when you take enough of it, has a specific helpful effect on your health.

Proteins

Your body uses protein to build and repair, particularly your muscles and bones. There are many types of protein, each made up from differently put-together protein building blocks called amino acids. There are 20 amino acids, and they act rather like Lego bricks – you can make a different model depending on how those bricks are arranged or which bricks you use. Your body can produce some of these amino acid building blocks by itself, but others must come from the food you eat. High-protein foods are meat, poultry, fish and seafood, eggs, dairy, nuts and seeds, and beans and legumes.

Short-chain fatty acids

Short-chain fatty acids are examples of metabolites produced by your gut bacteria when they ferment fibre. They have been linked to many health benefits.

Viruses

Your gut microbiome is also made up of viruses. They can interact with and influence your gut bacteria. We know less about them than about your gut bacteria.

Frequently Asked Questions

Should you take apple cider vinegar for your gut microbiome?

Apple cider vinegar is made through the fermentation of apples when making cider. Apple cider vinegar is a fermented food that contains a little bit of fibre in the form of pectin, some polyphenols (like you would find in apple juice), and can contain live microbes if it's unpasteurised (look for those with the 'mother' – it will be cloudy at the bottom). Apple cider vinegar gets a lot of airtime for its supposed health benefits, and while it has plenty of nutrition it's also been overhyped. We don't have any human studies yet to show that taking apple cider vinegar can help support your gut microbiome or digestion, unlike the evidence for other fermented foods like kimchi and kefir. There is some evidence that for those with type II diabetes, having some apple cider vinegar each day can help with blood sugar control and cholesterol levels[1] – but again, its effects tend to be overblown. There's no such thing as a silver bullet, unfortunately. That doesn't mean you can't enjoy apple cider vinegar in a delicious dressing or as part of a recipe. One thing to know – please don't take apple cider vinegar as a straight shot! It erodes the enamel on your teeth, and you'll have one very unhappy dentist.

Should you take medicinal mushrooms for your mind?

Mushrooms in any shape or form are fantastic for your health and for your gut bacteria. They're rich in fibre, polyphenols, vitamins and minerals. Medicinal mushrooms are types of mushrooms that have been suggested to help with your mood and in pre-venting or treating cancer. Medicinal mushrooms are another type of food with a lot of claims – though in truth the evidence is very thin on the ground or non-existent altogether. There are a few common types, including lion's mane, reishi, cordyceps, chaga and maitake. There are hints that these types of mush-rooms may help with your mood, ease anxiety and stress[2,3,4] and improve how well you think.[5] The evidence isn't strong enough yet to recommend them, but they do seem to be safe to take – so if you're interested in giving them a try then see how you feel, though your money might be better spent elsewhere.

Should you take a probiotic supplement?

If you're generally well and healthy, then you don't need to take a probiotic supplement – what you eat has a greater overall impact. Many of the probiotic supplements on the market haven't been rigorously tested and it's a bit of a wild west in terms of the claims many make. A study of commercial probiotic products available in Washington DC found that only 35 per cent of the probiotic supplements sold had the right type of bacteria linked to specific health effects and at the right dose for an effect.[6]

If you're looking for a probiotic that has a specific health effect, then you want to keep a beady eye out for how that bacteria is described. It needs its full name for you to know if it's the right bacteria and that it will do what it's promised to do. Have you ever tried to get a new email, only for your first name to already be taken? There are lots of other people with the same first name as you. It can be the same for bacteria too – if you're not specific enough then you're not going to get the right one. The key part to remember is that you want the postcode for that bacteria, called its 'strain' designation. This is found at the very end of the bacteria's name and usually is a bunch of numbers and/or letters. Bacteria can behave very differently so it's important to know which one is which.

Genus	Species	Strain
Bifidobacterium	*longum*	NCC3001
Lactobacillus	*rhamnosus*	GG

The first word is the 'genus' name of the bacteria. The second word is the bacteria's 'species' name. Sometimes there's even a subspecies, but not always. Then finally – you have the postcode – the 'strain' name. For *Bifidobacterium longum* NCC3001, *Bifidobacterium* is the genus, *Bifidobacterium longum* is the species and *Bifidobacterium longum* NCC3001 is the strain. It's this strain that's been shown to improve low mood and quality of life with those with irritable bowel syndrome.[7]

A great example of strains of bacteria behaving differently are those from the species *Escherichia coli*, or *E. coli* for short. There's a dangerous strain of *E. coli* called *E. coli* O157:H7 that produces a powerful poison, making you very sick with diarrhoea and stomach pain if it contaminates your food or water. This bacterial strain gets all the attention, yet its siblings aren't harmful at all, and some are even good for you, like *E. coli Nissle* 1917. Many of the *E. coli* strains in your gut help with digestion and protect you from other harmful microbes.

You also want to check on the label for how many viable bacteria it contains, called the total count of colony-forming units (CFU) per dose or serving. Ideally the product will tell you what the count is for each strain, so that you know that there's enough of each strain to have an effect rather than them chucking in a load of the cheapest ones and adding a teeny sprinkle of the others. Avoid the probiotics that say CFU 'at time of manufacture' as some bacterial strains are sensitive souls and can die off in storage, so by the time it arrives in your fridge or cupboard it can be severely depleted in numbers.

How to choose a probiotic cheat checklist

- *Is the strain described?*

Look for an odd collection of numbers and/or letters at the end

- *Does the strain have evidence for an effect?*

Check the company's website to see if there's a list of studies that have been conducted. You can also do a quick Google search and add 'pubmed' in the search bar. You want the participants to be similar to you to be confident

---

that it'll work for you, e.g. if you're healthy or have irritable bowel syndrome, and what effect you're looking for
- *What is the CFU count?*
While bigger doesn't necessarily mean better, you'll be more confident that you're getting enough of that bacterial strain for an effect. You want enough CFU that's been shown to have been beneficial in human studies
- *Avoid those who say CFU 'at time of manufacture'*
Their numbers may have deteriorated by the time you get your hands on them

As probiotics are transient visitors that can pass through your gut within a matter of days, you need to keep taking it to see a benefit. If you do want to try a probiotic, then try it for eight weeks. If you feel noticeably better then feel free to keep taking it, but if you don't – then your money is likely better spent elsewhere.

If you're taking a probiotic for a mood disorder, it shouldn't replace the standard treatment or medication, but it can act to complement it – probiotics have been shown to be effective alongside antidepressants in easing depressive symptoms, for example.[8] For a list of probiotics and prebiotics for stress, mood and cognition, see page 300.

Should you take a prebiotic supplement?

Prebiotics are a type of compound that feed specific 'good' bacteria and have been shown to have a resulting health effect. Most of those available on the market are inulin, fructo-oligosaccharides (FOS) and galacto-oligosaccharides (GOS). FOS and GOS, for example, have been shown to increase levels of 'good' gut bacteria and improve low mood and anxiety when taken in doses of 5g or more a day.[9] Prebiotics are often sold as supplements in pill form, but you can also often find them in food products like snack bars, biscuits, cereals and spreads – chicory root syrup contains inulin and is often used to sweeten foods instead of sugar.

If you would like to take a prebiotic supplement that you've seen has a particular effect you're looking for – then they're safe to try. Some key points to remember though. For some people, certain types of prebiotics can cause digestive issues and if you have irritable bowel syndrome some can trigger symptoms, while other types can help ease them. I would suggest talking to your dietitian or healthcare professional first.

Like with probiotics, more doesn't necessarily mean better and can also cause digestive issues. Most prebiotics need to be taken at a dose of at least 3g/day, or 5g/day for FOS or GOS.

What are synbiotics?

There are two different types of synbiotics. Complementary synbiotics are a combination of a prebiotic and a probiotic, paired together in a supplement or food product but not necessarily acting together as a team for your health but as two individuals. In synergistic synbiotics, though, the prebiotic and the probiotic do work together as a team. The prebiotic specifically feeds the probiotic, ensuring that the strain of bacteria has a food source and therefore giving it a better chance of survival in your gut microbiome.

The same advice applies as for prebiotics and probiotics – if you're generally well and healthy then you don't need to take one, and what you eat will have the biggest effect on your gut microbiome. If you do want to take one, find one that has the health effect you're looking for and try it for eight weeks; if you feel noticeably different then keep taking it, but if you don't, then it might not be worth continuing with it.

What about a short-chain fatty acid or postbiotic supplement?

You would think it would make sense to take a short-chain fatty acid supplement – considering how it's the short-chain fatty acids (along with other metabolites) produced by your gut microbiome that have powerful health effects. Postbiotic supplements are a relatively new concept, so we don't have much research yet on how they might, or might not, be helpful for your health. Some of the main concerns are whether the postbiotic supplements survive the acidic sloshing of your stomach and the alkaline secretions of bile into your small intestine, and if they do, whether they're even able to be fully absorbed into your body anyway.

If you're eating enough fibre, your gut microbiome will be producing enough short-chain fatty acids and other metabolites for your health – and there are around 50,000 metabolites that can be produced by your gut microbiome, compared to the few available within a supplement.

Should you cut out meat altogether for your health?

There's building scientific evidence that swapping out some animal-based foods for plant-based whole-food alternatives like beans is linked to many health benefits, lower risk of disease and longer life.[10] Should you go completely plant-based for your gut-brain connection? Not necessarily (for health reasons anyway). Many of the nutrients your brain needs, like iron and certain B vitamins like folate and B12, are most easily found in animal foods like meat, fish, eggs and dairy. That's not to say that you can't have a healthy brain by going fully plant-based, but it does mean that you'll need to be more conscious of how you're getting certain nutrients and being aware that some may be less easily absorbed than those in animal foods. For example, in a 12-week study, those who ate 30 per cent of their protein from animal sources like meat, dairy and eggs and 70 per cent from plant protein had lower vitamin B12 levels than those who ate more meat.[11] If you choose not to eat any animal products, then you'll need to take at least a B12 vitamin supplement and an algae omega-3 supplement.

Is meat bad for your gut microbiome?

Eating some meat isn't a problem for your gut microbiome. Meat is mostly absorbed in your small intestine with about 10 per cent of meat protein reaching the gut microbiome in your large intestine. Your microbiome is very adaptive, and can still produce some beneficial metabolites from meat. If you think back to caveman times – this was useful! Your body was able to adapt to make the most of what food sources were available.

What matters for your gut bacteria in terms of meat is the quality of the meat you're eating, and if you're eating enough plants with it. Many studies have shown that a diet high in processed red meat, fat and sugar, and low in fibre-rich and nutrient-dense plants – the standard Western diet – is bad for your gut bacteria. It can increase the number of 'bad' bacteria that can produce pro-inflammatory metabolites that don't support your health. If you eat a lot of processed red meat, like sausages, chorizo and bacon, then try to reduce how much you're having to 70g or less a day. Use them instead to occasionally flavour a veggie dish rather than making them 'the main event' – chickpeas and chorizo for example pair very well together. Eating processed meats with veggies also seems to prevent some of their conversion into potentially harmful metabolites.

For the most part – get your protein from oily fish, eggs and leaner cuts of meat like chicken or turkey rather than from fatty cuts of red or processed meat. You can also swap out some of your meat for plant proteins like lentils, beans and legumes, giving you that extra dose of fibre too.

Are nightshades bad for you?

Some people believe that nightshade foods – nightshade as in they like to grow at night or in shaded areas, like aubergine, tomatoes, peppers and potatoes – are inflammatory. That's simply not true. They've been confused with 'deadly nightshade', an inedible weed that's part of the same plant family. People who are worried about nightshade foods are concerned about a compound called solanine – a natural defence chemical produced by some plants to ward away insects. Solanine can develop in potatoes but only when they aren't properly stored and are exposed to light; they start turning green, which is why it's recommended not to eat potatoes with green areas on them. Solanine for the most part, though, is found in the leaves and stems of some nightshade members, and not in the parts we tend to eat. As well as containing lots of beneficial nutrients aubergines, tomatoes and peppers, alongside potatoes, are perfectly safe to eat and there's no evidence linking them with inflammation; in fact, the case is the opposite.

Are smoothies and juices good for you?

If you're choosing between your favourite smoothie or juice – pick the smoothie most days. Whizzing up fruit and veg into a smoothie breaks down the cell walls and releases the contents bound within – but you'll still get the fibre and polyphenols in there. With juice, though, a lot of the bulk is removed – the seeds, skins and pulp – and with it most of the fibre. To match the volume of drink you'd get with a smoothie, you need to use more fruits or veggies to get the same amount. This increases the polyphenol content, but it also increases how many free sugars are naturally present too (See Chapter 17). This is why 150ml (a small glass or just over half a regular glass) of juice only counts as one of your five a day – and not if you have more.

I like to add in some protein and fat to smoothies, like nut butters, Greek yoghurt, kefir, avocado and tofu, to help make them more filling and give you longer-lasting energy.

Is it bad to use the microwave?

The only danger a microwave presents is a risk of being scalded because food heats up so fast. Microwaves make the water molecules in food vibrate, making heat that cooks the food. While veggies cooked in the microwave don't always taste the best, it's a great way to reheat leftovers or cook some fresh from scratch without too much effort. Microwaving can prevent some of the nutrition being lost, as during steaming or boiling some small amounts of nutrients can be leached out into the surrounding water.[12]

Are dairy-free milks better for you?

Choose the milk you enjoy the most. Cow's milk provides a great source of protein and other micronutrients. In terms of plant milks, soy milk has the most similar nutritional profile, though there's limited but conflicting evidence on whether it helps increase your 'good' gut bacteria levels or not. For those who drink soy milk, likely you're having it in such small quantities, as a splash of milk in tea or coffee, that it's unlikely to have a significant effect on your gut microbiome anyway.

Should I take an intolerance test?

You can't test for intolerances apart from lactose intolerance, so avoid anyone that says otherwise, they're usually trying to sell you an expensive test that's not based on scientific evidence. You can test for allergies, and your doctor can help with that. If you think you have an intolerance a dietitian can guide you through an elimination diet that can help you pinpoint which foods are a trigger and how, if you can, to introduce them back into your diet in amounts that won't cause you symptoms.

Shouldn't I just eat loads of protein to feel happier?

It sounds simple that if you ate more protein, then, surely, you'd have more tryptophan and therefore more serotonin and feel happier? As ever – it's never quite as simple as that. While you need enough protein to get tryptophan in the first place, trying to eat loads of protein-rich foods like chicken, eggs and dairy to get more tryptophan doesn't make a great difference to how much serotonin your brain produces. To get to your brain, tryptophan must compete with other amino acids to cross your blood-brain barrier – these are all usually present in higher amounts than tryptophan, limiting how easily tryptophan can reach your brain. It's like everyone trying to pile into an elevator to reach the top floor, but there's a maximum capacity. So even if you're trying to flood the elevator with tryptophan, it can still only take up a certain amount at a time. While we don't yet fully understand the relationship between protein and mood, not eating enough protein means there's not enough tryptophan supplied to your brain to make your happy hormone serotonin. Eating a low-protein diet is linked to a 66 per cent greater likelihood of experiencing depressive symptoms.[13]

The Gut Store - Fridge, Store Cupboard, Freezer

These are some suggestions on what gut-friendly foods to stock up with. As always, choose the ones you enjoy and that work best for you.

Genius gut fridge hacks

Food	Notes/Ideas
Kefir/yoghurt	Use in salad dressings to add creaminess Have with berries, bran, nuts and seeds for breakfast Add to smoothies Make a kefir herb dip to go with salmon or chicken
Kimchi/other veggie ferments	Have with cheese and oatcakes as a snack Add as a condiment to lunch or dinner Spoon on top of avocado toast Stir through rice Add to an egg omelette or fritters

Food	Notes/Ideas
Berries	Have as a snack with nuts and dark chocolate Add to savoury salads for a hit of sweetness Blend into smoothies
Homemade/ shop-bought soups	Make a quick filling lunch by adding in beans, and sprinkle nuts and seeds and cheese on top with whole-grain seeded sourdough
Herbs	Nutrient powerhouses that elevate any meal by adding in extra flavour - try chopping them into salads or whizzing into dressings
Miso/gochujang/other fermented pastes or sauces	Great for salad dressings Add to soups Use to marinate chicken, tofu or fish
Onions, garlic and leeks	Rich in prebiotic fibres and a great base for most sauces, stews, soups and other dishes
Avocados	Add to smoothies Whizz into salad dressings for creaminess Have as a snack with sauerkraut, sliced apple and rye crackers
Rainbow veggies	Buy mixed packs where you can, e.g. pre-packaged bags of shredded stir-fry veggies Think of eating the five colour groups across your day
Other fruit	Keep your fruit bowl topped up Grab for a snack, bake for dessert or add to savoury dishes for some added sweetness

Food	Notes/Ideas
Hummus/other veggie dips	Have as a snack with cut-up veggie sticks Add on the side of lunch or dinner as a sauce or dip for extra flavour
Cut-up veggie sticks	Have as a snack while you're cooking, or, if you're feeling peckish mid-afternoon, with hummus and oatcakes or rye crackers
Tofu or tempeh	Blend tofu into smoothies for extra fibre and protein or scramble with spices and veggies Slice tempeh, fry until crispy and toss into a salad for extra texture
Cheese	Crumble into soups, salads or vegetable dishes Have with fruit as a snack

Genius gut store cupboard hacks

Food	Notes/Ideas
Beans and lentils	Swap half your mince for lentils when you're making a bolognese, lasagne or cottage pie If you're cooking beans or lentils from scratch, usually you need to soak them overnight before cooking. Red split lentils don't need soaking and can be added straight into stews and soups
Canned tuna/other oily fish	
Jarred artichokes	

Food	Notes/Ideas
Olives	
Capers	
Canned tomatoes/ passata	Make a really quick tomato sauce by blending canned tomatoes with a few sun-dried tomatoes, garlic and some herbs
Sun-dried tomatoes in oil	
Whole-grain pasta	
Brown/wild rice	
Quinoa/bulgar wheat/ pearl barley/spelt/ other grains	These are great to cook in advance, store in the fridge and reheat by adding to other dishes or gently warm or have cold by adding to salads for extra texture and satisfying fullness
Oatcakes and rye crackers	Both oatcakes and rye crackers are high in fibre, making them great for snacks with cheese and fruit, or with a dip like hummus
Wheat bran/other brans	Add to a mix of flaxseed, chia seeds and other nuts and seeds and sprinkle over veggie dishes or salads, or on fruit and yoghurt in the mornings for breakfast
Nuts and seeds	Stock up on different nuts, but also flaxseeds and chia seeds as they're especially high in fibre
85 per cent dark chocolate	
Coffee/green tea/other teas	
Spices and dried herbs	

Food	Notes/Ideas
Vinegars	Choose a vinegar that is unpasteurised, it should be a little cloudy at the bottom The darker the better as it'll generally contain more polyphenols
Pumpernickel bread	Pumpernickel bread often comes vacuum sealed and tends to be particularly high in fibre, making it great to keep in the store cupboard as a back-up (or main event!)
Nut butters	
Extra-virgin olive oil	
Rolled oats/steel-cut oats/oat groats	Have as porridge or overnight oats for breakfast with fruit, kefir and your nut and seed mix

Genius gut freezer hacks

Food	Notes/Ideas
Sliced sourdough wholegrain seeded bread (or your choice of bread)	Keeping bread in the freezer makes it last longer, and can increase the resistant starch for your gut bacteria
Peas	Add to soups, stews, pasta dishes
Frozen berries	Particularly when berries are out of season in the winter
Frozen veggies (e.g. spinach, mixed veg)	Great to add some extra veggies to bulk up leftovers or when you're running low on fresh veg

Food	Notes/Ideas
Plant-heavy ready meals or homemade frozen meals	There will be days when you don't feel like cooking. Great to know that you already have food ready in your freezer when you need it. Heat, add some extra veg and go
Frozen sustainable salmon/prawns/other oily fish	Easy to defrost to make a prawn stir-fry or baked salmon

The Genius Gut Tracker

Food diary

	Monday	Tuesday
Gut symptoms? Mood? Hunger level?		
Breakfast		
Gut symptoms? Mood? Hunger level?		
AM Snack (optional)		
Gut symptoms? Mood? Hunger level?		
Lunch		
Gut symptoms? Mood? Hunger level?		
PM Snack (optional)		
Gut symptoms? Mood? Hunger level?		
Dinner		
Gut symptoms? Mood? Hunger level?		

Poo diary

	Monday	Tuesday
Did you 'go' today? [Optimum is between 3 times a day and 3 times a week]		
Smooth or cracked sausage? (Y/N)		
Brown?		
Did it exit easily, completely and pain-free?		
Any other comments?		

Wednesday	Thursday	Friday	Saturday	Sunday

Wednesday	Thursday	Friday	Saturday	Sunday

Using the graph on the next page, how well do you feel on a scale from 0–10 each day, 1 being the lowest, and 10 being the highest?

Use a different coloured pencil for each, track the following and your mood of choice.

Orange – How much energy you had on average today

Yellow – Your average mood, or select a specific emotion or ability, e.g. happiness/anxiety/thinking well/stress

Green – How full and satisfied you felt on average today

Do you notice any food-mood patterns?

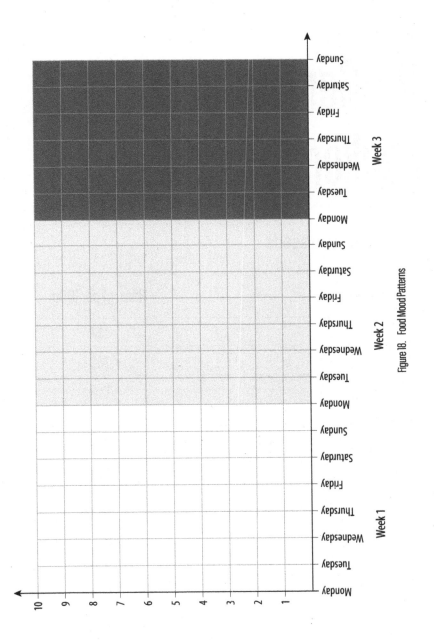

Figure 18. Food Mood Patterns

The Genius Gut Fibre Hacker

Genius nuts and seeds

Nuts and seeds	Fibre (g) per 100g
Chia seeds	34.4
Flaxseeds	27.3
Almonds	12.5
Sesame seeds	11.6
Sunflower seeds	11.1
Pistachios	10.3
Almond butter	10.3
Dried coconut flakes	9.9
Hazelnuts	9.7
Pecans	9.6
Peanuts	9.4
Tahini paste	9.3

Nuts and seeds	Fibre (g) per 100g
Raw coconut meat	9
Macadamias	8
Brazil nuts	7.5
Walnuts	6.7
Pumpkin seeds	6.5
Peanut butter	5.6
Chestnuts	5.1
Pine nuts	3.7
Cashews	3
Cashew butter	3

Genius beans

Bean	Bean colour	Fibre (g) per 100g (cooked)
Pinto beans	Pink	9
Black beans	Black	8.7
Split peas	Yellow/beige	8.3
Lentils	Brown	7.9
Chickpeas	Yellow/beige	7.6
Mung beans	Green	7.6
Kidney beans	Red	7.4

Bean	Bean colour	Fibre (g) per 100g (cooked)
Adzuki beans	Red	7
Butter beans	Yellow/beige	7
Cowpeas	Yellow/beige	6.5
White beans	White	6.3
Soy beans	Yellow/beige	6
Baked (haricot) beans	White	5.5
Broad beans	Yellow/beige	5.4
Miso	Yellow/beige/brown	5.4
Natto	Yellow/beige	5.4
Hummus	Yellow/beige	5.4
Pink beans	Pink	5.3
Edamame beans	Green	5.2
Great northern beans	White	4.9

Genius grains

Grain	Fibre (g) per 100g
Wheat bran	44.5
Oat bran	16.1
Barley flakes	16
Rye flakes	15

Grain	Fibre (g) per 100g
Rye crackers	14.3
Rye flour	14
Oatcakes	10.4
Popcorn	10.1
Oats	10
Pumpernickel bread	9.6
Wholemeal flour	9.1
Rye bread	8.2
Wholemeal bread	6.6
Wild rice	6.2
Pearl barley	4.9
Pearled spelt	4.9
Freekeh	4.5
Whole-wheat bulgar	4.2
Whole-wheat pasta	3.9
Spelt	3.3
Buckwheat flour	3.1
Whole-wheat couscous	3.1
Refined wheat flour	3
White pasta	2.9
Quinoa	2.8
White bread	2.4

Grain	Fibre (g) per 100g
Bulgar wheat	2.1
Buckwheat	1.6
Brown rice	1.4
Couscous	1.3
Egg noodles	0.9
Basmati rice	0.6

Genius vegetables

Vegetable	Vegetable Colour	Fibre (g) per 100g
Avocado	Green	6.7
Artichoke	Green	5.7
Green peas	Green	4.5
Brussel sprouts	Green	4.1
Kale	Green	4.1
Taro	White/Brown	4.1
Collard greens	Green	4
Beet greens	Green	3.7
Cooked spinach	Green	3.7
Kohlrabi	Green	3.6
Parsnips	White/Pale Yellow	3.6
Dandelion greens	Green	3.5

Vegetable	Vegetable Colour	Fibre (g) per 100g
Turnip greens	Green	3.5
Olives	Green	3.3
Carrots	Yellow/Orange	3.3
Parsley	Green	3.3
Sweet potato	Yellow/Orange	3.3
Mustard greens	Green	3.2
Cauliflower	Green/white	3.2
Savoy cabbage	Green	3.1
Lotus root	White	3.1
Salsify	White	3.1
Fennel	White/Pale green	3.1
Green snap peas	Green	3
Broccoli	Green	3
Aubergine	Purple	3
Pumpkin	Orange	2.9
Sauerkraut	White/Pale green	2.9
Beetroot	Red	2.8
Squash	Yellow/Orange	2.8
Garlic	White	2.7
Spring onions	White/Pale green	2.6
Water chestnuts	White	2.5
Baked potato	White	2.2
Red onion	Red	2.2

Vegetable	Vegetable Colour	Fibre (g) per 100g
Asparagus	Green	2.1
Red cabbage	Red	2.1
Mushrooms	Brown	2.1
Okra	Green	2.1
Peppers	Red/Yellow/Green	2.1
Sweetcorn	Yellow	2
Raw ginger	Yellow	2
Tinned tomatoes	Red	1.9
Mashed potatoes	White	1.9
Coleslaw	White	1.9
Yellow onions	White/Pale yellow	1.9
Leeks	Green	1.8
Cos or Romaine lettuce	Green	1.8
Turnip	White/Pale yellow	1.8
Kimchi	White	1.6
Celery	Green	1.6
Swiss chard	Green	1.6
Radishes	Red	1.6
Spinach	Green	1.6
Rocket	Green	1.6
Bamboo shoots	White	1.4
Kelp seaweed	Green	1.3
Cucumber	Green	0.5

Genius fruits

Fruit	Fruit Colour	Fibre (g) per 100g
Passionfruit	Orange	10.4
Dried fig	Purple	9.8
Dried apple	Green	8.7
Dates	Purple	8
Dried blueberries	Purple	7.5
Dried apricot	Orange	7.3
Prunes	Purple	7.1
Kumquats	Yellow/Orange	6.5
Raspberries	Red	6.5
Guavas	Pink	5.4
Blackberries	Purple	5.3
Dried cranberries	Red	5.3
Dried currants	Purple	4.4
Pomegranate	Red	4
Persimmon	Orange	3.6
Asian pear	Green	3.6
Pear	Green	3.1
Kiwi fruit	Green	3
Fig	Purple	2.9

Fruit	Fruit Colour	Fibre (g) per 100g
Starfruit	Yellow/Orange	2.8
Lemon	Yellow/Orange	2.8
Lime	Green	2.8
Blueberries	Purple	2.7
Cherries	Red	2.5
Apple	Green	2.5
Strawberries	Red	2.1
Apricot	Orange	2
Orange	Orange	2
Tangerine	Orange	1.8
Rhubarb	Pink	1.8
Banana	Yellow	1.7
Papaya	Orange	1.7
Grapefruit	Pink	1.6
Mango	Yellow/Orange	1.6
Nectarines	Yellow/Orange	1.5
Peaches	Yellow/Orange	1.5
Pineapple	Yellow	1.4
Plum	Purple	1.4
Melon	Yellow	0.8

The Genius Gut
Polyphenol Hacker

The 50 highest polyphenol-containing foods

Group	Food	Polyphenol (mg/100g)
Spices	Cloves	16,048
Spices	Cinnamon	9,700
Herbs	Dried marjoram	9,306
Beans and pulses	Adzuki bean	8,970
Herbs	Dried spearmint	6,575
Cocoa and chocolate	Cocoa powder	5,624
Beans	Black bean	4,846
Herbs	Dried summer savory	4,512
Herbs	Dried basil	4,318
Herbs	Dried bay leaves	4,170
Beans and pulses	Lentils	3,697
Spices	Capers	3,600

Group	Food	Polyphenol (mg/100g)
Herbs	Dried oregano	3,117
Herbs	Dried sage	2,920
Spices	Caraway seeds	2,913
Nuts	Chestnut	2,757
Herbs	Dried rosemary	2,519
Herbs	Dried camomile	2,483
Herbs	Dried coriander	2,260
Herbs	Dried fenugreek	2,250
Spices	Dried turmeric	2,117
Spices	Cumin seeds	2,038
Fruit – berries	Black elderberry	1,950
Spices	Nutmeg	1,905
Herbs	Dried winter savory	1,880
Cocoa and chocolate	Dark chocolate	1,860
Herbs	Dried thyme	1,815
Spices	Star anise	1,810
Fruit – berries	Black chokeberry	1,752
Herbs	Dried lemon balm	1,700
Herbs	Dried hyssop	1,623
Herbs	Dried parsley	1,585
Nuts	Walnut	1,575
Nuts	Pistachio	1,420

Group	Food	Polyphenol (mg/100g)
Vegetable	Red Swiss chard leaves	1,320
Nuts	Pecan	1,284
Herbs	Dried dill	1,250
Fruit – dried	Prune	1,195
Herbs	Fresh thyme	1,173
Herbs	Fresh oregano	1,165
Vegetable	Globe artichoke	1,142
Herbs	Fresh rosemary	1,082
Spices	Curry powder	1,075
Fruit – dried	Raisin	1,065
Beans and pulses	Broad bean	1,039
Spices	Black pepper	1,000
Herbs	Fresh peppermint	980
Fruit – berries	Black raspberry	980
Fruit – dried	Dried fig	960
Herbs	Fresh oregano	935

The Genius Gut BFF Recommendations

Genius Gut BFF	Recommendation
Sleeping well	• Sleep for 7–9 hours[1] • Sleep quality is equally important; try a wind-down bedtime routine and regular sleep and wake times
Exercise	• At least 2½ hours of moderate intensity movement that raises your heart rate, e.g. walking fast, hiking, cycling, or 1¼ hours of high intensity movement where you're out of breath and/or sweating, e.g. jogging, swimming, team sports, in (or across) a week[2] • Muscle-building exercises twice a week, e.g. lifting weights, working with resistance bands, rock climbing, bodyweight exercises
Not sitting too much during the day	• Both sitting for a long time without moving and being sedentary for a large part of the day aren't great for your health[3] • If you're sitting down for a while, try and move your body every 30 minutes even if it's only for a minute or two[4]

Genius Gut BFF	Recommendation
	• If you are sitting at a desk for work every weekday, then it's recommended to try and work standing up for 2 hours (and progress to 4 hours) a day[5]
Not drinking too much alcohol	• It's recommended to drink no more than six glasses of wine or six pints of beer a week for your health, equivalent to 14 units[6]
Time in nature	• Spending a total of 2 hours or more across the week outside in nature is linked with better health and well-being[7]
Managing stress	• See Hack 9: Zen Out Your Brain, Zen Out Your Gut

Recap: Your 10 Gut-Brain Hacks to Superpower Your Second Brain

Genius Gut Hack 1: Half Your Plate With Veggies
Genius Gut Hack 2: Go for the Colourful Five
Genius Gut Hack 3: Eat the BGBGs
Genius Gut Hack 4: Opt for a Daily Ferment
Genius Gut Hack 5: Make Early Dinner Your Friend
Genius Gut Hack 6: Oily Fish Twice a Week
Genius Gut Hack 7: Join the Dark Side
Genius Gut Hack 8: Protein- and Fibre-Power Your Breakfast
Genius Gut Hack 9: Zen Out Your Brain, Zen Out Your Gut
Genius Gut Hack 10: Drink Up!

Acknowledgements

My biggest heartfelt thank you has to go to you – the reader. This book is for you. Otherwise, why write it? I hope you've enjoyed reading it as much as I've had writing *Genius Gut*. And that you've taken something from the information within these pages that makes your life (and your gut-brain!) that bit better.

My wonderful family – now extended with my brilliant sisters-in-law Zoe and Amelia, and including my too-good-to-be-true godmother Amelia F-H – a huge thank you for your support, laughter and cheerleading to get this book over the finish line. Also to my grandfather Christopher, the true writer of the family, and my grandmother Victoria – whose sharp behind-the-scenes editing of my grandfather's poetry and short stories highlights that no great feat is ever achieved alone. On that note – *Genius Gut* wouldn't be anywhere near the book it is today without the guidance, support and expertise of my fantastic editor Karolina Kaim, and my wonderful agent Matilda Forbes Watson, and the talented team at Penguin Michael Joseph and WME. I am forever grateful for having the complete joy of working with you both.

I feel very lucky to have some phenomenal friends who, in some shape or form, have been part of this book – including glasses of wine, supportive phone chats, useful advice and reading through chapters. Particularly Freya Berry, V Hodgson, Ellie Knight, Erris de

Stacpoole, Kat Kimber, Zoe James, Eddie Foster, Mark Tsirekas, Lauren Everet, Isabella Birch-Reynardson, Camilla Mossop, Ruth Bowyer, Alice Carson, Hannah Knight, Ashley Forbes Reville, Erin Barnes, Amrita Vijay and Margot Eliason – thank you.

Science really is a field where you stand upon the shoulders of those who came before you, where your research contributes another drop to the ocean, in the hope that collectively it becomes a new wave. For that and more I want to thank my research colleagues past and present, and also Professor Felice Jacka, Dr Caroline Le Roy, Professor Claire Steves, Dr Anna Rodriguez Mateos, Dr Sophie Mort, Dr Sarah Berry and Professor Tim Spector for their valuable insights either when writing *Genius Gut* or for their mentorship at various points in my career.

And finally to my four-legged comrade in arms, my whippet Mavis. She sat quietly, watching me type away, and mostly patiently, while I wrote the entirety of this book. Many walks, new toys and adventures with other furry friends are promised in thanks.

References

Preface

1   Nes RB, Røysamb E. Happiness in Behaviour Genetics: An Update on Heritability and Changeability. *Journal of Happiness Studies*. 2017/10/01 2017;18(5):1533-1552. doi:10.1007/s10902-016-9781-6

2   Breit S, Kupferberg A, Rogler G, Hasler G. Vagus Nerve as Modulator of the Brain-Gut Axis in Psychiatric and Inflammatory Disorders. *Front Psychiatry*. 2018;9:44. doi:10.3389/fpsyt.2018.00044

3   Yu QJ, Yu SY, Zuo LJ, Lian TH, Hu Y, Wang RD, Piao YS, Guo P, Liu L, Jin Z, Li LX, Chan P, Chen SD, Wang XM, Zhang W. Parkinson disease with constipation: clinical features and relevant factors. *Scientific Reports*. 2018 Jan 12;8(1):567. doi:10.1038/s41598-017-16790-8

4   Zamani M, Alizadeh-Tabari S, Zamani V. Systematic review with meta-analysis: the prevalence of anxiety and depression in patients with irritable bowel syndrome. *Alimentary Pharmacology & Therapeutics*. 2019;50(2): 132-143. doi:10.1111/apt.15325

Chapter 2. Your Gut Microbiome

1   Ogbonnaya ES, Clarke G, Shanahan F, Dinan TG, Cryan JF, O'Leary OF. Adult Hippocampal Neurogenesis Is Regulated by the Microbiome. *Biological Psychiatry*. 2015;78(4):e7-e9. doi:10.1016/j.biopsych.2014.12.023

2   Goodrich JK, Waters JL, Poole AC, et al. Human Genetics Shape the Gut Microbiome. *Cell*. 2014;159(4):789-799. doi:10.1016/j.cell.2014.09.053

3   Parrish A, Boudaud M, Grant ET, et al. Akkermansia muciniphila exacerbates food allergy in fibre-deprived mice. *Nature Microbiology*. 2023/10/01 2023;8(10):1863-1879. doi:10.1038/s41564-023-01464-1

4   Francesco A, Leeming ER, Eirini D, et al. Blue poo: impact of gut transit time on the gut microbiome using a novel marker. *Gut*. 2021;70(9):1665. doi:10.1136/gutjnl-2020-323877

5   Wu J, Wang K, Wang X, Pang Y, Jiang C. The role of the gut microbiome and its metabolites in metabolic diseases. *Protein & Cell*. 2021/05/01 2021;12(5): 360-373. doi:10.1007/s13238-020-00814-7

6   Frost G, Sleeth ML, Sahuri-Arisoylu M, et al. The short-chain fatty acid acetate reduces appetite via a central homeostatic mechanism. *Nature Communications*. 2014/04/29 2014;5(1):3611. doi:10.1038/ncomms4611

7   David LA, Maurice CF, Carmody RN, et al. Diet rapidly and reproducibly alters the human gut microbiome. *Nature*. Jan 23 2014;505(7484):559-63. doi:10.1038/nature12820

Chapter 3. The Gut-Brain Conversation

1   Gorczyca K, Obuchowska A, Kimber-Trojnar Ż, Wierzchowska-Opoka M, Leszczyńska-Gorzelak B. Changes in the Gut Microbiome and Pathologies in Pregnancy. *Int J Environ Res Public Health*. Aug 12 2022;19(16). doi:10.3390/ijerph19169961

2   Jašarević E, Bale TL. Prenatal and postnatal contributions of the maternal microbiome on offspring programming. *Frontiers in Neuroendocrinology*. 2019/10/01/ 2019;55:100797. doi:10.1016/j.yfrne.2019.100797

3   Zhou L, Qiu W, Wang J, et al. Effects of vaginal microbiota transfer on the neurodevelopment and microbiome of cesarean-born infants: A blinded randomized controlled trial. *Cell Host & Microbe*. 2023/07/12/ 2023;31(7): 1232-1247.e5. doi:10.1016/j.chom.2023.05.022

4   Sun Z, Lee-Sarwar K, Kelly RS, et al. Revealing the importance of prenatal gut microbiome in offspring neurodevelopment in humans. *eBioMedicine*. 2023;90doi:10.1016/j.ebiom.2023.104491

5   Dawson SL, O'Hely M, Jacka FN, et al. Maternal prenatal gut microbiota composition predicts child behaviour. *eBioMedicine*. 2021;68doi:10.1016/j. ebiom.2021.103400

6   Ogbonnaya ES, Clarke G, Shanahan F, Dinan TG, Cryan JF, O'Leary OF. Adult Hippocampal Neurogenesis Is Regulated by the Microbiome. *Biological Psychiatry*. 2015;78(4): e7-e9. doi:10.1016/j.biopsych.2014.12.023

7   Carlson AL, Xia K, Azcarate-Peril MA, et al. Infant Gut Microbiome Associated With Cognitive Development. *Biol Psychiatry*. Jan 15 2018;83(2): 148-159. doi:10.1016/j.biopsych.2017.06.021

8   Sordillo JE, Korrick S, Laranjo N, et al. Association of the Infant Gut Microbiome With Early Childhood Neurodevelopmental Outcomes: An Ancillary Study to the VDAART Randomized Clinical Trial. *JAMA Netw Open*. Mar 1 2019;2(3):e190905. doi:10.1001/jamanetworkopen.2019.0905

9   Kevin SB, Guilherme Fahur B, Shelley Hoeft M, et al. Gut-resident microorganisms and their genes are associated with cognition and neuroanatomy in children. *bioRxiv*. 2023:2020.02.13.944181. doi:10.1101/2020.02.13.944181

10   Oluwagbemigun K, Schnermann ME, Schmid M, Cryan JF, Nöthlings U. A prospective investigation into the association between the gut microbiome composition and cognitive performance among healthy young adults. *Gut Pathogens*. 2022/04/19 2022;14(1):15. doi:10.1186/s13099-022-00487-z

11   Boehme M, Guzzetta KE, Bastiaanssen TFS, et al. Microbiota from young mice counteracts selective age-associated behavioral deficits. *Nature Aging.* 2021/08/01 2021;1(8):666-676. doi:10.1038/s43587-021-00093-9

12   Ma C, Li Y, Mei Z, et al. Association Between Bowel Movement Pattern and Cognitive Function: Prospective Cohort Study and a Metagenomic Analysis of the Gut Microbiome. *Neurology.* Nov 14 2023;101(20):e2014-e2025. doi:10.1212/wnl.0000000000207849

13   Agus A, Planchais J, Sokol H. Gut Microbiota Regulation of Tryptophan Metabolism in Health and Disease. *Cell Host & Microbe.* 2018;23(6):716-724. doi:10.1016/j.chom.2018.05.003

14   Cryan JF, Dinan TG. Mind-altering microorganisms: the impact of the gut microbiota on brain and behaviour. *Nature Reviews Neuroscience.* 2012/10/01 2012;13(10):701-712. doi:10.1038/nrn3346

15   Agus A, Planchais J, Sokol H. Gut Microbiota Regulation of Tryptophan Metabolism in Health and Disease. *Cell Host & Microbe.* 2018;23(6): 716-724. doi:10.1016/j.chom.2018.05.003

16   Waclawiková B, El Aidy S. Role of Microbiota and Tryptophan Metabolites in the Remote Effect of Intestinal Inflammation on Brain and Depression. *Pharmaceuticals.* 2018;11(3):63.

17   Kan Gao, Chun-long Mu, Aitak Farzi, Wei-yun Zhu, Tryptophan Metabolism: A Link Between the Gut Microbiota and Brain, *Advances in Nutrition,* 2020;11(3):709–723. doi:10.1093/advances/nmz127

18   Madison A, Kiecolt-Glaser JK. Stress, depression, diet, and the gut microbiota: human-bacteria interactions at the core of psychoneuroimmunology and nutrition. *Curr Opin Behav Sci.* Aug 2019;28: 105-110. doi:10.1016/j.cobeha.2019.01.011

19   Dalile B, Van Oudenhove L, Vervliet B, Verbeke K. The role of short-chain fatty acids in microbiota–gut–brain communication. *Nature Reviews Gastroenterology & Hepatology.* 2019/08/01 2019;16(8):461-478. doi:10.1038/s41575-019-0157-3

20   O'Riordan KJ, Collins MK, Moloney GM, et al. Short chain fatty acids: Microbial metabolites for gut-brain axis signalling. *Mol Cell Endocrinol.* Apr 15 2022;546:111572. doi:10.1016/j.mce.2022.111572

21   Unger MM, Spiegel J, Dillmann K-U, et al. Short chain fatty acids and gut microbiota differ between patients with Parkinson's disease and age-matched controls. *Parkinsonism & Related Disorders.* 2016;32:66-72. doi:10.1016/j.parkreldis.2016.08.019

22   Zhang L, Wang Y, Xiayu X, et al. Altered Gut Microbiota in a Mouse Model of Alzheimer's Disease. *Journal of Alzheimer's Disease.* 2017;60:1241-1257. doi:10.3233/JAD-170020

23   Maltz RM, Keirsey J, Kim SC, et al. Prolonged restraint stressor exposure in outbred CD-1 mice impacts microbiota, colonic inflammation, and short chain fatty acids. *PLOS ONE.* 2018;13(5):e0196961. doi:10.1371/journal.pone.0196961

24   Byrne CS, Chambers ES, Alhabeeb H, et al. Increased colonic propionate reduces anticipatory reward responses in the human striatum to high-energy foods. *Am J Clin Nutr.* Jul 2016;104(1):5-14. doi:10.3945/ajcn.115.126706

25   Kristina SF, Madelief W, Max N, Richard GI. Potential of butyrate to influence food intake in mice and men. *Gut.* 2018;67(7):1203. doi:10.1136/gutjnl-2017-315543

Chapter 4. The Female Gut-Brain Connection

1   Bailey P. Hysteria: The History of a Disease. *Archives of General Psychiatry.* 1966;14(3):332-333. doi:10.1001/archpsyc.1966.01730090108024

2   Stricker R, Eberhart R, Chevailler M-C, Quinn FA, Bischof P, Stricker R. Establishment of detailed reference values for luteinizing hormone, follicle stimulating hormone, estradiol, and progesterone during different phases of the menstrual cycle on the Abbott ARCHITECT® analyzer. *Clinical Chemistry and Laboratory Medicine (CCLM).* 2006;44(7):883-887. doi:10.1515/CCLM.2006.160

3   Baker JM, Al-Nakkash L, Herbst-Kralovetz MM. Estrogen & gut microbiome axis: Physiological and clinical implications. *Maturitas.* 2017;103:45–53. doi:o.1016/j.maturitas.2017.06.025

4   Shobeiri P, Kalantari A, Teixeira AL, Rezaei N. Shedding light on biological sex differences and microbiota–gut–brain axis: a comprehensive review of its roles in neuropsychiatric disorders. *Biology of Sex Differences.* 2022/03/25 2022;13(1):12. doi:10.1186/s13293-022-00422-6

5   Korpela K, Kallio S, Salonen A, et al. Gut microbiota develop towards an adult profile in a sex-specific manner during puberty. *Scientific Reports.* 2021/12/02 2021;11(1):23297. doi:10.1038/s41598-021-02375-z

6   Reiman EM, Armstrong SM, Matt KS, Mattox JH. The application of positron emission tomography to the study of the normal menstrual cycle. *Human Reproduction.* 1996;11(12):2799-2805. doi:10.1093/oxfordjournals.humrep.a019214

7   McVay MA, Copeland AL, Geiselman PJ. Eating disorder pathology and menstrual cycle fluctuations in eating variables in oral contraceptive users and non-users. *Eat Behav.* Jan 2011;12(1):49-55. doi:10.1016/j.eatbeh.2010.11.005

8   Natale V, Albertazzi P, Cangini A. The Effects of Menstrual Cycle on Dreaming. *Biological Rhythm Research.* 2003/07/01 2003;34(3):295-303. doi:10.1076/brhm.34.3.295.18808

9   Li T, Shao W, Wang Y, et al. A two-sample mendelian randomization analysis investigates associations between gut microbiota and infertility. *Scientific Reports.* 2023/07/15 2023;13(1):11426. doi:10.1038/s41598-023-38624-6

10   Koren O, Goodrich Julia K, Cullender Tyler C, et al. Host Remodeling of the Gut Microbiome and Metabolic Changes during Pregnancy. *Cell.* 2012;150(3):470-480. doi:10.1016/j.cell.2012.07.008

11   Dahl C, Stanislawski M, Iszatt N, et al. Gut microbiome of mothers delivering prematurely shows reduced diversity and lower relative abundance of

Bifidobacterium and Streptococcus. *PLOS ONE*. 2017;12(10):e0184336. doi:10.1371/journal.pone.0184336

12   Sharma A, Davies R, Kapoor A, Islam H, Webber L, Jayasena CN. The effect of hormone replacement therapy on cognition and mood. *Clin Endocrinol (Oxf)*. 2023;98: 285–295. doi:10.1111/cen.14856

13   Mayneris-Perxachs J, Arnoriaga-Rodríguez M, Luque-Córdoba D, et al. Gut microbiota steroid sexual dimorphism and its impact on gonadal steroids: influences of obesity and menopausal status. *Microbiome*. 2020/09/20 2020;8(1):136. doi:10.1186/s40168-020-00913-x

14   Setchell KD, Brown NM, Desai PB, et al. Bioavailability, disposition, and dose-response effects of soy isoflavones when consumed by healthy women at physiologically typical dietary intakes. *J Nutr*. Apr 2003;133(4): 1027-35. doi:10.1093/jn/133.4.1027

15   Joshu E. Man who performed 'DIY' fecal transplants from his mom after Crohn's disease left him hospitalized experienced her menopause symptoms. www.dailymail.co.uk/health/article-12754413/mom-fecal-transplant-son-crohns-disease-hospitalized-menopause-symptoms.html

Chapter 5. The Male Gut-Brain Connection

1   Wallis A, Butt H, Ball M, Lewis DP, Bruck D. Support for the Microgenderome: Associations in a Human Clinical Population. *Scientific Reports*. 2016/01/13 2016;6(1):19171. doi:10.1038/srep19171

2   Shobeiri P et al., Shedding light on biological sex differences and microbiota–gut–brain axis. *Biology of Sex Differences*

3   Levkovich T, Poutahidis T, Smillie C, et al. Probiotic bacteria induce a 'glow of health'. *PLoS One*. 2013;8(1):e53867. doi:10.1371/journal.pone.0053867

4   Yurkovetskiy L, Burrows M, Khan AA, et al. Gender bias in autoimmunity is influenced by microbiota. *Immunity*. Aug 22 2013;39(2):400-12. doi:10.1016/j.immuni.2013.08.013

5   Li X, Cheng W, Shang H, Wei H, Deng C. The Interplay between Androgen and Gut Microbiota: Is There a Microbiota-Gut-Testis Axis. *Reprod Sci*. Jun 2022;29(6):1674-1684. doi:10.1007/s43032-021-00624-0

6   Zhang P, Feng Y, Li L, et al. Improvement in sperm quality and spermatogenesis following faecal microbiota transplantation from alginate oligosaccharide dosed mice. *Gut*. Jan 2021;70(1):222-225. doi:10.1136/gutjnl-2020-320992

7   Molina NM, Plaza-Díaz J, Vilchez-Vargas R, et al. Assessing the testicular sperm microbiome: a low-biomass site with abundant contamination. *Reproductive BioMedicine Online*. 2021/09/01 2021;43(3):523-531. doi:10.1016/j.rbmo.2021.06.021

8   Dixon R, Egan S, Hughes S, Chapman B. The Sexome – A proof of concept study into microbial transfer between heterosexual couples after sexual

intercourse. *Forensic Science International*. 2023/07/01/ 2023;348:111711. doi:10.1016/j.forsciint.2023.111711

9   Toh E, Xing Y, Gao X, et al. Sexual behavior shapes male genitourinary microbiome composition. *Cell Rep Med*. Mar 21 2023;4(3):100981. doi:10.1016/j.xcrm.2023.100981

10   Noguera-Julian M, Rocafort M, Guillén Y, et al. Gut Microbiota Linked to Sexual Preference and HIV Infection. *eBioMedicine*. 2016;5:135-146. doi:10.1016/j.ebiom.2016.01.032

Chapter 6. The Diverse Gut-Brain

1   Ahrens AP, Hyötyläinen T, Petrone JR, Igelström K, George CD, Garrett TJ, et al. Infant microbes and metabolites point to childhood neurodevelopmental disorders. *Cell*. 2024;187(8):1853-73.e15. doi:10.1016/j.cell.2024.02.035

2   Tengeler AC, Dam SA, Wiesmann M, et al. Gut microbiota from persons with attention-deficit/hyperactivity disorder affects the brain in mice. *Microbiome*. 2020/04/01 2020;8(1):44. doi:10.1186/s40168-020-00816-x

3   Stiernborg M, Debelius JW, Yang LL, et al. Bacterial gut microbiome differences in adults with ADHD and in children with ADHD on psychostimulant medication. *Brain, Behavior, and Immunity*. 2023/05/01/ 2023;110:310-321. doi:10.1016/j.bbi.2023.03.012

4   Morton JT, Jin D-M, Mills RH, et al. Multi-level analysis of the gut–brain axis shows autism spectrum disorder-associated molecular and microbial profiles. *Nature Neuroscience*. 2023/07/01 2023;26(7):1208-1217. doi:10.1038/s41593-023-01361-0

Chapter 7. Starving Gut Bacteria

1   Carter MM, Olm MR, Merrill BD, et al. Ultra-deep sequencing of Hadza hunter-gatherers recovers vanishing gut microbes. *Cell*. 2023/07/06/ 2023;186(14):3111-3124.e13. doi:10.1016/j.cell.2023.05.046

2   Reynolds A, Mann J, Cummings J, Winter N, Mete E, Te Morenga L. Carbohydrate quality and human health: a series of systematic reviews and meta-analyses. *The Lancet*. 2019;393(10170):434-445. doi:10.1016/S0140-6736(18)31809-9

3   Fernanda R, Maria Laura da Costa L, Euridice Martinez S, et al. Ultra-processed foods and excessive free sugar intake in the UK: a nationally representative cross-sectional study. *BMJ Open*. 2019;9(10):e027546. doi:10.1136/bmjopen-2018-027546

4   Monteiro CA, Cannon G, Levy RB, et al. Ultra-processed foods: what they are and how to identify them. *Public Health Nutrition*. 2019;22(5):936-941. doi:10.1017/S1368980018003762

5   Cordova R, Viallon V, Fontvieille E, et al. Consumption of ultra-processed foods and risk of multimorbidity of cancer and cardiometabolic diseases:

multinational cohort study. *The Lancet Regional Health – Europe.* 2023;35 doi:10.1016/j.lanepe.2023.100771

6   Wang L, Du M, Wang K, et al. Association of ultra-processed food consumption with colorectal cancer risk among men and women: results from three prospective US cohort studies. *BMJ.* 2022;378:e068921. doi:10.1136/bmj-2021-068921

7   Naimi S, Viennois E, Gewirtz AT, Chassaing B. Direct impact of commonly used dietary emulsifiers on human gut microbiota. *Microbiome.* 2021/03/22 2021;9(1):66. doi:10.1186/s40168-020-00996-6

8   Sandall A, Smith L, Svensen E, Whelan K. Emulsifiers in ultra-processed foods in the UK food supply. *Public Health Nutr.* Nov 2023;26(11):2256-2270. doi:10.1017/s1368980023002021

9   Um CY, Hodge RA, Tran HQ, Campbell PT, Gewirtz AT, McCullough ML. Association of Emulsifier and Highly Processed Food Intake with Circulating Markers of Intestinal Permeability and Inflammation in the Cancer Prevention Study-3 Diet Assessment Sub-Study. *Nutr Cancer.* 2022;74(5): 1701-1711. doi:10.1080/01635581.2021.1957947

10 Knüppel A, Shipley MJ, Llewellyn CH, Brunner EJ. Sugar intake from sweet food and beverages, common mental disorder and depression: prospective findings from the Whitehall II study. *Scientific Reports.* 2017/07/27 2017;7(1):6287. doi:10.1038/s41598-017-05649-7

11 Thomson P, Santibañez R, Aguirre C, Galgani JE, Garrido D. Short-term impact of sucralose consumption on the metabolic response and gut microbiome of healthy adults. *Br J Nutr.* Oct 28 2019;122(8):856-862. doi:10.1017/s0007114519001570

12 Serrano J, Smith KR, Crouch AL, et al. High-dose saccharin supplementation does not induce gut microbiota changes or glucose intolerance in healthy humans and mice. *Microbiome.* Jan 12 2021;9(1):11. doi:10.1186/s40168-020-00976-w

13 Suez J, Cohen Y, Valdés-Mas R, et al. Personalized microbiome-driven effects of non-nutritive sweeteners on human glucose tolerance. *Cell.* Sep 1 2022;185(18):3307-3328.e19. doi:10.1016/j.cell.2022.07.016

14 Afshin A, Sur PJ, Fay KA, et al. Health effects of dietary risks in 195 countries, 1990–2017: a systematic analysis for the Global Burden of Disease Study 2017. *The Lancet.* 2019;393(10184):1958-1972. doi:10.1016/S0140-6736(19) 30041-8

15 Gesch CB, Hammond SM, Hampson SE, Eves A, Crowder MJ. Influence of supplementary vitamins, minerals and essential fatty acids on the antisocial behaviour of young adult prisoners: Randomised, placebo-controlled trial. *The British Journal of Psychiatry.* 2002;181(1):22-28. doi:10.1192/ bjp.181.1.22

16 Barabási A-L, Menichetti G, Loscalzo J. The unmapped chemical complexity of our diet. *Nature Food.* 2020/01/01 2020;1(1):33-37. doi:10.1038/ s43016-019-0005-1

Chapter 8. A Sanitised Gut Isn't a Happy One

1   Hutchings MI, Truman AW, Wilkinson B. Antibiotics: past, present and future. *Current Opinion in Microbiology*. 2019;51:72–80 doi.org/10.1016/j.mib.2019.10.008

2   Neuman H, Forsythe P, Uzan A, Avni O, Koren O. Antibiotics in early life: dysbiosis and the damage done. *FEMS Microbiology Reviews*. 2018;42(4): 489-499. doi:10.1093/femsre/fuy018

3   Slykerman RF, Neumann D, Underwood L, et al. Age at first exposure to antibiotics and neurodevelopmental outcomes in childhood. *Psychopharmacology*. 2023;240: 1143–1150. doi.org 10.1007/s00213-023-06351-5

4   Mehta RS, Lochhead P, Wang Y, et al. Association of midlife antibiotic use with subsequent cognitive function in women. *PLoS One*. 2022;17(3):e0264649. doi:10.1371/journal.pone.0264649

5   Dethlefsen L, Huse S, Sogin ML, Relman DA. The Pervasive Effects of an Antibiotic on the Human Gut Microbiota, as Revealed by Deep 16S rRNA Sequencing. *PLOS Biology*. 2008;6(11):e280. doi:10.1371/journal.pbio.0060280

6   Suez J, Zmora N, Zilberman-Schapira G, et al. Post-Antibiotic Gut Mucosal Microbiome Reconstitution Is Impaired by Probiotics and Improved by Autologous FMT. *Cell*. Sep 6 2018;174(6):1406-1423.e16. doi:10.1016/j.cell.2018.08.047

7   Penumutchu S, Korry BJ, Hewlett K, Belenky P. Fiber supplementation protects from antibiotic-induced gut microbiome dysbiosis by modulating gut redox potential. *Nature Communications*. 2023/08/24 2023;14(1):5161. doi:10.1038/s41467-023-40553-x

8   Suez J, Zmora N, Zilberman-Schapira G, et al. Post-Antibiotic Gut Mucosal Microbiome Reconstitution Is Impaired by Probiotics and Improved by Autologous FMT. *Cell*. Sep 6 2018;174(6): 1406-1423. e16. doi:10.1016/j.cell.2018.08.047

9   Singh S, Sharma P, Pal N, et al. Impact of Environmental Pollutants on Gut Microbiome and Mental Health via the Gut-Brain Axis. *Microorganisms*. Jul 19 2022;10(7). doi:10.3390/microorganisms10071457

Chapter 9. In a Lonely Body, Lonely . . . Gut?

1   Kannan VD, Veazie PJ. US trends in social isolation, social engagement, and companionship – nationally and by age, sex, race/ethnicity, family income, and work hours, 2003–2020. *SSM - Population Health*. 2023/03/01/2023;21:101331. doi:https://doi.org/10.1016/j.ssmph.2022.101331

2   Gallup. Loneliness in U.S. Subsides From Pandemic High. https://news.gallup.com/poll/473057/loneliness-subsides-pandemic-high.aspx%5D

3   Nguyen TT, Zhang X, Wu T-C, et al. Association of Loneliness and Wisdom With Gut Microbial Diversity and Composition: An Exploratory Study. Brief

Research Report. *Frontiers in Psychiatry*. 2021-March-25 2021;12. doi:10.3389/fpsyt.2021.648475

4   National Academies of Sciences, Engineering, and Medicine. 2020. Social Isolation and Loneliness in Older Adults: Opportunities for the Health Care System. Washington, DC: The National Academies Press. doi. org/10.17226/25663

5   Wu W-L, Adame MD, Liou C-W, et al. Microbiota regulate social behaviour via stress response neurons in the brain. *Nature*. 2021/07/01 2021;595(7867): 409-414. doi:10.1038/s41586-021-03669-y

6   Johnson KVA. Gut microbiome composition and diversity are related to human personality traits. *Human Microbiome Journal*. 2020/03/01/ 2020;15:100069. doi:10.1016/j.humic.2019.100069

7   Valles-Colomer M, Blanco-Míguez A, Manghi P, et al. The person-to-person transmission landscape of the gut and oral microbiomes. *Nature*. 2023/02/01 2023;614(7946):125-135. doi:10.1038/s41586-022-05620-1

8   Kort R, Caspers M, van de Graaf A, van Egmond W, Keijser B, Roeselers G. Shaping the oral microbiota through intimate kissing. *Microbiome*. 2014/11/17 2014;2(1):41. doi:10.1186/2049-2618-2-41

9   Kort R, Caspers M, van de Graaf A, van Egmond W, Keijser B, Roeselers G. Shaping the oral microbiota through intimate kissing. *Microbiome*. 2014/11/17 2014;2(1):41. doi:10.1186/ 2049-2618-2-41

Chapter 10. Gut-Brain Burnout

1   Stressed nation: 74% of UK 'overwhelmed or unable to cope' at some point in the past year. www.mentalhealth.org.uk/about-us/news/survey-stressed-nation-UK-overwhelmed-unable-to-cope

2   Gheorghe CE, Leigh S-J, Tofani GSS, Bastiaanssen TFS, Lyte JM, Gardellin E, et al. The microbiota drives diurnal rhythms in tryptophan metabolism in the stressed gut. *Cell Reports*. 2024;43(4). doi: 10.1016/j.celrep.2024.114079

3   Mariotti A. The effects of chronic stress on health: new insights into the molecular mechanisms of brain-body communication. *Future Sci OA*. Nov 2015;1(3):Fso23. doi:10.4155/fso.15.21

4   Laudani S, Torrisi SA, Alboni S, et al. Gut microbiota alterations promote traumatic stress susceptibility associated with p-cresol-induced dopaminergic dysfunctions. *Brain Behav Immun*. Jan 2023;107:385-396. doi:10.1016/j.bbi.2022.11.004

5   Houtz JL, Taff CC, Vitousek MN. Gut Microbiome as a Mediator of Stress Resilience: A Reactive Scope Model Framework. *Integrative and Comparative Biology*. 2022;62(1):41-57. doi:10.1093/icb/icac030

6   Ménard C, Pfau ML, Hodes GE, Russo SJ. Immune and Neuroendocrine Mechanisms of Stress Vulnerability and Resilience. *Neuropsychopharmacology*. 2017/01/01 2017;42(1):62-80. doi:10.1038/npp.2016.90

7   Gianaros PJ, Jennings JR, Sheu LK, Greer PJ, Kuller LH, Matthews KA. Prospective reports of chronic life stress predict decreased grey matter volume in the hippocampus. *NeuroImage*. 2007/04/01/ 2007;35(2):795-803. doi:10.1016/j.neuroimage.2006.10.045

8   Kulshreshtha A, Alonso A, McClure LA, Hajjar I, Manly JJ, Judd S. Association of Stress With Cognitive Function Among Older Black and White US Adults. *JAMA Network Open*. 2023;6(3):e231860-e231860. doi:10.1001/jamanetworkopen.2023.1860

9   Yau YH, Potenza MN. Stress and eating behaviors. *Minerva Endocrinol*. Sep 2013;38(3):255-67.

10   Foundation TMH. Mental Health Statistics. www.mentalhealth.org.uk/explore-mental-health/statistics/stress-statistics

11   Zhang X, Ravichandran S, Gee GC, et al. Social Isolation, Brain Food Cue Processing, Eating Behaviors, and Mental Health Symptoms. *JAMA Netw Open*. 2024;7(4):e244855. doi:10.1001/jamanetworkopen.2024.4855

12   Kelly JR, Borre Y, O'Brien C, et al. Transferring the blues: Depression-associated gut microbiota induces neurobehavioural changes in the rat. *J Psychiatr Res*. Nov 2016;82:109-18. doi:10.1016/j.jpsychires.2016.07.019

13   Valles-Colomer M, Falony G, Darzi Y, et al. The neuroactive potential of the human gut microbiota in quality of life and depression. *Nature Microbiology*. 2019/04/01 2019;4(4):623-632. doi:10.1038/s41564-018-0337-x

14   Kelly JR, Borre Y, O'Brien C, et al. Transferring the blues: Depression-associated gut microbiota induces neurobehavioural changes in the rat. J Psychiatr Res. Nov 2016;82: 109-18. doi:10.1016/j.jpsychires.2016.07.019

15   Liu L, Wang H, Chen X, Zhang Y, Zhang H, Xie P. Gut microbiota and its metabolites in depression: from pathogenesis to treatment. *eBioMedicine*. 2023;90 doi:10.1016/j.ebiom.2023.104527

16   Bercik P, Denou E, Collins J, et al. The Intestinal Microbiota Affect Central Levels of Brain-Derived Neurotropic Factor and Behavior in Mice. *Gastroenterology*. 2011/08/01/ 2011;141(2):599-609.e3. doi:10.1053/j.gastro.2011.04.052

17   Johnstone N, Milesi C, Burn O, et al. Anxiolytic effects of a galacto-oligosaccharides prebiotic in healthy females (18-25 years) with corresponding changes in gut bacterial composition. *Scientific Reports*. Apr 15 2021;11(1):8302. doi:10.1038/s41598-021-87865-w

18   Tarar ZI, Farooq U, Zafar Y, et al. Burden of anxiety and depression among hospitalized patients with irritable bowel syndrome: a nationwide analysis. *Irish Journal of Medical Science*. 2023/10/01 2023;192(5):2159-2166. doi:10.1007/s11845-022-03258-6

19   Peters SL, Yao CK, Philpott H, Yelland GW, Muir JG, Gibson PR. Randomised clinical trial: the efficacy of gut-directed hypnotherapy is similar to that of the low FODMAP diet for the treatment of irritable bowel syndrome. *Aliment Pharmacol Ther*. Sep 2016;44(5):447-59. doi:10.1111/apt.13706

20 Staudacher HM, Mahoney S, Canale K, et al. Clinical trial: A Mediterranean diet is feasible and improves gastrointestinal and psychological symptoms in irritable bowel syndrome. *Alimentary Pharmacology & Therapeutics*. n/a(n/a). doi:10.1111/apt.17791

Chapter 11. Gut-Brain Power

1 Tooley KL. Effects of the Human Gut Microbiota on Cognitive Performance, Brain Structure and Function: A Narrative Review. *Nutrients*. Sep 30 2020;12(10). doi:10.3390/nu12103009

2 Gareau MG, Wine E, Rodrigues DM, et al. Bacterial infection causes stress-induced memory dysfunction in mice. *Gut*. 2011;60(3):307-317. doi:10.1136/gut.2009.202515

3 Sarkar A, Harty S, Lehto SM, et al. The Microbiome in Psychology and Cognitive Neuroscience. *Trends in Cognitive Sciences*. 2018/07/01/ 2018;22(7):611-636. doi:10.1016/j.tics.2018.04.006

4 Ni Lochlainn M, Bowyer RCE, Moll JM, et al. Effect of gut microbiome modulation on muscle function and cognition: the PROMOTe randomised controlled trial. *Nat Commun*.2024;15.1859. doi.org/10.1038/ s41467-024-46116-y

5 Thapa M, Kumari A, Chin CY, et al. Translocation of gut commensal bacteria to the brain. *bioRxiv*. Sep 1 2023. doi:10.1101/2023.08.30.555630

6 Boehme M, Guzzetta KE, Bastiaanssen TFS, et al. Microbiota from young mice counteracts selective age-associated behavioral deficits. *Nature Aging*. 2021/08/01 2021;1(8): 666-676. doi:10.1038/ s43587-021-00093-9

7 Adewuyi EO, O'Brien EK, Nyholt DR, Porter T, Laws SM. A large-scale genome-wide cross-trait analysis reveals shared genetic architecture between Alzheimer's disease and gastrointestinal tract disorders. *Commun Biol*. Jul 18 2022;5(1):691. doi:10.1038/s42003-022-03607-2

8 Zhan Y, Al-Nusaif M, Ding C, Zhao L, Dong C. The potential of the gut microbiome for identifying Alzheimer's disease diagnostic biomarkers and future therapies. *Front Neurosci*. 2023;17:1130730. doi:10.3389/ fnins.2023.1130730

9 Grabrucker S, Marizzoni M, Silajdžić E, et al. Microbiota from Alzheimer's patients induce deficits in cognition and hippocampal neurogenesis. *Brain*. 2023:awad303. doi:10.1093/brain/awad303

10 Okunoye O, Marston L, Walters K, Schrag A. Change in the incidence of Parkinson's disease in a large UK primary care database. *npj Parkinson's Disease*. 2022/03/15 2022;8(1):23. doi:10.1038/s41531-022-00284-0

11 Tremlett H, Bauer KC, Appel-Cresswell S, Finlay BB, Waubant E. The gut microbiome in human neurological disease: A review. *Annals of Neurology*. 2017;81(3):369-382. doi:10.1002/ana.24901

12 Schaeffer E, Kluge A, Böttner M, et al. Alpha Synuclein Connects the Gut-Brain Axis in Parkinson's Disease Patients – A View on Clinical Aspects,

Cellular Pathology and Analytical Methodology. *Front Cell Dev Biol.* 2020;8:573696. doi:10.3389/fcell.2020.573696

Chapter 13. How to Make Your Gut-Brain Happier

1   Mujcic R, Oswald AJ. Evolution of Well-Being and Happiness After Increases in Consumption of Fruit and Vegetables. *American Journal of Public Health.* 2016/08/01 2016;106(8):1504-1510. doi:10.2105/AJPH.2016.303260

2   Ocean N, Howley P, Ensor J. Lettuce be happy: A longitudinal UK study on the relationship between fruit and vegetable consumption and well-being. *Social Science & Medicine.* 2019/02/01 2019;222:335-345. doi:10.1016/j.socscimed.2018.12.017

3   Lee S-H, Yoon S-H, Jung Y, et al. Emotional well-being and gut microbiome profiles by enterotype. *Scientific Reports.* 2020/11/26 2020;10(1):20736. doi:10.1038/s41598-020-77673-z

4   Kan Gao, Chun-long Mu, Aitak Farzi, Wei-yun Zhu. Tryptophan Metabolism: A Link Between the Gut Microbiota and Brain. *Advances in Nutrition.*2020;11(3):709–723. doi.org/10.1093/advances/nmz127

5   Hamamah S, Aghazarian A, Nazaryan A, Hajnal A, Covasa M. Role of Microbiota-Gut-Brain Axis in Regulating Dopaminergic Signaling. *Biomedicines.* 2022;10(2):436. doi:10.3390/biomedicines10020436

6   de Wouters d'Oplinter A, Huwart SJP, Cani PD, Everard A. Gut Microbes and Food Reward: From the Gut to the Brain. *Front Neurosci.* 2022;16:947240. doi: 10.3389/fnins.2022.947240

7   Chen Y, Xu J, Chen Y. Regulation of Neurotransmitters by the Gut Microbiota and Effects on Cognition in Neurological Disorders. *Nutrients.* Jun 19 2021;13(6)doi:10.3390/nu13062099

8   Ke S, Guimond AJ, Tworoger SS, et al. Gut feelings: associations of emotions and emotion regulation with the gut microbiome in women. *Psychol Med.* Mar 21 2023:1-10. doi:10.1017/s0033291723000612

9   Cowan CSM, Hoban AE, Ventura-Silva AP, Dinan TG, Clarke G, Cryan JF. Gutsy Moves: The Amygdala as a Critical Node in Microbiota to Brain Signaling. *Bioessays.* Jan 2018;40(1)doi:10.1002/bies.201700172

10 Schmidt K, Cowen PJ, Harmer CJ, Tzortzis G, Errington S, Burnet PWJ. Prebiotic intake reduces the waking cortisol response and alters emotional bias in healthy volunteers. *Psychopharmacology.* 2015/05/01 2015;232(10): 1793-1801.doi:10.1007/ s00213-014-3810-0

11 Gheorghe CE, Leigh SJ, Tofani GSS. The microbiota drives diurnal rhythms in tryptophan metabolism in the stressed gut. *Cell Reports.* 2024;43(4):114079. doi.org/10.1016/j.celrep.2024.114079

12 Bangsgaard Bendtsen KM, Krych L, Sørensen DB, et al. Gut Microbiota Composition Is Correlated to Grid Floor Induced Stress and Behavior in the BALB/c Mouse. *Plos One.* 2012;7(10):e46231. doi:10.1371/journal.pone.0046231

13 Jacka FN, Cherbuin N, Anstey KJ, Sachdev P, Butterworth P. Western diet is associated with a smaller hippocampus: a longitudinal investigation. *BMC Medicine*. 2015/09/08 2015;13(1):215. doi:10.1186/s12916-015-0461-x

14 Liang X, Fu Y, Cao W-t, et al. Gut microbiome, cognitive function and brain structure: a multi-omics integration analysis. *Translational Neurodegeneration*. 2022/11/14 2022;11(1):49. doi:10.1186/s40035-022-00323-z

15 Beibei Y, Jinbao W, Peijun J, Jinghong C. Effects of regulating intestinal microbiota on anxiety symptoms: A systematic review. *General Psychiatry*. 2019;32(2):e100056. doi:10.1136/gpsych-2019-100056

16 Gorka SM, Fitzgerald DA, Labuschagne I, et al. Oxytocin Modulation of Amygdala Functional Connectivity to Fearful Faces in Generalized Social Anxiety Disorder. *Neuropsychopharmacology*. 2015/01/01 2015;40(2):278-286. doi:10.1038/npp.2014.168

17 Varian BJ, Weber KT, Erdman SE. Oxytocin and the microbiome. *Comprehensive Psychoneuroendocrinology*. 2023/11/01/ 2023;16:100205. doi:10.1016/j.cpnec.2023.100205

18 Madison A, Kiecolt-Glaser JK. Stress, depression, diet, and the gut microbiota: human-bacteria interactions at the core of psychoneuroimmunology and nutrition. *Curr Opin Behav Sci*. Aug 2019;28:105-110. doi:10.1016/j.cobeha.2019.01.011

19 Johnson KVA, Foster KR. Why does the microbiome affect behaviour? *Nature Reviews Microbiology*. 2018/10/01 2018;16(10):647-655. doi:10.1038/s41579-018-0014-3

20 Jacka FN, O'Neil A, Opie R, et al. A randomised controlled trial of dietary improvement for adults with major depression (the 'SMILES' trial). *BMC Medicine*. 2017/01/30 2017;15(1):23. doi:10.1186/s12916-017-0791-y

21 Firth J, Solmi M, Wootton RE, et al. A meta-review of "lifestyle psychiatry": the role of exercise, smoking, diet and sleep in the prevention and treatment of mental disorders. *World Psychiatry*. 2020/10/01 2020;19(3):360-380. doi:10.1002/wps.20773

22 van de Rest O, Berendsen AA, Haveman-Nies A, de Groot LC. Dietary patterns, cognitive decline, and dementia: a systematic review. *Adv Nutr*. Mar 2015;6(2):154-168. doi:10.3945/an.114.007617

23 McEvoy CT, Guyer H, Langa KM, Yaffe K. Neuroprotective Diets Are Associated with Better Cognitive Function: The Health and Retirement Study. *J Am Geriatr Soc*. Aug 2017;65(8):1857-1862. doi:10.1111/jgs.14922

24 Saghafian F, Hajishafiee M, Rouhani P, Saneei P. Dietary fiber intake, depression, and anxiety: a systematic review and meta-analysis of epidemiologic studies. *Nutritional Neuroscience*. 2023/02/01 2023;26(2):108-126. doi:10.1080/1028415X.2021.2020403

25 Sun W, Li S, Chen C, Lu Z, Zhang D. Dietary fiber intake is positively related with cognitive function in US older adults. *Journal of Functional Foods.* 2022/03/01/ 2022;90:104986. doi:10.1016/j. jff.2022.104986

Chapter 14. Your Gut's BFFs

1 Blumenthal JA, Babyak MA, Doraiswamy PM, et al. Exercise and pharmacotherapy in the treatment of major depressive disorder. *Psychosom Med.* Sep-Oct 2007;69(7):587-96. doi:10.1097/ PSY.0b013e318148c19a

2 Badawy AAB. Tryptophan availability for kynurenine pathway metabolism across the life span: Control mechanisms and focus on aging, exercise, diet and nutritional supplements. *Neuropharmacology.* 2017/01/01/ 2017;112: 248-263. doi:10.1016/j.neuropharm.2015.11.015

3 Basso JC, Suzuki WA. The Effects of Acute Exercise on Mood, Cognition, Neurophysiology, and Neurochemical Pathways: A Review. *Brain Plast.* Mar 28 2017;2(2):127-152. doi:10.3233/bpl-160040

4 Dohnalová L, Lundgren P, Carty JRE, et al. A microbiome-dependent gut–brain pathway regulates motivation for exercise. *Nature.* 2022/12/01 2022;612(7941):739-747. doi:10.1038/s41586-022-05525-z

5 Ludyga S, Gerber M, Pühse U, Looser VN, Kamijo K. Systematic review and meta-analysis investigating moderators of long-term effects of exercise on cognition in healthy individuals. *Nature Human Behaviour.* 2020/06/01 2020;4(6):603-612. doi:10.1038/s41562-020-0851-8

6 Parvin E, Mohammadian F, Amani-Shalamzari S, Bayati M, Tazesh B. Dual-Task Training Affect Cognitive and Physical Performances and Brain Oscillation Ratio of Patients With Alzheimer's Disease: A Randomized Controlled Trial. *Front Aging Neurosci.* 2020;12:605317. doi:10.3389/ fnagi.2020.605317

7 Collins KA, Huffman KM, Wolever RQ, et al. Determinants of Dropout from and Variation in Adherence to an Exercise Intervention: The STRRIDE Randomized Trials. *Transl J Am Coll Sports Med.* Winter 2022;7(1). doi:10.1249/tjx.0000000000000190

8 Singh B, Olds T, Curtis R, et al. Effectiveness of physical activity interventions for improving depression, anxiety and distress: an overview of systematic reviews. *Br J Sports Med.* 2023;57(18):1203. doi:10.1136/bjsports-2022-106195

9 Campion M, Levita L. Enhancing positive affect and divergent thinking abilities: Play some music and dance. *The Journal of Positive Psychology.* 2014/03/04 2014;9(2):137-145. doi:10.1080/17439760.2013.848376

10 Greer SM, Goldstein AN, Walker MP. The impact of sleep deprivation on food desire in the human brain. *Nature Communications.* 2013/08/06 2013;4(1):2259. doi:10.1038/ncomms3259

11   Taheri S, Lin L, Austin D, Young T, Mignot E. Short sleep duration is associated with reduced leptin, elevated ghrelin, and increased body mass index. *PLoS Med*. Dec 2004;1(3):e62. doi:10.1371/journal.pmed.0010062

12   Han M, Yuan S, Zhang J. The interplay between sleep and gut microbiota. *Brain Research Bulletin*. 2022/03/01/ 2022;180:131-146. doi:10.1016/j.brainresbull.2021.12.016

13   Bermingham KM, Stensrud S, Asnicar F, et al. Exploring the relationship between social jetlag with gut microbial composition, diet and cardiometabolic health, in the ZOE PREDICT 1 cohort. *Eur J Nutr*. Dec 2023;62(8):3135-3147. doi:10.1007/s00394-023-03204-x

14   Carasso S, Fishman B, Lask LS, Shochat T, Geva-Zatorsky N, Tauber E. Metagenomic analysis reveals the signature of gut microbiota associated with human chronotypes. *Faseb j*. Nov 2021;35(11):e22011. doi:10.1096/fj.202100857RR

15   Stretton B, Eranki A, Kovoor J, et al. Too Sour to be True? Tart Cherries (Prunus cerasus) and Sleep: a Systematic Review and Meta-analysis. *Current Sleep Medicine Reports*. 2023/09/01 2023;9(3):225-233. doi:10.1007/s40675-023-00261-w

16   Howatson G, Bell PG, Tallent J, Middleton B, McHugh MP, Ellis J. Effect of tart cherry juice (Prunus cerasus) on melatonin levels and enhanced sleep quality. *Eur J Nutr*. 2012 Dec;51(8):909-16. doi:10.1007/s00394-011-0263-7

17   Valles-Colomer M, Blanco-Míguez A, Manghi P, et al. The person-to-person transmission landscape of the gut and oral microbiomes. *Nature*. 2023/02/01 2023;614(7946): 125-135. doi:10.1038/ s41586-022-05620-1

18   Schloss PD, Iverson KD, Petrosino JF, Schloss SJ. The dynamics of a family's gut microbiota reveal variations on a theme. *Microbiome*. 2014;2:25. doi:10.1186/2049-2618-2-25

19   Valles-Colomer M, Blanco-Míguez A, Manghi P, et al. The person-to-person transmission landscape of the gut and oral microbiomes. *Nature*. 2023/02/01 2023;614(7946): 125-135. doi:10.1038/ s41586-022-05620-1

20   Harvard Study of Adult Development. www.adultdevelopmentstudy.org

21   Hall JA, Holmstrom AJ, Pennington N, Perrault EK, Totzkay D. Quality Conversation Can Increase Daily Well-Being. *Communication Research*. 2023:00936502221139363. doi:10.1177/00936502221139363

22   Cohen S, Janicki-Deverts D, Turner RB, Doyle WJ. Does Hugging Provide Stress-Buffering Social Support? A Study of Susceptibility to Upper Respiratory Infection and Illness. *Psychological Science*. 2015/02/01 2014;26(2):135-147. doi:10.1177/0956797614559284

23   Diener E, Seligman MEP. Very Happy People. *Psychological Science*. 2002/01/01 2002;13(1):81-84. doi:10.1111/1467-9280.00415

24   Degges-White S, Kepic M. Friendships, Subjective Age, and Life Satisfaction of Women in Midlife. *Adultspan Journal*. 2020/04/01 2020;19(1): 39-53. doi:10.1002/adsp.12086

25 Sandstrom GM, Dunn EW. Social Interactions and Well-Being: The Surprising Power of Weak Ties. *Personality and Social Psychology Bulletin.* 2014/07/01 2014;40(7):910-922. doi:10.1177/0146167214529799
26 Meredith GR, Rakow DA, Eldermire ERB, Madsen CG, Shelley SP, Sachs NA. Minimum Time Dose in Nature to Positively Impact the Mental Health of College-Aged Students, and How to Measure It: A Scoping Review. *Front Psychol.* 2019;10:2942. doi:10.3389/fpsyg.2019.02942
27 Nurminen N, Lin J, Grönroos M, et al. Nature-derived microbiota exposure as a novel immunomodulatory approach. *Future Microbiol.* Jun 1 2018;13: 737-744. doi:10.2217/fmb-2017-0286

Chapter 15. How to Make an Unhappy Gut Happy

1 Koloski NA, Jones M, Kalantar J, Weltman M, Zaguirre J, Talley NJ. The brain–gut pathway in functional gastrointestinal disorders is bidirectional: a 12-year prospective population-based study. *Gut.* Sep 2012;61(9):1284-90. doi:10.1136/gutjnl-2011-300474
2 Ma C, Li Y, Mei Z, et al. Association Between Bowel Movement Pattern and Cognitive Function: Prospective Cohort Study and a Metagenomic Analysis of the Gut Microbiome. *Neurology.* Nov 14 2023;101(20): e2014-e2025. doi:10.1212/wnl.0000000000207849
3 Chey SW, Chey WD, Jackson K, Eswaran S. Exploratory Comparative Effectiveness Trial of Green Kiwifruit, Psyllium, or Prunes in US Patients With Chronic Constipation. *Am J Gastroenterol.* Jun 1 2021;116(6):1304-1312. doi:10.14309/ajg.0000000000001149
4 Attaluri A, Donahoe R, Valestin J, Brown K, Rao SS. Randomised clinical trial: dried plums (prunes) vs. psyllium for constipation. *Aliment Pharmacol Ther.* Apr 2011;33(7):822-8. doi:10.1111/j.1365-2036.2011.04594.x
5 Bellini M, Tonarelli S, Barracca F, et al. Chronic Constipation: Is a Nutritional Approach Reasonable? *Nutrients.* Sep 26 2021;13(10). doi:10.3390/nu13103386
6 Dimidi E, Christodoulides S, Fragkos KC, Scott SM, Whelan K. The effect of probiotics on functional constipation in adults: a systematic review and meta-analysis of randomized controlled trials. *Am J Clin Nutr.* 2014;100(4): 1075-1084. doi:10.3945/ajcn.114.089151
7 Zhang C, Jiang J, Tian F, et al. Meta-analysis of randomized controlled trials of the effects of probiotics on functional constipation in adults. *Clinical Nutrition.* 2020/10/01/ 2020;39(10):2960-2969. doi:10.1016/j.clnu.2020.01.005
8 Dimidi E, Christodoulides S, Fragkos KC, Scott SM, Whelan K. The effect of probiotics on functional constipation in adults: a systematic review and meta-analysis of randomized controlled trials. *Am J Clin Nutr.* 2014;100(4): 1075-1084. doi:10.3945/ajcn.114.089151

9   Favretto DC, Pontin B, Moreira TR. Effect of the consumption of a cheese enriched with probiotic organisms (Bifidobacterium Lactis Bi-07) in improving symptoms of constipation. *Arquivos de Gastroenterologia.* 2013;50(3):196-201. doi:10.1590/S0004-28032013000200035. PMID: 24322191

10   Yang YX, He M, Hu G, et al. Effect of a fermented milk containing Bifidobacterium lactis DN-173010 on Chinese constipated women. *World J Gastroenterol.* Oct 28 2008;14(40):6237-43. doi:10.3748/wjg.14.6237

11   Ford AC, Talley NJ, Spiegel BMR, et al. Effect of fibre, antispasmodics, and peppermint oil in the treatment of irritable bowel syndrome: systematic review and meta-analysis. *BMJ.* 2008;337:a2313. doi:10.1136/bmj.a2313

12   Salazar-Parra MAG, Cruz-Neri RU, Trujillo-Trujillo XAR, et al. Effectiveness of Saccharomyces Boulardii CNCM I-745 probiotic in acute inflammatory viral diarrhoea in adults: results from a single-centre randomized trial. *BMC Gastroenterology.* 2023/07/03 2023;23(1):229. doi:10.1186/s12876-023-02863-8

Chapter 16. A New Way of Eating

1   Linardon J, Tylka TL, Fuller-Tyszkiewicz M. Intuitive eating and its psychological correlates: A meta-analysis. *Int J Eat Disord.* Jul 2021;54(7):1073-1098. doi:10.1002/eat.23509

2   Owens BA, Sabik NJ, Tovar A, et al. Higher morning cortisol is associated with lower intuitive eating in midlife women. *Psychoneuroendocrinology.* Jan 9 2024;162:106958. doi:10.1016/j.psyneuen.2024.106958

3   Hawley G, Horwath C, Gray A, et al. Sustainability of health and lifestyle improvements following a non-dieting randomised trial in overweight women. *Preventive Medicine.* 2008/12/01 2008;47(6):593-599. doi:10.1016/j.ypmed.2008.08.008

4   Adams, CE, & Leary, MR. Promoting self-compassionate attitudes toward eating among restrictive and guilty eaters. *Journal of Social and Clinical Psychology.* 2007;26(10),1120-1144. doi:10.1521/jscp.2007.26.10.1120

5   Massey A, Hill AJ. Dieting and food craving. A descriptive, quasi-prospective study. *Appetite.* 2012/06/01 2012;58(3):781-785. doi:10.1016/j.appet.2012.01.020

6   Polivy J, Coleman J, Herman CP. The effect of deprivation on food cravings and eating behavior in restrained and unrestrained eaters. *Int J Eat Disord.* Dec 2005;38(4):301-9. doi:10.1002/eat.20195

7   Ledochowski L, Ruedl G, Taylor AH, Kopp M. Acute effects of brisk walking on sugary snack cravings in overweight people, affect and responses to a manipulated stress situation and to a sugary snack cue: a crossover study. *PLoS One.* 2015;10(3):e0119278. doi:10.1371/journal.pone.0119278

Chapter 17. Sugar, Baby

1   Di Rienzi SC, Britton RA. Adaptation of the Gut Microbiota to Modern Dietary Sugars and Sweeteners. *Adv Nutr*. May 1 2020;11(3):616-629. doi:10.1093/advances/nmz118

2   Ruxton CHS, Myers M. Fruit Juices: Are They Helpful or Harmful? An Evidence Review. *Nutrients*. 2021;13(6):1815. doi:10.3390/nu13061815

3   Toews T, Lohner S, Küllenberg de Gaudry, Sommer H, Meerpohl JJ. Association between intake of non-sugar sweeteners and health outcomes: systematic review and meta-analyses of randomised and non-randomised controlled trials and observational studies. *BMJ*. 2019;364:k4718. doi:10.1136/bmj.k4718

4   Ahmad SY, Friel J, Mackay D. The Effects of Non-Nutritive Artificial Sweeteners, Aspartame and Sucralose, on the Gut Microbiome in Healthy Adults: Secondary Outcomes of a Randomized Double-Blinded Crossover Clinical Trial. *Nutrients*. Nov 6 2020;12(11). doi:10.3390/nu12113408

Chapter 18. In Tune With Your Body

1   Bushman BJ, DeWall CN, Pond RS, Hanus MD. Low glucose relates to greater aggression in married couples. *Proceedings of the National Academy of Sciences*. 2014/04/29 2014;111(17):6254-6257. doi:10.1073/pnas.1400619111

2   Page KA, Seo D, Belfort-DeAguiar R, et al. Circulating glucose levels modulate neural control of desire for high-calorie foods in humans. *J Clin Invest*. Oct 2011;121(10):4161-9. doi:10.1172/jci57873

3   Bray GA, Flatt JP, Volaufova J, Delany JP, Champagne CM. Corrective responses in human food intake identified from an analysis of 7-d food-intake records. *Am J Clin Nutr*. Dec 2008;88(6):1504-10. doi:10.3945/ajcn.2008.26289

Chapter 19. Feeling Energised, Feeling Great

1   Mishra S, Singh AK, Rajotiya S, et al. Exploring the risk of glycemic variability in non-diabetic depressive individuals: a cross-sectional GlyDep pilot study. Original Research. *Frontiers in Psychiatry*. 2023-September-15 2023;14 doi:10.3389/fpsyt.2023.1196866

2   Dhillon J, Craig BA, Leidy HJ, et al. The Effects of Increased Protein Intake on Fullness: A Meta-Analysis and Its Limitations. *J Acad Nutr Diet*. Jun 2016;116(6):968-83. doi:10.1016/j.jand.2016.01.003

3   Dekker IM, van Rijssen NM, Verreijen A, et al. Calculation of protein requirements; a comparison of calculations based on bodyweight and fat free mass. *Clin Nutr ESPEN*. Apr 2022;48:378-385. doi:10.1016/j.clnesp.2022.01.014

4   Goltz SR, Campbell WW, Chitchumroonchokchai C, Failla ML, Ferruzzi MG. Meal triacylglycerol profile modulates postprandial absorption of

carotenoids in humans. *Molecular Nutrition & Food Research*. 2012/06/01 2012;56(6):866-877. doi:10.1002/mnfr.201100687

Chapter 21. Small Changes are Successful

1   Santini ZI, Nelausen MK, Kusier AO, et al. Impact evaluation of the 'ABCs of Mental Health' in Denmark and the role of mental health-promoting beliefs and actions. *Mental Health and Social Inclusion*. 2022;26(3):271-291. doi:10.1108/MHSI-03-2022-0014

Hack 1: Half Your Plate With Veggies

1   Aune D, Giovannucci E, Boffetta P, Fadnes LT, Keum N, Norat T, Greenwood DC, Riboli E, Vatten LJ, Tonstad S. Fruit and vegetable intake and the risk of cardiovascular disease, total cancer and all-cause mortality – a systematic review and dose-response meta-analysis of prospective studies, *International Journal of Epidemiology*. 46. Jun 3 2017; 46: 1029–1056. doi:10.1093/ije/dyw319

2   Wicaksono WA, Cernava T, Wassermann B, et al. The edible plant microbiome: evidence for the occurrence of fruit and vegetable bacteria in the human gut. *Gut Microbes*. Dec 2023;15(2):2258565. doi:10.1080/194909 76.2023.2258565

3   Wassermann B, Müller H, Berg G. An Apple a Day: Which Bacteria Do We Eat With Organic and Conventional Apples? Original Research. *Frontiers in Microbiology*. 2019;10. doi:10.3389/fmicb.2019.01629

4   De Leon A, Jahns L, Roemmich JN, Duke SE, Casperson SL. Consumption of Dietary Guidelines for Americans Types and Amounts of Vegetables Increases Mean Subjective Happiness Scale Scores: A Randomized Controlled Trial. *Journal of the Academy of Nutrition and Dietetics*. 2022/07/01/ 2022;122(7): 1355-1362. doi:10.1016/j.jand.2021.11.009

5   White BA, Horwath CC, Conner TS. Many apples a day keep the blues away – Daily experiences of negative and positive affect and food consumption in young adults. *British Journal of Health Psychology*. 2013;18(4):782-798. doi:10.1111/bjhp.12021

6   Morris MC, Evans DA, Tangney CC, Bienias JL, Wilson RS. Associations of vegetable and fruit consumption with age-related cognitive change. *Neurology*. 2006;67(8):1370-1376. doi:10.1212/01.wnl.0000240224 .38978.d8

7   Xu M, Ke P, Wang C, et al. Association of food groups with the risk of cognitive impairment in Chinese older adults. *Journal of Affective Disorders*. 2022/07/15/ 2022;309:266-273. doi:10.1016/j.jad.2022. 04.113

8   Crinnion WJ. Organic foods contain higher levels of certain nutrients, lower levels of pesticides, and may provide health benefits for the consumer. *Altern Med Rev*. Apr 2010;15(1):4–12.

9   Matsuzaki R, Gunnigle E, Geissen V, Clarke G, Nagpal J, Cryan JF. Pesticide exposure and the microbiota-gut-brain axis. *The ISME Journal.* 2023/08/01 2023;17(8):1153-1166. doi:10.1038/s41396-023-01450-9

10 Roe LS, Meengs JS, Rolls BJ. Salad and satiety: The effect of timing of salad consumption on meal energy intake. *Appetite.* Feb 2012;58(1):242-8. doi:10.1016/j.appet.2011.10.003

11 Holt SH, Miller JC, Petocz P, Farmakalidis E. A satiety index of common foods. *Eur J Clin Nutr.* Sep 1995;49(9):675-90.

12 Muir JG, O'Dea K. Measurement of resistant starch: factors affecting the amount of starch escaping digestion in vitro. *Am J Clin Nutr.* Jul 1992;56(1): 123-7. doi:10.1093/ajcn/56.1.123

Hack 2: Go for the Colourful Five

1   Lee S-H, Yoon S-H, Jung Y, et al. Emotional well-being and gut microbiome profiles by enterotype. *Scientific Reports.* 2020/11/26 2020;10(1):20736. doi:10.1038/ s41598-020-77673-z

2   Ghosh S, Whitley CS, Haribabu B, Jala VR. Regulation of Intestinal Barrier Function by Microbial Metabolites. *Cell Mol Gastroenterol Hepatol.* 2021;11(5):1463-1482. doi:10.1016/j.jcmgh.2021.02.007

3   Spragge F, Bakkeren E, Jahn MT, et al. Microbiome diversity protects against pathogens by nutrient blocking. *Science.* 2023;382(6676):eadj3502. doi:10.1126/science.adj3502

4   So D, Whelan K, Rossi M, et al. Dietary fiber intervention on gut microbiota composition in healthy adults: a systematic review and meta-analysis. *Am J Clin Nutr.* Jun 1 2018;107(6):965-983. doi:10.1093/ajcn/nqy041

5   Evelyn M, Frauke B, Ronja T, et al. Prebiotic diet changes neural correlates of food decision-making in overweight adults: a randomised controlled within-subject cross-over trial. *Gut.* 2023:gutjnl-2023-330365. doi:10.1136/ gutjnl-2023-330365

6   Hiel S, Bindels LB, Pachikian BD, et al. Effects of a diet based on inulin-rich vegetables on gut health and nutritional behavior in healthy humans. *Am J Clin Nutr.* Jun 1 2019;109(6):1683-1695. doi:10.1093/ajcn/nqz001

7   Leyrolle Q, Cserjesi R, Mulders DGH, Zamariola G, Hiel S, Gianfrancesco MA, et al. Prebiotic effect on mood in obese patients is determined by the initial gut microbiota composition: A randomized, controlled trial. *Brain Behav Immun.* 2021;94:289-98. doi: 10.1016/j.bbi.2021.01.014

8   Schmidt K, Cowen PJ, Harmer CJ, Tzortzis G, Errington S, Burnet PWJ. Prebiotic intake reduces the waking cortisol response and alters emotional bias in healthy volunteers. *Psychopharmacology.* 2015/05/01 2015;232(10): 1793-1801. doi:10.1007/s00213-014-3810-0

9   Berding K, Bastiaanssen TFS, Moloney GM, et al. Feed your microbes to deal with stress: a psychobiotic diet impacts microbial stability and perceived stress in a healthy adult population. *Molecular Psychiatry.* 2023/02/01 2023;28(2):601-610. doi:10.1038/s41380-022-01817-y

10 Johnstone N, Milesi C, Burn O, et al. Anxiolytic effects of a galacto-oligosaccharides prebiotic in healthy females (18–25 years) with corresponding changes in gut bacterial composition. *Scientific Reports.* Apr 15 2021;11(1):8302. doi:10.1038/ s41598-021-87865-w

11 Ni Lochlainn M, Bowyer RCE, Moll JM, et al. Effect of gut microbiome modulation on muscle function and cognition: the PROMOTe randomised controlled trial. *Nature Communications.* 2024/02/29 2024;15(1):1859. doi:10.1038/s41467-024-46116-y

12 Bellumori M, Cecchi L, Innocenti M, Clodoveo ML, Corbo F, Mulinacci N. The EFSA Health Claim on Olive Oil Polyphenols: Acid Hydrolysis Validation and Total Hydroxytyrosol and Tyrosol Determination in Italian Virgin Olive Oils. *Molecules.* Jun 10 2019;24(11). doi:10.3390/molecules24112179

13 Chang SC, Cassidy A, Willett WC, Rimm EB, O'Reilly EJ, Okereke OI. Dietary flavonoid intake and risk of incident depression in midlife and older women. *Am J Clin Nutr.* Sep 2016;104(3):704-14. doi:10.3945/ajcn.115.124545

14 Davinelli S, Ali S, Solfrizzi V, Scapagnini G, Corbi G. Carotenoids and Cognitive Outcomes: A Meta-Analysis of Randomized Intervention Trials. *Antioxidants.* 2021;10(2):223. doi:10.3390/antiox10020223

15 Ziauddeen N, Rosi A, Del Rio D, et al. Dietary intake of (poly)phenols in children and adults: cross-sectional analysis of UK National Diet and Nutrition Survey Rolling Programme (2008–2014). *Eur J Nutr.* 2019/12/01 2019;58(8):3183-3198. doi:10.1007/s00394-018-1862-3

16 Khine, WWT, Haldar, S, De Loi, S et al. A single serving of mixed spices alters gut microflora composition: a dose–response randomised trial. *Scientific Reports.* 2021;11:11264. doi:10.1038/s41598-021-90453-7

17 McDonald D, Hyde E, Debelius JW, et al. American Gut: an Open Platform for Citizen Science Microbiome Research. *mSystems.* May-Jun 2018;3(3) doi:10.1128/mSystems.00031-18

Hack 3: Eat the BGBGs

1 Silva YP, Bernardi A, Frozza RL. The Role of Short-Chain Fatty Acids From Gut Microbiota in Gut-Brain Communication. *Front Endocrinol (Lausanne).* 2020;11:25. doi:10.3389/fendo.2020.00025

2 Darmadi-Blackberry I, Wahlqvist ML, Kouris-Blazos A, et al. Legumes: the most important dietary predictor of survival in older people of different ethnicities. *Asia Pac J Clin Nutr.* 2004;13(2):217-20.

3 Yeh T-S, Yuan C, Ascherio A, Rosner BA, Blacker D, Willett WC. Long-term dietary protein intake and subjective cognitive decline in US men and women. *Am J Clin Nutr.* 2022;115(1):199-210. doi:10.1093/ajcn/nqab236

4 Zhang X, Irajizad E, Hoffman KL, et al. Modulating a prebiotic food source influences inflammation and immune-regulating gut microbes and metabolites: insights from the BE GONE trial. *eBioMedicine.* 2023;98. doi:10.1016/j.ebiom.2023.104873

5   Di Noia J. Defining powerhouse fruits and vegetables: a nutrient density approach. *Prev Chronic Dis*. Jun 5 2014;11:E95. doi:10.5888/pcd11.130390

6   Hanson BT, Dimitri Kits K, Löffler J, et al. Sulfoquinovose is a select nutrient of prominent bacteria and a source of hydrogen sulfide in the human gut. *The ISME Journal*. 2021/09/01 2021;15(9):2779-2791. doi:10.1038/s41396-021-00968-0

7   Baharzadeh E, Siassi F, Qorbani M, Koohdani F, Pak N, Sotoudeh G. Fruits and vegetables intake and its subgroups are related to depression: a cross-sectional study from a developing country. *Ann Gen Psychiatry*. 2018;17:46. doi:10.1186/s12991-018-0216-0

8   Morris MC, Wang Y, Barnes LL, Bennett DA, Dawson-Hughes B, Booth SL. Nutrients and bioactives in green leafy vegetables and cognitive decline: Prospective study. *Neurology*. Jan 16 2018;90(3):e214-e222. doi:10.1212/wnl.0000000000004815

9   Marino M, Venturi S, Gargari G, et al. Berries-Gut Microbiota Interaction and Impact on Human Health: A Systematic Review of Randomized Controlled Trials. *Food Reviews International*.1-23. doi:10.1080/87559129.2023.2276765

10 Miller MG, Rutledge GA, Scott TM, Shukitt-Hale B, Thangthaeng N. Dietary strawberry improves cognition in a randomised, double-blind, placebo-controlled trial in older adults. *Br J Nutr*. 2021;126(2):253-263. doi:10.1017/S0007114521000222

11 Khalid S, Barfoot KL, May G, Lamport DJ, Reynolds SA, Williams CM. Effects of Acute Blueberry Flavonoids on Mood in Children and Young Adults. *Nutrients*. Feb 20 2017;9(2). doi:10.3390/nu9020158

12 Bourassa MW, Alim I, Bultman SJ, Ratan RR. Butyrate, neuroepigenetics and the gut microbiome: Can a high fiber diet improve brain health? *Neurosc Lett*. 2016;625: 56-63. doi:10.1016/j.neulet.2016.02.009

13 Ross AB, Shertukde SP, Livingston Staffier K, Chung M, Jacques PF, McKeown NM. The Relationship between Whole-Grain Intake and Measures of Cognitive Decline, Mood, and Anxiety-A Systematic Review. *Adv Nutr*. Jul 2023;14(4):652-670. doi:10.1016/j.advnut.2023.04.003

14 Liu X, Beck T, Dhana K, et al. Association of Whole Grain Consumption and Cognitive Decline. *Neurology*. 2023;101(22):e2277-e2287. doi:10.1212/WNL.0000000000207938

15 Burton P, Lightowler HJ. The impact of freezing and toasting on the glycaemic response of white bread. *Eur J Clin Nutr*. 2008/05/01 2008;62(5):594-599. doi:10.1038/sj.ejcn.1602746

16 Cordova R, Viallon V, Fontvieille E, et al. Consumption of ultra-processed foods and risks of multimorbidity of cancer and cardiometabolic diseases: a multinational cohort study. *The Lancet Regional Health – Europe*. 2023;35. doi:10.1016/j.lanepe.2023.100771

17 Tindall AM, McLimans CJ, Petersen KS, Kris-Etherton PM, Lamendella R. Walnuts and Vegetable Oils Containing Oleic Acid Differentially Affect the Gut Microbiota and Associations with Cardiovascular Risk Factors: Follow-up

of a Randomized, Controlled, Feeding Trial in Adults at Risk for Cardiovascular Disease. *J Nutr.* Apr 1 2020;150(4):806-817. doi:10.1093/jn/nxz289

18   Haskell-Ramsay CF, Dodd FL, Smith D, et al. Mixed Tree Nuts, Cognition, and Gut Microbiota: A 4-Week, Placebo-Controlled, Randomized Crossover Trial in Healthy Nonelderly Adults. *J Nutr.* Jan 14 2023;152(12): 2778-2788. doi:10.1093/jn/nxac228

Hack 4: Opt for a Daily Ferment

1   Bryant KL, Hansen C, Hecht EE. Fermentation technology as a driver of human brain expansion. *Communications Biology*. 2023/11/23 2023;6(1):1190. doi:10.1038/s42003-023-05517-3

2   Xia T, Kang C, Qiang X, et al. Beneficial effect of vinegar consumption associated with regulating gut microbiome and metabolome. *Current Research in Food Science*. 2024/01/01 2024;8:100566. doi:10.1016/j. crfs.2023.100566

3   Wastyk HC, Fragiadakis GK, Perelman D, et al. Gut-microbiota-targeted diets modulate human immune status. *Cell*. Aug 5 2021;184(16):4137-4153. e14. doi:10.1016/j.cell.2021.06.019

4   Milani C, Duranti S, Napoli S, et al. Colonization of the human gut by bovine bacteria present in Parmesan cheese. *Nature Communications*. 2019/03/20 2019;10(1):1286. doi:10.1038/s41467-019-09303-w

5   Wastyk HC, Fragiadakis GK, Perelman D, et al. Gut-microbiota-targeted diets modulate human immune status. *Cell*. Aug 5 2021;184(16): 4137-4153. e14. doi:10.1016/j.cell.2021.06.019

6   Hilimire MR, DeVylder JE, Forestell CA. Fermented foods, neuroticism, and social anxiety: An interaction model. *Psychiatry Research*.2015;228(2): 203-208. doi:10.1016/j.psychres.2015.04.023

7   Tillisch K, Labus J, Kilpatrick L, et al. Consumption of fermented milk product with probiotic modulates brain activity. *Gastroenterology*. 2013;144(7): 1394-401,1401. doi:10.1053/j.gastro.2013.02.043

8   Porras-García E, Fernández-Espada Calderón I, Gavala-González J, Fernández-García JC. Potential neuroprotective effects of fermented foods and beverages in old age: a systematic review. Systematic Review. *Frontiers in Nutrition*. 2023;10. doi:10.3389/fnut.2023.1170841

9   Van de Wouw M, Walsh AM, Crispie F, et al. Distinct actions of the fermented beverage kefir on host behaviour, immunity and microbiome gut-brain modules in the mouse. *Microbiome*. 2020/05/18 2020;8(1):67. doi:10.1186/s40168-020-00846-5

10   Cannavale CN, Mysonhimer AR, Bailey MA, Cohen NJ, Holscher HD, Khan NA. Consumption of a fermented dairy beverage improves hippocampal-dependent relational memory in a randomized, controlled cross-over trial. *Nutritional Neuroscience*. 2023/03/04 2023;26(3):265-274. doi:10.1080/1028 415X.2022.2046963

11 Rezac S, Kok CR, Heermann M, Hutkins R. Fermented Foods as a Dietary Source of Live Organisms. *Front Microbiol*. 2018;9:1785. doi:10.3389/fmicb.2018.01785

12 Brassard D, Tessier-Grenier M, Allaire J, et al. Comparison of the impact of SFAs from cheese and butter on cardiometabolic risk factors: a randomized controlled trial. *Am J Clin Nutr*. Apr 2017;105(4):800-809. doi:10.3945/ajcn.116.150300

13 Cho YA, Kim J. Effect of Probiotics on Blood Lipid Concentrations: A Meta-Analysis of Randomized Controlled Trials. *Medicine (Baltimore)*. Oct 2015;94(43):e1714. doi:10.1097/md.0000000000001714

14 Chen G-C, Wang Y, Tong X, et al. Cheese consumption and risk of cardiovascular disease: a meta-analysis of prospective studies. *Eur J Nutr*. 2017/12/01 2017; 56(8):2565-2575. doi:10.1007/s00394-016-1292-z

15 Jy K, Ey C. Changes in Korean Adult Females' Intestinal Microbiota Resulting from Kimchi Intake. *Journal of Nutrition & Food Sciences*. 01/01 2016;06. doi:10.4172/2155-9600.1000486

Hack 5. Make Early Dinner Your Friend

1 Montagner A, Korecka A, Polizzi A, et al. Hepatic circadian clock oscillators and nuclear receptors integrate microbiome-derived signals. *Scientific Reports*. Feb 16 2016;6:20127. doi:10.1038/srep20127

2 Voigt RM, Forsyth CB, Green SJ, Engen PA, Keshavarzian A. Circadian Rhythm and the Gut Microbiome. *Int Rev Neurobiol*. 2016;131:193-205. doi:10.1016/bs.irn.2016.07.002

3 Gu C, Brereton N, Schweitzer A, et al. Metabolic Effects of Late Dinner in Healthy Volunteers—A Randomized Crossover Clinical Trial. *The Journal of Clinical Endocrinology & Metabolism*. 2020;105(8):2789-2802. doi:10.1210/clinem/dgaa354

4 Currenti W, Godos J, Castellano S, et al. Association between Time Restricted Feeding and Cognitive Status in Older Italian Adults. *Nutrients*. Jan 9 2021;13(1). doi:10.3390/nu13010191

5 Bermingham KM, Pushilal A, Polidori L, Wolf J, Bulsiewicz W, Spector TD, Berry SE. Ten Hour Time-Restricted Eating (TRE) Is Associated with Improvements in Energy, Mood, Hunger and Weight in Free-Living Settings: The ZOE BIG IF Study. *Proceedings*. 2023; 91(1):120. doi:10.3390/proceedings2023091120

6 Zhang Y, Li Y, Barber AF, et al. The microbiome stabilizes circadian rhythms in the gut. *Proceedings of the National Academy of Sciences*. 2023/01/31 2023;120(5):e2217532120. doi:10.1073/pnas.2217532120

Hack 6: Oily Fish Twice a Week

1 Vijay A, Astbury S, Le Roy C, Spector TD, Valdes AM. The prebiotic effects of omega-3 fatty acid supplementation: A six-week randomised intervention trial. *Gut Microbes*. Jan-Dec 2021;13(1):1-11. doi:10.1080/19490976.2020.1863133

2   Menni C, Zierer J, Pallister T, et al. Omega-3 fatty acids correlate with gut microbiome diversity and production of N-carbamylglutamate in middle aged and elderly women. *Scientific Reports*. Sep 11 2017;7(1):11079. doi:10.1038/s41598-017-10382-2

3   Mateos R, Pérez-Correa J R, Domínguez H. Bioactive Properties of Marine Phenolics. *Marine Drugs*. 2020;18(10). doi:10.3390/md18100501

4   Liao Y, Xie B, Zhang H, et al. Efficacy of omega-3 PUFAs in depression: A meta-analysis. *Translational Psychiatry*. 2019/08/05 2019;9(1):190. doi:10.1038/s41398-019-0515-5

5   Jacka FN, O'Neil A, Opie R, et al. A randomised controlled trial of dietary improvement for adults with major depression (the 'SMILES' trial). *BMC Medicine*. 2017/01/30 2017;15(1):23. doi:10.1186/ s12916-017-0791-y

6   Raji CA, Erickson KI, Lopez OL, et al. Regular Fish Consumption and Age-Related Brain Gray Matter Loss. *American Journal of Preventive Medicine*. 2014/10/01 2014;47(4):444-451. doi:10.1016/j.amepre. 2014.05.037

7   Samieri C, Morris MC, Bennett DA, et al. Fish Intake, Genetic Predisposition to Alzheimer Disease, and Decline in Global Cognition and Memory in 5 Cohorts of Older Persons. *Am J Epidemiol*. May 1 2018;187(5): 933-940. doi:10.1093/aje/kwx330

8   Keenan TD, Agrón E, Mares JA, et al. Adherence to a Mediterranean diet and cognitive function in the Age-Related Eye Disease Studies 1 & 2. *Alzheimer's & Dementia*. 2020;16(6):831-842. doi:10.1002/ alz.12077

Hack 7: Join the Dark Side

1   Bruinsma K, Taren DL. Chocolate: food or drug? *J Am Diet Assoc*. Oct 1999;99(10):1249-56. doi:10.1016/s0002-8223(99)00307-7

2   Shin J-H, Kim C-S, Cha L, et al. Consumption of 85% cocoa dark chocolate improves mood in association with gut microbial changes in healthy adults: a randomized controlled trial. *The Journal of Nutritional Biochemistry*. 2022/01/01 2022;99:108854. doi:10.1016/j.jnutbio.2021.108854

Hack 8: Protein- and Fibre-Power Your Breakfast

1   Leeming ER, Mompeo O, Turk P, et al. Characterisation, procedures and heritability of acute dietary intake in the Twins UK cohort: an observational study. *Nurt J*. 2022/02/27 2022;21(1):13. doi:10.1186/ s12937-022-00763-3

2   Chang Z-S, Boolani A, Conroy DA, Dunietz T, Jansen EC. Skipping breakfast and mood: The role of sleep. *Nutrition and Health*. 2021/12/01 2021;27(4): 373-379. doi:10.1177/0260106020984861

3   Deshmukh-Taskar PR, Nicklas TA, O'Neil CE, Keast DR, Radcliffe JD, Cho S. The relationship of breakfast skipping and type of breakfast consumption with nutrient intake and weight status in children and adolescents: the National Health and Nutrition Examination Survey 1999-2006. *J Am Diet Assoc.* Jun 2010;110(6):869-78. doi:10.1016/j.jada.2010.03.023

4   Gibney MJ, Barr SI, Bellisle F, et al. Breakfast in Human Nutrition: The International Breakfast Research Initiative. *Nutrients.* May 1 2018;10(5). doi:10.3390/nu10050559

5   Lesani A, Mohammadpoorasl A, Javadi M, Esfeh JM, Fakhari A. Eating breakfast, fruit and vegetable intake and their relation with happiness in college students. *Eating and Weight Disorders - Studies on Anorexia, Bulimia and Obesity.* 2016/12/01 2016;21(4):645-651. doi:10.1007/s40519-016-0261-0

6   Piqueras JA, Kuhne W, Vera-Villarroel P, van Straten A, Cuijpers P. Happiness and health behaviours in Chilean college students: a cross-sectional survey. *BMC Public Health.* Jun 7 2011;11:443. doi:10.1186/1471-2458-11-443

7   Zahedi H, Djalalinia S, Sadeghi O, et al. Breakfast consumption and mental health: a systematic review and meta-analysis of observational studies. *Nutritional Neuroscience.* 2022/06/03 2022;25(6):1250-1264. doi:10.1080/1028415X.2020.1853411

8   Hoertel HA, Will MJ, Leidy HJ. A randomized crossover, pilot study examining the effects of a normal protein vs. high protein breakfast on food cravings and reward signals in overweight/obese 'breakfast skipping', late-adolescent girls. *Nurt J.* 2014;13:80. doi.org/10.1186/1475-2891-13-80

9   Leidy HJ, Lepping RJ, Savage CR, Harris CT. Neural responses to visual food stimuli after a normal vs. higher-protein breakfast in breakfast-skipping teens: A pilot fMRI study. *Obesity,* 2011;19: 2019-25. doi:10.1038/oby.2011.108

Hack 9: Zen Out Your Brain, Zen Out Your Gut

1   Wang Z, Liu S, Xu X, et al. Gut Microbiota Associated With Effectiveness And Responsiveness to Mindfulness-Based Cognitive Therapy in Improving Trait Anxiety. *Front Cell Infect Microbiol.* 2022;12:719829. doi:10.3389/fcimb.2022.719829

2   Khine WWT, Voong ML, Ng TKS, et al. Mental awareness improved mild cognitive impairment and modulated gut microbiome. *Aging (Albany NY).* Dec 9 2020;12(23):24371-24393. doi:10.18632/aging.202277

3   Mai FM. Beaumont's contribution to gastric psychophysiology: a reappraisal. *Can J Psychiatry.* Oct 1988;33(7):650-3. doi:10.1177/070674378803300715

4   Ying S, Peijun J, Ting X, Usman A, Donghong C, Jinghong C. Alteration of faecal microbiota balance related to long-term deep meditation. *General Psychiatry.* 2023;36(1):e100893. doi:10.1136/gpsych-2022-100893

5   Balban MY, Neri E, Kogon MM, et al. Brief structured respiration practices enhance mood and reduce physiological arousal. *Cell Rep Med.* Jan 17 2023;4(1):100895. doi:10.1016/j.xcrm.2022.100895

6   Magnon V, Dutheil F, Vallet GT. Benefits from one session of deep and slow breathing on vagal tone and anxiety in young and older adults. *Scientific Reports.* 2021/09/29 2021;11(1):19267. doi:10.1038/s41598-021-98736-9

7   Balban MY, Neri E, Kogon MM, et al. Brief structured respiration practices enhance mood and reduce physiological arousal. *Cell Rep Med.* Jan 17 2023;4(1):100895. doi:10.1016/j.xcrm.2022.100895

8   Christina Z, Heidi J, Guangyu Z, et al. Nasal Respiration Entrains Human Limbic Oscillations and Modulates Cognitive Function. *The Journal of Neuroscience.* 2016;36(49):12448. doi:10.1523/jneurosci. 2586-16.2016

9   Bernardi L, Gabutti A, Porta C, Spicuzza L. Slow breathing reduces chemoreflex response to hypoxia and hypercapnia, and increases baroreflex sensitivity. *J Hypertens.* Dec 2001;19(12):2221-9. doi:10.1097/ 00004872-200112000-00016

10 Saoji AA, Raghavendra BR, Manjunath NK. Effects of yogic breath regulation: A narrative review of scientific evidence. *Journal of Ayurveda and Integrative Medicine.* 2019/01/01/ 2019;10(1):50-58. doi:10.1016/j. jaim.2017.07.008

11 Smith RP, Easson C, Lyle SM, et al. Gut microbiome diversity is associated with sleep physiology in humans. *PLoS One.* 2019;14(10):e0222394. doi:10.1371/journal.pone.0222394

Hack 10: Drink Up!

1   Popkin BM, D'Anci KE, Rosenberg IH. Water, hydration, and health. *Nutrition Reviews.* 2010;68(8):439-458. doi:10.1111/j.1753-4887.2010.00304.x

2   Stookey JD. Analysis of 2009–2012 Nutrition Health and Examination Survey (NHANES) Data to Estimate the Median Water Intake Associated with Meeting Hydration Criteria for Individuals Aged 12–80 in the US Population. *Nutrients.* Mar 18 2019;11(3). doi:10.3390/nu11030657

3   Ganio MS, Armstrong LE, Casa DJ, et al. Mild dehydration impairs cognitive performance and mood of men. *Br J Nutr.* 2011;106(10):1535-1543. doi:10.1017/S0007114511002005

4   Kempton MJ, Ettinger U, Foster R, et al. Dehydration affects brain structure and function in healthy adolescents. *Human Brain Mapping.* 2011;32(1): 71-79. doi:10.1002/hbm.20999

5   Edmonds C, Crombie R, Gardner M. Subjective thirst moderates changes in speed of responding associated with water consumption. Original Research. *Frontiers in Human Neuroscience.* 2013-July-16 2013;7. doi:10.3389/fnhum.2013.00363

6   Popova NK, Ivanova LN, Amstislavskaya TG, et al. Brain Serotonin Metabolism during Water Deprivation and Hydration in Rats. *Neuroscience*

and *Behavioral Physiology*. 2001/05/01 2001;31(3):327-332.
doi:10.1023/A:1010346904526

7 Pross N, Demazières A, Girard N, et al. Influence of progressive fluid restriction on mood and physiological markers of dehydration in women. *Br J Nutr*. Jan 28 2013;109(2):313-21. doi:10.1017/s0007114512001080

8 Zhang J, Zhang N, He H, Du S, Ma G. Different Amounts of Water Supplementation Improved Cognitive Performance and Mood among Young Adults after 12 h Water Restriction in Baoding, China: A Randomized Controlled Trial (RCT). *Int J Environ Res Public Health*. Oct 24 2020;17(21). doi:10.3390/ijerph17217792

9 Daniel H. Diet and the gut microbiome: from hype to hypothesis. *Br J Nutr*. Sep 28 2020;124(6):521-530. doi:10.1017/s0007114520001142

10 Vanhaecke T, Bretin O, Poirel M, Tap J. Drinking Water Source and Intake Are Associated with Distinct Gut Microbiota Signatures in US and UK Populations. *J Nutr*. Jan 11 2022;152(1):171-182. doi:10.1093/jn/nxab312

11 Willis NB, Muñoz CX, Mysonhimer AR, et al. Hydration Biomarkers Are Related to the Differential Abundance of Fecal Microbiota and Plasma Lipopolysaccharide-Binding Protein in Adults. *Annals of Nutrition and Metabolism*. 2022;77(Suppl. 4):37-45. doi:10.1159/000520478

12 Asnicar F, Berry SE, Valdes AM, et al. Microbiome connections with host metabolism and habitual diet from 1,098 deeply phenotyped individuals. *Nature Medicine*. 2021/02/01 2021;27(2): 321-332. doi:10.1038/s41591-020-01183-8

13 Díaz-Rubio ME, Saura-Calixto F. Dietary Fiber in Brewed Coffee. *Journal of Agricultural and Food Chemistry*. 2007/03/01 2007;55(5):1999-2003. doi:10.1021/jf062839p

14 Pham K, Mulugeta A, Zhou A, O'Brien JT, Llewellyn DJ, Hyppönen E. High coffee consumption, brain volume and risk of dementia and stroke. *Nutritional Neuroscience*. 2022/10/03 2022;25(10):2111-2122. doi:10.1080/1028415X.2021.1945858

15 Jeon J-S, Kim H-T, Jeong I-H, et al. Contents of chlorogenic acids and caffeine in various coffee-related products. *Journal of Advanced Research*. 2019/05/01/ 2019;17:85-94. doi:10.1016/j.jare.2019.01.002

16 Saitou K, Ochiai R, Kozuma K, et al. Effect of Chlorogenic Acids on Cognitive Function: A Randomized, Double-Blind, Placebo-Controlled Trial. *Nutrients*. 2018;10(10):1337

17 Umeda M, Tominaga T, Kozuma K, et al. Preventive effects of tea and tea catechins against influenza and acute upper respiratory tract infections: a systematic review and meta-analysis. *Eur J Nutr*. 2021/12/01 2021;60(8):4189-4202. doi:10.1007/s00394-021-02681-2

18 Kochman J, Jakubczyk K, Antoniewicz J, Mruk H, Janda K. Health Benefits and Chemical Composition of Matcha Green Tea: A Review. *Molecules*. Dec 27 2020;26(1). doi:10.3390/molecules26010085

19   Weiss DJ, Anderton CR. Determination of catechins in matcha green tea by micellar electrokinetic chromatography. *Journal of Chromatography A*. 2003/09/05/ 2003;1011(1):173-180. doi:10.1016/S0021-9673(03)01133-6

20   Sokary S, Al-Asmakh M, Zakaria Z, Bawadi H. The therapeutic potential of matcha tea: A critical review on human and animal studies. *Current Research in Food Science*. 2023/01/01/ 2023;6:100396. doi:10.1016/j.crfs.2022.11.015

21   Wang J, Dong L, Hu J-q, et al. Differential regulation and preventive mechanisms of green tea powder with different quality attributes on high-fat diet-induced obesity in mice. Original Research. *Frontiers in Nutrition*. 2022-September-29 2022;9doi:10.3389/fnut.2022.992815

22   Drink Less. NHS. www.nhs.uk/ better-health/drink-less#:~:text=Alcohol%20guidelines,risk%20of%20harming%20your%20health

23   Daviet R, Aydogan G, Jagannathan K, et al. Associations between alcohol consumption and gray and white matter volumes in the UK Biobank. *Nature Communications*. 2022/03/04 2022;13(1):1175. doi:10.1038/s41467-022-28735-5

24   Le Roy CI, Wells PM, Si J, Raes J, Bell JT, Spector TD. Red Wine Consumption Associated With Increased Gut Microbiota α-Diversity in 3 Independent Cohorts. *Gastroenterology*. Jan 2020;158(1):270-272.e2. doi:10.1053/j.gastro.2019.08.024

25   Queipo-Ortuño MI, Boto-Ordóñez M, Murri M, et al. Influence of red wine polyphenols and ethanol on the gut microbiota ecology and biochemical biomarkers1234. *Am J Clin Nutr*. 2012/06/01/ 2012;95(6):1323-1334. doi:10.3945/ajcn.111.027847

Frequently Asked Questions

1   Hadi A, Pourmasoumi M, Najafgholizadeh A, Clark CCT, Esmaillzadeh A. The effect of apple cider vinegar on lipid profiles and glycemic parameters: a systematic review and meta-analysis of randomized clinical trials. *BMC Complement Med Ther*. Jun 29 2021;21(1):179. doi:10.1186/s12906-021-03351-w

2   Nagano M, Shimizu K, Kondo R, et al. Reduction of depression and anxiety by 4 weeks Hericium erinaceus intake. *Biomed Res*. Aug 2010;31(4):231-7. doi:10.2220/biomedres.31.231

3   Vigna L, Morelli F, Agnelli GM, et al. Hericium erinaceus Improves Mood and Sleep Disorders in Patients Affected by Overweight or Obesity: Could Circulating Pro-BDNF and BDNF Be Potential Biomarkers? *Evid Based Complement Alternat Med*. 2019;2019:7861297. doi:10.1155/2019/7861297

4   Docherty S, Doughty FL, Smith EF. The Acute and Chronic Effects of Lion's Mane Mushroom Supplementation on Cognitive Function, Stress and

Mood in Young Adults: A Double-Blind, Parallel Groups, Pilot Study. *Nutrients*. 2023;15(22). doi:10.3390/nu15224842

5   Li IC, Chang HH, Lin CH, et al. Prevention of Early Alzheimer's Disease by Erinacine A-Enriched Hericium erinaceus Mycelia Pilot Double-Blind Placebo-Controlled Study. *Front Aging Neurosci*. 2020;12:155. doi:10.3389/fnagi.2020.00155

6   Merenstein D, Guzzi J, Sanders ME. More Information Needed on Probiotic Supplement Product Labels. *Journal of General Internal Medicine*. 2019/12/01 2019;34(12):2735-2737. doi:10.1007/s11606-019-05077-5

7   Pinto-Sanchez MI, Hall GB, Ghajar K, et al. Probiotic Bifidobacterium longum NCC3001 Reduces Depression Scores and Alters Brain Activity: A Pilot Study in Patients With Irritable Bowel Syndrome. *Gastroenterology*. 2017/08/01 2017;153(2):448-459.e8. doi:10.1053/j.gastro.2017.05.003

8   Nikolova VL, Cleare AJ, Young AH, Stone JM. Updated Review and Meta-Analysis of Probiotics for the Treatment of Clinical Depression: Adjunctive vs. Stand-Alone Treatment. *J Clin Med*. Feb 8 2021;10(4). doi:10.3390/jcm10040647

9   Taylor AM, Holscher HD. A review of dietary and microbial connections to depression, anxiety, and stress. *Nutritional Neuroscience*. 2020/03/03 2020;23(3):237-250. doi:10.1080/1028415X.2018.1493808

10   Neuenschwander M, Stadelmaier J, Eble J, et al. Substitution of animal-based with plant-based foods on cardiometabolic health and all-cause mortality: a systematic review and meta-analysis of prospective studies. *BMC Medicine*. 2023/11/16 2023;21(1):404. doi:10.1186/s12916-023-03093-1

11   Pellinen T, Päivärinta E, Isotalo J, et al. Replacing dietary animal-source proteins with plant-source proteins changes dietary intake and status of vitamins and minerals in healthy adults: a 12-week randomized controlled trial. *Eur J Nutr*. Apr 2022;61(3):1391-1404. doi:10.1007/s00394-021-02729-3

12   Lee S, Choi Y, Jeong HS, Lee J, Sung J. Effect of different cooking methods on the content of vitamins and true retention in selected vegetables. *Food Sci Biotechnol*. Apr 2018;27(2):333-342. doi:10.1007/s10068-017-0281-1

13   Li Y, Li S, Zhang C, Zhang D. Association between dietary protein intake and the risk of depressive symptoms in adults. *Br J Nutr*. 2020;123(11): 1290-1301. doi:10.1017/S0007114520000562

Genius Gut BFF Recommendations

1   Hirshkowitz M, Whiton K, Albert SM, et al. National Sleep Foundation's updated sleep duration recommendations: final report. *Sleep Health*. Dec 2015;1(4):233-243. doi:10.1016/j.sleh.2015.10.004

2   Physical activity guidelines for adults aged 19 to 64. NHS. www.nhs.uk/live-well/exercise/physical-activity-guidelines-for-adults-aged-19-to-

64/#:~:text=do%20at%20least%20150%20minutes,not%20moving%20
with%20some%20activity

3   Wilmot EG, Edwardson CL, Achana FA, et al. Sedentary time in adults and
    the association with diabetes, cardiovascular disease and death: systematic
    review and meta-analysis. *Diabetologia*. Nov 2012;55(11):2895-905.
    doi:10.1007/s00125-012-2677-z

4   Diaz KM, Howard VJ, Hutto B, et al. Patterns of Sedentary Behavior and
    Mortality in U.S. Middle-Aged and Older Adults. *Annals of Internal
    Medicine*. 2017/10/03 2017;167(7):465-475. doi:10.7326/M17-0212

5   Buckley JP, Hedge A, Yates T, et al. The sedentary office: an expert statement
    on the growing case for change towards better health and productivity. *Br J
    Sports Med*. Nov 2015;49(21):1357-62. doi:10.1136/bjsports-2015-094618

6   Drink Less. NHS. www.nhs.uk/ better-health/drink-less#:~:text=Alcohol%20
    guidelines,risk%20of%20harming%20your%20health

7   White MP, Alcock I, Grellier J, et al. Spending at least 120 minutes a week in
    nature is associated with good health and wellbeing. *Scientific Reports*.
    2019/06/13 2019;9(1):7730. doi:10.1038/s41598-019-44097-3

Permissions